THE CHALLENGES OF ROGER WILLIAMS

BAPTISTS

HISTORY, LITERATURE, THEOLOGY, HYMNS

GENERAL EDITOR: WALTER B. SHURDEN

This series explores Baptists in all facets of Baptist life and thought. Open-ended and inclusive, this series seeks to publish works that advance understanding of where Baptists have been, where they are, and where they are tending. It will promote the exploration and investigation of Baptist history; publish classics of Baptist literature including letters, diaries, and other writings; offer analyses of Baptist theologies; and examine the role of Baptists in societies and cultures both in the US and abroad.

Walter B. Shurden is the Callaway Professor of Christianity in the Roberts Department of Christianity and Executive Director of the Center for Baptist Studies, Mercer University, Macon, Georgia.

Books in the series

Richard Groves (Wake Forest Baptist Church) ed., Roger Williams's *The Bloody Tenant of Persecution for Cause of Conscience*

Richard Groves, ed., Thomas Helwys's *A Short Declaration of the Mystery of Iniquity*

Keith Harper, ed., *Send the Light: Letters and Other Writings of Lottie Moon*

Chester Raymond Young, ed., John Taylor's *Baptists on the American Frontier: A History of Ten Baptist Churches of Which the Author Has Been Alternately a Member*

James A. Rogers,† *Richard Furman: Life and Legacy*

The Challenges of Roger Williams

Williams

Religious Liberty, Violent Persecution, and the Bible

James P. Byrd, Jr.

MERCER

ISBN 0-86554-771-8
MUP/H582

First Edition.

Library of Congress Cataloging-in-Publication Data

Byrd, James P., 1965-
The challenges of Roger Williams:
Religious liberty, violent persecution, and the Bible /
James P. Byrd, Jr.—1st ed.
    p. cm.
Includes bibliographical references and index.
  ISBN 0-86554-771-8 (alk. paper)
  1. Persecution—United States—History—17th century.
2. Freedom of religion—United States—History—17th
century. 3. United States—Church history—17th
century. 4. Williams, Roger, 1604?-1683.
I. Title.
  BR1608.U6 B97 2002
  261.7'2'092—dc21

                                                                    2002004823

For

Ray E. Byrd (1917-1992),

Ruby H. Byrd (1919-1987),

Karen M. Byrd,

and

Olivia M. Byrd

Table of Contents

Preface

I became interested in Roger Williams through a graduate seminar taught by Dale Johnson at Vanderbilt University. The seminar focused on how historians have written about American religion. Such a course led me to an interest in Roger Williams because historians and others have written about him a great deal since the seventeenth century, but the abundance of books has not led to a consensus about who he really was and what impact he had on America. To Puritans in the Massachusetts Bay Colony, Williams was a heretic—and a particularly dangerous one because he threatened both the church and the state with his radical idea of religious liberty. Over a century later, however, when Americans founded a new nation and talk of "freedom" permeated almost every area of society, including religion, Roger Williams the heretic was hailed as a hero—a prophet who proclaimed the gospel of religious liberty in hostile circumstances. This reversal in Williams's reputation presented an interesting historical problem. Depending upon which book one happed to read, Williams was either a dangerous radical who attacked the religious foundations of society or a liberating prophet who contested religious persecution and advocated the freedom of every individual to worship as he or she pleased. While many disagreed about Williams, nearly all agreed that he was interesting, and he remains so in the twenty-first century. While I have no illusions that my work will be the final statement on Roger Williams, I found it productive to view him from the perspective of his biblical interpretation—an approach that no one had considered in its entirety.

My interest in Williams, therefore, soon awakened a new interest in the importance of the Bible in American history. One would have difficulty overestimating the Bible's influence in America from the colonial period to the present. Throughout American history the Bible is nearly everywhere, serving as an- authoritative Word of truth for churches, a fountain of symbols for the national culture, and a never-depleted quote book for politicians. The Bible has been reverenced and reviled, but seldom ignored. America's captivation with the Bible began in the colonial period and the "Bible Commonwealths" founded by the New England Puritans led the way. Puritans looked to the Bible for truth in all areas of life, named many of their children after biblical figures, and founded America's first college—Harvard—in large part so that young people could learn to read the Bible and equip themselves against Satan's temptations in the vast "wilderness." It therefore makes sense that, to investigate the importance of the Bible in America, we should begin with these seventeenth-century Bible-readers.

Williams provides a fascinating entrée into study of the Bible in colonial America. He did not write commentaries, and the sermons he preached are lost. He did not compose a systematic theology or theological treatises per se. His theology focused on political issues, especially religious war, persecution, and the relations between church and state. How was one to negotiate the claims of these two authorities? Williams was typical in his day in believing that the Bible held the key. But deriving that key from scripture was another problem. Moreover, Williams was sensitive to the persecution and the violent possibilities in religious exercises, including reading the Bible and evangelism. He recognized that the Bible not only opened the way to salvation, for many the Bible provided a justification for unjust violence. He knew that the Bible, when misconstrued, could disrupt the world, leading to war, bloody persecutions, and the violent "conversion" of Native Americans to Christianity. Such fears upped the ante on biblical interpretation, and Williams played his hand with skill. Thus my goal is to shed light on Williams, helping to answer the perennial questions of who he really was and why, as well as to emphasize the importance of scripture to all of life in colonial America—a biblically-saturated society in which the Bible held the key to worldly knowledge and heavenly speculations.

Many people have contributed to my pursuit of Roger Williams. In my studies at Vanderbilt University, I received guidance from the Graduate Department of Religion faculty, especially John Fitzmier, Dale Johnson, Eugene TeSelle, Howard Harrod, Victor Anderson, and Fernando Segovia. Beyond their assistance with this project, the probing questions and pedagogical expertise of these scholars have made me a better scholar and teacher. Since I have made the transition from student to teacher at Vanderbilt, several of these professors are now my colleagues, though they continue to teach me much and for that I am grateful.

I have benefited from many good friends whose support has made this study possible. I would never have considered an academic career if it were not for the inspiration and encouragement of my teacher and friend, Richard F. Wilson of Mercer University. My interest in the history of Christianity was awakened in divinity school classes with Ted Campbell, who presented the landscape of Church History in a lively, intriguing manner. In addition to academicians, I have relied on friends whose expertise lay in the realm of computer technology. This study would not have been possible without a database that I used to uncover Williams's most cited biblical passages. My longtime friend Eric Hood made this difficult task more bearable by generously lending his expertise.

I owe a dept of gratitude to the Vanderbilt University Library for providing many of the resources for this study. I am thankful for the help of Anne Womack and Bill Hook, who kindly offered their expert advice in the ever-expanding fields of research and bibliography. I am also grateful for the assistance of William Harris, the director of archives and special collections at the Luce Library at Princeton Theological Seminary. Mr. Harris and his student assistant, Peter Haas, were very gracious hosts who allowed me access to their impressive collection of seventeenth-century texts.

I received much assistance in preparing the manuscript for publication. I benefited from correspondences with Edwin S. Gaustad and Walter B. Shurden, outstanding scholars whose books have long guided my understanding of Roger Williams and American religious history. Michael S. Stephens, a graduate student in American religion at Vanderbilt, read the manuscript several times and offered very helpful comments. He was a valuable conversation partner throughout the process of bringing this book to print. The publication of this book is, of course, primarily due to the support of Mercer University Press. I am especially grateful to Marc Jolley and Marsha Luttrell, who supported this project and worked diligently to bring it to fruition.

While Roger Williams was not officially a Baptist for very long, he maintained his sympathy for Baptist theology, and he repeatedly quoted from Baptist works in his writings. I would never have understood Williams's fascination with Baptist life if it were not for my upbringing in the Southern Baptist Church of Rutherfordton, North Carolina. This church, led by my pastor and friend, John Perry, has shown me why Baptists who advocate liberty of conscience are as interesting in the twenty-first century as they were in the seventeenth.

My family has tirelessly supported my work in many ways. While their careers are in homemaking, nursing, public relations, farming, electrical engineering, accounting, and other fields, they are also experts in Roger Williams, whether they intended to be or not. I am grateful for the many gifts they give me in my life and the perspectives that they provide on my work. Some of those who made this book possible are unfortunately not here to see its fruition. Most of all I am thankful for my grandparents, Ray E. Byrd and Ruby H. Byrd, who made my life possible and taught me to live it rightly. This book would not have been possible without the encouragement of my wife, Karen Byrd. Her character and love enrich my life daily. Included in the dedication is our daughter, Olivia—the one person I cherish who has never heard of Roger Williams, since she is too busy celebrating her first birthday. When she learns to read, I hope she will find this book worthy of her time.

March 2002
Nashville, Tennessee

INTRODUCTION

This book examines how biblical interpretation promoted both violent persecution and religious liberty in colonial America. Frequently the Bible was a violent force in Puritan New England, where ministers and magistrates used biblical passages to justify the punishment of religious radicals. Puritans whipped and imprisoned Baptists, banished a variety of radicals from the Puritan colonies, and even sent Quakers to the gallows. Puritans believed that the Bible demonstrated that Baptists, Quakers, and other so-called heretics and pagans deserved punishment because they threatened both civil peace and religious orthodoxy in the "Bible Commonwealths" of New England. Roger Williams objected to this Puritan vision of society, prompting Puritan leaders to expel him from the Massachusetts Bay Colony in 1635. Following his banishment, Williams wrote continually on behalf of religious liberty, founded the colony of Rhode Island, established the first Baptist church in America, and became one of the more knowledgeable colonists on Native American cultures. In making his case for religious liberty, Williams ignited a struggle with Puritans over the Bible that held vast implications for society. He adamantly opposed the Puritans' use of the Bible to persecute religious outsiders who did not accept the state's established religion. In retaliation against the use of scripture for violent purposes, Williams argued that religious liberty was the only biblical means of securing civil peace and curtailing the religious wars and persecution that plagued the seventeenth century. Empowered by his radical interpretation of scripture, Williams posed a serious challenge to a Puritan society in which the Bible was the paramount guide in every area of life, from individual piety to public policy. By focusing on Williams's biblical opposition to religious persecution, this book examines the importance of the Bible to issues such as violence, religious liberty, and the relationship between church and state in early American history.

Williams's use of scripture provides insight into how Christianity both supported and opposed violence in colonial America. Critics of Christian missions to Native Americans often have commented that Christianity was an inherently intolerant, violent influence—an exclusivist faith that missionaries imposed upon indigenous peoples.[1] As one who experienced persecution firsthand, Roger Williams recognized that Christianity was a potentially violent force in the American colonies. He asserted that Christianity, when allied with civil states, committed heinous acts of violence and injustice against those who opposed the "orthodox" faith. Williams also lamented the cruelty that "Christian" nations inflicted upon Native Americans. Yet, while mourning the alliance of churches with coercive states, he denied that Christianity was an essentially intolerant, persecuting faith. Indeed, he argued that true, biblical Christianity opposed religious persecution and endorsed religious liberty for all, including heretics and so-called "pagans." This book investigates the biblical resources that Williams enlisted in opposition to the perverted gospel of persecution. Such an examination of Williams's biblical interpretation reveals a complex view of Christianity as a violent force. Christianity was not an intrinsically persecuting religion, despite all appearances to the contrary in the Puritans' treatment of heretics and in missionaries' oppression of Native Americans. Christianity was an ambiguous influence, often used to inflict violence, but also called upon to oppose coercion in religious matters. Williams believed that authentic Christianity asserted a redemptive, peaceful witness in opposition to the perverted alliances of church and state that falsely claimed biblical sanction for their acts of persecution.

---

[1] For example, James Axtell concludes his study of missionary conquests in North America with the assessment that "by its very nature, Christianity is exclusive and intolerant" (*The Invasion Within: The Contest of Cultures in Colonial North America* [New York: Oxford University Press, 1985] 329).

My primary purpose is to highlight biblical arguments that were central to Williams's thought, especially his famous defense of religious freedom and the separation of church and state. His advocacy of these convictions required not only that he wrestle with Puritans such as John Cotton, but that he also struggle to comprehend biblical figures such as Nebuchadnezzar, Ezra, Naboth, Jezebel, Paul, and Jesus. Williams's attention to scriptural authority was commonplace in the seven-teenth century, especially in Puritan settlements. Despite Puritan New England's familiar description as a collection of "Bible Commonwealths," however, surprisingly few books focus on Puritan biblical interpretation and its influence.[2] This is a significant omission because biblical texts and ideas influenced nearly everything the Puritans wrote, including poems, diaries, civil ordinances, and, of course, sermons. In his published appeals for religious liberty, Williams quoted scripture incessantly, fully aware that the Bible was the authoritative basis for any argument that needed to persuade the widest possible audience.[3] Although Williams and his Puritan

---

[2] Several historians have commented on this neglect of Puritan exegesis. For example, see Theodore Dwight Bozeman, *To Live Ancient Lives: The Primitivist Dimension in Puritanism* (Chapel Hill: University of North Carolina Press, 1988) 13; Harry S. Stout, "Word and Order in Colonial New England," in *The Bible in America: Essays in Cultural History,* ed. Nathan O. Hatch and Mark A. Noll (New York: Oxford University Press, 1982) 19. Although exegesis was not his primary focus, Stout helped to fill this void in his extensive study of the Puritan sermon in which he asserted that "scriptural texts were always the last word in New England culture" (*The New England Soul: Preaching and Religious Culture in Colonial New England* [New York: Oxford University Press, 1986] 8). The few studies that do concentrate on some aspect of Puritan exegesis include John R. Knott, Jr., *The Sword of the Spirit: Puritan Responses to the Bible* (Chicago: University of Chicago Press, 1980); and John S. Coolidge, *The Pauline Renaissance in England: Puritanism and the Bible* (London: Clarendon, 1970).

[3] In his own biblical study, Williams probably used both the Authorized Version and the popular Geneva Bible, although he, like most Puritans, apparently preferred the latter. See LaFantasie's editorial comment in Roger Williams, *The Correspondence of Roger Williams,* ed. Glenn W. LaFantasie, 2 vols. (Hanover: Brown University Press, 1988) lxxiv. In most cases, it is difficult to

opponents disagreed over biblical interpretation, they waged their arguments with vigor because of their shared conviction that no case was fully convincing without the support of the Bible, whether the subject was religion, politics, or even the weather. The "Scriptures," according to Williams, are "heavenly righteous scales, wherein all our controversies must be tried" and proven.[4]

Williams believed that, in the hands of educated and godly interpreters, the Bible provided both an invaluable instrument for the improvement of church and society and a formidable weapon against iniquity. Yet biblical authority also could be dangerous. If a properly interpreted Bible held infinite promise for good, then a misread Bible was an equally potent weapon for evil. Williams reminded his contemporaries of the destructive potential of scripture, pointing out that, if distorted, the godly and peaceful Bible could inspire contemptible violence. For him, the religious wars and oppression that plagued the seventeenth century were the tragic consequences of biblical misinterpretation and perversion. As Williams stated in the title of his most famous book, religious persecution began with a "bloody tenet"—an evil teaching. He believed that this "doctrine of persecution for cause of conscience" was "lamentably contrary to the doctrine of Christ Jesus the Prince of Peace."[5] Williams complained that the religious violence

---

determine which version Williams quoted from since the two versions rarely differ in wording. As Christopher Hill noted, "the A. V. normally took over the Geneva wording, just as the Geneva translators had followed Tyndale" (*The English Bible and the Seventeenth-Century Revolution* [London: Penguin, 1993] ix). In this essay, I will use the following abbreviations to denote versions of the Bible: GB (Geneva Bible), KJV (Authorized Version), and NRSV (New Revised Standard Version).

[4] Roger Williams, *Mr. Cottons Letter Lately Printed, Examined and Answered*, in vol. 1 of *The Complete Writings of Roger Williams* (Providence: Narragansett Club Publications, 1874; reprint, New York: Russell & Russell, 1963) 359–60.

[5] Roger Williams, *The Bloudy Tenent, of Persecution, for Cause of Conscience, discussed, in A Conference Betweene Truth and Peace*, in vol. 3 of *The Complete Writings of Roger Williams* (Providence: Narragansett Club Publications, 1867;

marring the political scene was primarily a biblical problem—a perversion of scripture. *— religious violence = scripture perversion*

Williams recognized the consequences of disastrous biblical interpretation in the association between church and state that devastated the seventeenth century, resulting in religious wars and unjust persecution. He disparagingly referred to this kind of government as "Christendom," a septic combination of civil and religious authority that corrupted the church and disrupted the state. He blamed the alliance of religion with civil authority for much of the war and brutality in the seventeenth century. People not only lived their religion, they killed for it, using violence to promote their religious faith. In graphic detail, Williams catalogued the dangers of forcing religious observance upon a civil state, arguing that "to force the consciences of the unwilling" into religious observance "is a Soul-rape," an example of "tyranny, and a mere policy of Satan."[6] He blamed this confusion of patriotism and piety for religious conflicts such as the Thirty Years' War, which pitted Protestants against Catholics, slaughtering "each other in their blinded zeal" on behalf of their religious convictions.[7] Williams found equally perilous mixtures of politics and religion in his homeland, where it was "England's sinful shame" to change its national religion as easily as one changes clothes, adopting the religious preference of each successive king or queen. Williams despaired that, in England, religious truth was not determined by argument or persuasion but by which ruler wielded "the stronger sword." In reviewing England's recent history, Williams lamented that the national religion had fluctuated from Catholicism under Henry VII to Protestantism under Henry VIII and Edward VI, and then back to Catholicism under Mary Tudor before returning to

---

reprint, New York: Russell & Russell, 1963) 425. I have modernized the spelling and capitalization of primary texts, except in the titles of books.

[6] Roger Williams, *The Examiner Defended in a Fair and Sober Answer*, in vol. 7 of *The Complete Writings of Roger Williams* (New York: Russell & Russell, 1963) 268, 210.

[7] Williams, *Bloudy Tenent*, in vol. 3 of *Complete Writings*, 60.

Protestantism under Elizabeth I. Such civil enforcement of religion, Williams argued, transformed the civil state into "a nation of hypocrites" populated by citizens who obeyed the state's religion in their practices but did not believe it in their hearts.[8] The situation was no better in New England, where Williams personally felt the sting of religious persecution when the Massachusetts Bay Colony banished him for publicizing radical ideas. Williams's reading of the Bible convinced him that, whether in Europe, old or New England, use of the sword to enforce religious obedience was unjust and un-christian. As he said, a "religion cannot be true which needs such instruments of violence to uphold it."[9]

One of the greatest obstacles to Williams's defense of religious liberty was Christendom's apparently sturdy biblical foundation. Williams therefore had the unenviable task of defying the seventeenth century's dominant political interpretation of the Bible. In taking up this challenge, he redefined scripture as the enemy of Christendom rather than its ally, arguing that religious persecution was an immense tragedy that called for religious freedom in civil governments. He relied upon the power of scripture to persuade everyone from Puritans in Boston to members of Parliament in London that religious liberty was a biblical truth. In his reading of the Bible, Williams portrayed Christ as an enemy of persecution who commanded magistrates to "see that none of their subjects be persecuted and oppressed for their conscience and worship"—no matter how heretical or scandalous.[10]

This book concerns points of contention between Williams and some of the most revered biblical interpreters in the sixteenth and seventeenth centuries. Williams lamented that many respected Christian leaders were actually "bloody Persecutors" who drew arrows from "the Quiver of Scripture" and used them "to pierce

---

[8] Ibid., 136–37.
[9] Ibid., 139.
[10] Ibid., 188.

the tender heart of Christ Jesus" in their errant exegesis.[11] Due to Williams's participation in these conflicts over the proper interpretation of scripture, an accurate evaluation of his thought cannot view his biblical interpretation in isolation. My purpose, therefore, is to assess Williams's reading of scripture in comparison with the biblical interpretation of Protestant Reformers, Ana- *purpose* baptists, English Separatists, Baptists, and New England Puritans. Since representatives from all of these groups wrestled with some of the same biblical passages that captivated Williams, he joined these exegetical conversations and controversies, and his interpretive contributions reveal much about his revolutionary ideas.

I begin with an analysis of modern interpretations of Roger Williams. Throughout the twentieth century, historians have praised Williams for his courageous advocacy of religious liberty in hostile times. But despite the many books written about Williams, he remains an enigma, with historians offering various and often conflicting assessments of his thought. In chapter one, a review of the diverse historical portraits of Williams reveals that scholars have given insufficient attention to his use of the Bible. Approaching Williams from the perspective of his biblical interpretation is essential to understanding his radical ideas because the Bible was the universal basis for authority in Puritan New England. Biblical images and ideas saturated the culture, crossing boundaries of social class, education, and gender. Thus a compelling assessment of Williams within his historical milieu must account for his position on the biblical landscape of the seventeenth century.

---

[11] Williams, *Examiner Defended*, in vol. 7 of *Complete Writings*, 207–208. In challenging the Puritan understanding of the Bible, calling it violent and anti-Christian, Williams could hardly have offended Massachusetts Bay leaders more. As Janice Knight observes, Puritan ministers "trusted in a single 'right reading' of scripture." Consequently, when Roger Williams offered a variant reading of the Bible, an exegetical war resulted. (Knight, *Orthodoxies in Massachusetts: Rereading American Puritanism* [Cambridge: Harvard University Press, 1994] 73.)

The widespread neglect of the biblical dimensions of Williams's thought was due in part to the lack of a biblical index to Williams's published works, which would have provided an organized way to locate the biblical texts that were crucial in the formulation of his controversial ideas. An appendix to this book fills the void with "A Reference Guide to Roger Williams's Biblical Interpretation," which includes indices that reveal the biblical citations in his published works, and rankings of Williams's most cited biblical books, chapters, and genre. With the assistance of the reference guide, this book reveals the major biblical texts and themes that Williams used to oppose religious persecution in the seventeenth century. The implications of these biblical confrontations are immense for a contemporary understanding of Williams as a pioneer of religious liberty, his theories regarding Native American cultures, his theology, the cultural influence of the Bible in Puritan New England, and the history of the relationship between church and state in America.

Williams's biblical defiance of Christendom was multifaceted, covering a wide range of biblical texts and themes that often were used to support alliances of churches and states. In the seventeenth century, many Protestants, including Puritan ministers and magistrates, agreed on the political interpretation of the Bible in four key areas. First, the Old Testament narratives of divine rule through Israel's kings authorized contemporary rulers to govern religion in the state. Second, the Jesus of the Gospels kept a safe distance from politics, focusing instead on spiritual concerns. Third, Paul, a Roman citizen, defended the authority of the civil magistrate in religious matters and appealed to the judgment of Caesar in both political and religious disputes. Fourth, the mysterious symbols in the book of Revelation captivated interpreters in the seventeenth century, but few acknowledged their relevance to religious liberty. Williams engaged the dominant understanding of the Bible in each of these important areas.

In contrast to previous interpretations of Williams, chapter two reveals that Williams was not a narrow interpreter who limited his scope to the New Testament and disregarded the Old. Williams

nifts focus
from rule of
od to seeing
edience
God
pite
ctons
ters

embraced the Old Testament's political importance in a way that challenged the Puritan establishment. Rather than focusing on the rule of God through national covenants in ancient Israel, Williams highlighted the passages that described God's people in bondage to foreign rulers. These texts depicted times in which God's people were not in control of the government, and yet they adhered faithfully to their religious convictions, witnessing courageously on behalf of their faith while serving foreign masters who often were hostile to the Israelite religion. Williams asserted that this approach to the Old Testament was more relevant to his own time, when no particular civil state could claim God's endorsement, and many states were hostile to certain varieties of Christianity. In Williams's radical view, the Old Testament provided vivid examples of religious liberty and courageous opposition to malicious kings and governments.

Chapter three examines Williams's interpretation of Jesus' parable of the wheat and weeds (Matthew 13:24–30, 36–43).[12] Much to Williams's dismay, many interpreters, including Protestant Reformers and Puritan ministers, used this passage to justify persecution in defense of Christendom.[13] In contrast, Williams argued that this parable was Christ's most vivid denouncement of the evils of Christendom and assertion of the virtues of religious liberty. A reinterpretation of this parable was vital to Williams

---

[12] For references to this passage in Williams's published works, see *Bloudy Tenent*, in vol. 3 of *Complete Writings*, 16–17, 29, 43, 97–119, 169–70, 178–79, 184–85, 208, 285, 373; *The Bloody Tenent Yet More Bloody*, in vol. 4 of *The Complete Writings of Roger Williams* (Providence: Narragansett Club Publications, 1870; reprint, New York: Russell & Russell, 1963) 14–155, 159, 305–307, 340, 437; *George Fox Digg'd Out of His Burrowes*, in vol. 5 of *The Complete Writings of Roger Williams* (Providence: Narragansett Club Publications, 1872; reprint, New York: Russell & Russell, 1963), 196, 207; *Queries of Highest Consideration*, in vol. 2 of *The Complete Writings of Roger Williams* (Providence: Narragansett Club Publications, 1867; reprint, New York: Russell & Russell, 1963) 274; *Examiner Defended*, in vol. 7 of *Complete Writings*, 247; *The Fourth Paper, Presented by Major Butler*, in vol. 7 of *Complete Writings*, 132.

[13] Williams, *Bloudy Tenent*, in vol. 3 of *Complete Writings*, 97–98.

because he believed that much of the controversy, persecution, forced conversion, and religious war resulted from an interpretative stance that misread this parable and neglected its implications. Williams's interpretation of the parable emphasized the centrality of Jesus to the defense of religious liberty in the seventeenth century.

Chapter four considers Williams's interpretation of Paul's teaching on the civil magistrate in Romans 13 and other texts.[14] Williams recognized that many interpreters cited Paul's teachings to justify Christendom and its practice of religious persecution. In his engagement with these interpreters, Williams argued that Paul rejected the power of the civil magistrate in religious issues. In Williams's view, Paul distinguished between civil and religious authorities and emphasized the power of spiritual persuasion in combating heretics and pagans while rejecting the use of physical weapons to coerce the conscience. This Pauline distinction was essential to Williams's arguments for the separation of church and state and for religious liberty.

In chapter five, I examine how Williams used the book of Revelation to frame such critical issues as the relationship between church and state, the dangerous "doctrine" of religious persecution, and Christ's teaching of religious freedom. The discussion begins with Williams's use of Revelation 2–3 in his arguments for religious freedom.[15] These apocalyptic messages from Christ to the

---

[14] See *Bloudy Tenent*, in vol. 3 of *Complete Writings*, 18, 45–46, 59, 109, 146–47, 150–64, 211, 222, 226, 232, 268, 312, 355, 373, 387–89, 398, 403; *Bloody Tenent Yet More Bloody*, in vol. 4 of *Complete Writings*, 144, 243–44, 262–72, 280–84, 420, 440–41, 447; *Examiner Defended*, in vol. 7 of *Complete Writings*, 232; *The Hireling Ministry None of Christs*, in vol. 7 of *Complete Writings*, 180; *Queries*, in vol. 2 of *Complete Writings*, 266.

[15] For references to this passage in Williams's published works, see *Bloudy Tenent*, in vol. 3 of *Complete Writings*, 13, 18, 43, 46, 50, 74, 109, 127, 134, 165–66, 172–74, 190, 197–98, 208, 251–52, 273, 276, 281, 263, 303, 328, 354, 363, 403, 408; *Mr. Cottons Letter*, in vol. 1 of *Complete Writings*, 338–39, 385; *Experiments of Spiritual Life and Health*, in vol. 7 of *Complete Writings*, 57–58;

seven churches of Asia provided the context for an important exegetical disagreement between Williams and John Cotton that revealed their conflicting perspectives. In his challenge to Cotton's interpretation, Williams argued that Revelation 2–3 contained valuable instruction on issues such as the liberty of heretics in society, the sword as a religious weapon, and the influence of religious freedom on civil peace. I continue my assessment of Williams's use of Revelation by considering his interpretation of the whore and the beast in Revelation 17.[16] Like many Protestants of his day, Williams interpreted the whore as a symbol for the Roman Church. But Williams expanded the whore's application to include all nations that used civil force to maintain religious uniformity. Williams used this text to issue specific condemnations of the persecuting governments of King Charles I of England and the Massachusetts Bay Colony, arguing that there were no "Christian" princes and that civil rulers had no authority to use violence to enforce religious orthodoxy. Williams considered the book of Revelation to be the ultimate consolation to those who endured civil persecution for their religious convictions.

In the concluding chapter, I examine Williams's significance for America. Various historians in the twentieth century struggled with this issue, attempting to understand Williams in his own world while simultaneously identifying his importance to the modern age. The struggle continues in this book. While America at the dawn of the twenty-first century is drastically different from colonial New England, Williams's ideas are as challenging now as they were in the past. The concluding essay examines how Williams

---

Bloody Tenent Yet More Bloody, in vol. 4 of *Complete Writings*, 43–45, 86, 146–47, 159, 294, 349.

[16] For references to this passage in Williams's published works, see: *Bloudy Tenent*, in vol. 3 of *Complete Writings*, 112, 145, 150, 192, 228, 262–63, 320, 335–36, 349, 361, 421, 423; *Bloody Tenent Yet More Bloody*, in vol. 4 of *Complete Writings*, 128–29, 329–31, 353–54; *Examiner Defended*, in vol. 7 of *Complete Writings*, 234, 249, 268–69, 277; *George Fox Digg'd*, in vol. 5 of *Complete Writings*, 205, 207, 239, 262, 348; *Mr. Cottons Letter*, in vol. 1 of *Complete Writings*, 362.

remains relevant to contemporary discussions of religious liberty and the place of the Bible in American society.

𝔖

We glean what we know of Williams's biblical interpretation from the books and tracts that he published over a thirty-three year period, 1643–1676. It should be useful, therefore, to introduce this study with an overview of some of his major works and the circumstances of their publication.[17] By the time Williams published his first book, he already had lived a turbulent life. He was an Anglican minister who had apparently adopted Puritan views while a student at Pembroke College, Cambridge, a major center of Puritan activity. In 1630, he and his wife, Mary Barnard Williams, migrated to New England to join their Puritan colleagues in the Massachusetts Bay Colony. Soon after Williams's arrival in 1631, Puritan leaders offered him the position of teacher at the Boston church. Surprisingly, he rejected the offer, citing his unwillingness to minister to a church that had not officially separated from the Church of England. In so doing, Williams indicated that he was a "Separatist." Unlike Puritans, who strove to "purify" the Church of England, Separatists such as Williams "separated" from the Church because they believed it was fully corrupt and beyond the possibility of reform. So began Williams's disagreements with Puritan leaders in New England.

Throughout the next few years, his controversies with Massachusetts Puritans continued, leading to his banishment from the colony in October 1635. The General Court of Massachusetts Bay issued four charges as grounds for his dismissal. First, he

---

[17] The following is a brief overview of Williams's career. For a more complete account of his life, see the excellent biography, Edwin S. Gaustad, *Liberty of Conscience: Roger Williams in America*, ed. Mark A. Noll and Nathan O. Hatch, Library of Religious Biography (Grand Rapids: William B. Eerdmans, 1991). An earlier but still valuable work is Ola Elizabeth Winslow, *Master Roger Williams* (New York: Macmillan, 1957).

rejected the legitimacy of the patent whereby King Charles I had granted Massachusetts territory to the Bay Colony. Williams had denied Charles's right to grant the land, arguing instead that "the Natives are the true owners of it." Second, Williams insisted that civil courts should not force non-Christians to swear oaths or pray since these were activities of worship, not political duties owed to the state. The third offense was his Separatist argument that the Church of England was a false church and, therefore, colonial visitors to England should neither associate with Anglican ministers nor attend their services. The final charge was the most serious: Williams argued that civil officers did not have authority over the consciences and religious activities of their subjects. Magistrates and other civil leaders, Williams claimed, had jurisdiction over civil concerns only—"the bodies and goods, and outward state" of the commonwealth.[18] Following his banishment, the General Court allowed Williams to remain in the colony through the winter under the condition that he would refrain from championing his views publicly. When he violated that order by preaching to anyone who would listen, colonial leaders attempted to arrest him. Williams successfully evaded Massachusetts authorities and headed south to Narragansett Bay where he purchased land from the Narragansett sachems and established the settlement he called Providence, which would be a colonial experiment of religious liberty.

Along with his experiment in government, in 1638 Williams set another precedent by establishing the first Baptist church in America. Soon afterward, however, he rejected the Baptist church along with all others because he had come to believe that no church was truly faithful to the New Testament model. Such was Williams's life before he published his first book. His turbulent wanderings as a banished radical, a student of Native American cultures, a civil magistrate, and a sometime church leader were pivotal in shaping his ideas, which came to fruition in his published works.

---

[18] Roger Williams, *Mr. Cottons Letter*, in vol. 1 of *Complete Writings*, 41.

To be sure, Williams had little chance of publishing anything in America. Certainly no Boston press would bring this radical's ideas to print. Thus, his first opportunity to publish came in 1643 while he was in London attempting to secure a charter for his new colony. Williams's first book had to do, not with religious liberty, but with Native American language and culture. As the title indicated, *A Key into the Language of America* was a linguistic study of the Narragansett dialect. But the book also featured information on Native American life, including religious beliefs, customs, and attitudes toward "peace and war" and "life and death."[19] Much of the *Key* was a defense of the Natives Americans' integrity and civility, especially when compared to the hostilities of English society. Amid his discussion of various topics, Williams interspersed some of his poetry, including the following ominous and prophetic lines: "Oft have I heard these Indians say, / These English will deceive us. / Of all that's ours, our lands and lives. / In th' end they will bereave us."[20] Tragically, the history of colonists' relationship with Native Americans would fulfill this prediction.

Williams's *Key* was an unqualified success in England, where it profited from English curiosity about Native Americans. The *Key* appeared only thirty years after Pocahontas, the "Indian Princess," had fascinated English society and had been received at the court of King James I. Thus, English readers were intrigued by Williams's account of the details of Native American life, and the interest in the book aided Williams's development of social and political connections in London. As Edwin Gaustad observed, Williams's "*Key* opened more doors than he knew."[21] Williams's connections in English society and his lobbying efforts with Parliament paid off; in 1644, he received an official charter for "Providence Plantations," which would soon be known as the colony of Rhode Island.

---

[19] Roger Williams, *A Key Into the Language of America*, in vol. 1 of *Complete Writings*, 17.

[20] Williams, *Key*, in vol. 1 of *Complete Writings*, 185.

[21] Gaustad, *Liberty of Conscience*, 62.

The *Key* did not exhaust everything that Williams had to say about Native Americans. He also published a short work that confronted a great topic of discussion among English: the conversion of indigenous people to Christianity. Williams' title for his tract, *Christenings Make Not Christians*, reveals his belief that many of the so-called "conversions" of native peoples that missionaries boasted of were only outward baptisms—forced rites that did not represent the native peoples' free acceptance of Christianity. The culprits in the forced conversions were the missionary representatives of Christendom who used physical coercion and intimidation to compel indigenous peoples to accept Christianity. Williams claimed that, because of his close relations with native peoples, he could have easily forced "many thousands of these Natives, yea the whole country" to an "Antichristian" conversion the likes of which America had never seen.[22] Yet he refused because of his respect for both native peoples and the gospel. Forced conversion, Williams argued, made a mockery of true conversion because "the will in worship, if true, is like a free vote." Thus "Jesus Christ compels by the mighty persuasions of his messengers to come in, but otherwise" he never forcibly converted anyone "with earthly weapons."[23] The subtitle of *Christenings* is also revealing: *A Briefe Discourse concerning that name Heathen; commonly given to the Indians*. Williams had often "heard both the English and Dutch" say that Native Americans were "heathen dogs" and that it would be better to "kill a thousand of them than that we Christians should be endangered or troubled with them." Further, such Europeans said that, since Indians "have spilt our Christian blood," we should "cut them all off, and so make way for Christians."[24] Williams objected, arguing that Europeans were wrong to call indigenous peoples "heathen" merely because they "go naked" and have not heard of the Christian God. "Heathen,"

---

[22] Roger Williams, *Christenings Make Not Christians*, in vol. 7 of *Complete Writings*, 36.

[23] Ibid., 38.

[24] Ibid., 31.

Williams argued, properly applies to anyone not truly converted to Christianity, regardless of their level of civilization. Thus, since not only the Native Americans but many English men and women were unconverted, England was just as "heathen" a nation as any of the indigenous peoples of America.[25]

In addition to his writings on Native Americans, Williams used his trip to London to publish his arguments on behalf of religious liberty. These publications reached England during a turbulent period. The nation was in the midst of a civil war in which the "Cavaliers" of King Charles I battled the "Roundheads" of the Puritan-controlled Parliament. There was never any love lost between Charles and the Puritans. Charles wanted a church that resembled Catholicism, while Puritans abhorred "popish" traditions and sought a return to the church described in the New Testament. Charles had also commissioned William Laud, the Archbishop of Canterbury, to enforce the official worship of the Church of England against Puritan objections. This strict enforcement of "popish" worship motivated many Puritans to migrate to New England, where they would have the freedom to worship according to the New Testament model without the interference of king and bishop. Many Puritans, however, remained in England to oppose Charles in civil war, creating a volatile political and religious situation. Contributing to the volatility was a disagreement among English Puritans over the kind of polity that the Church should adopt. While Presbyterians stressed the need for synods and assemblies to oversee church activities, Independents insisted on the right of each local church to govern itself without outside supervision. Both Presbyterians and Independents opposed the tyrannical control of bishops, yet both groups also feared the anarchy of complete religious liberty and the proliferation of uncontrollable sectarian groups. When a small group of Independents endorsed a policy of compromise, Williams issued his book, *Queries of Highest Consideration,* which opposed compromise and argued for complete religious liberty. In addition

---

[25] Ibid., 31–32.

to this group of Independents, Williams addressed *Queries* to Parliament itself. In his preface, Williams acknowledged that Parliament sat "at the helm in as great a storm as ever poor England's commonwealth was lost in." But he cautioned members of Parliament to concern themselves only with the political government of England without suffering the delusion that they were also responsible for reforming the Church.[26]

While *Queries* provided a rapid-fire summary of some of Williams's main conclusions, he published his fully developed arguments in his pamphlet war with Puritan minister John Cotton. This debate raged for almost two decades and is recognized as a classic confrontation between religious liberty and religious establishment. The stakes were high because the debate was not only a personal quarrel; through their publications, Williams and Cotton waged their controversy in a public forum, convinced that the issues they debated were significant for church and state in old and New England. In 1644, Williams published two books in his confrontation with Cotton. The first was a response to a letter that Cotton wrote soon after Williams's banishment. While Williams had received the letter earlier, he was not able to respond promptly because of his "distressed wanderings" in the wilderness where he was "destitute of food, of cloths, of time"—thanks to Cotton and his Puritan associates.[27] Cotton's letter, which appeared in print in 1643, defended the Bay Colony's treatment of Williams, given his Separatist radicalism that threatened the Puritan commonwealths. This letter appeared in England at an opportune time because the Puritans in the Westminster Assembly were working to defend the Church of England against Separatism's rampant expansion.[28]

Williams published his response to Cotton with the title, *Mr. Cottons Letter Lately Printed, Examined and Answered.* While this letter provided a point-by-point confrontation between Cotton

---

[26] Williams, *Queries,* in vol. 2 of *Complete Writings,* 14.

[27] Williams, *Mr. Cottons Letter,* in vol. 1 of *Complete Writings,* 31.

[28] W. Clark Gilpin, *The Millenarian Piety of Roger Williams* (Chicago: University of Chicago Press, 1979) 85–86.

and Williams on essential issues, it was a brief treatment when compared to Williams's next book, *The Bloudy Tenent, of Persecution, for cause of Conscience.* This became his most famous book though, as Edwin Gaustad observes, the recognition is due "more from a quoting of the title than from a reading of the contents, for it is a messy book."[29] Indeed, the book is long, scattered, and consists mostly of Williams's defense of religious liberty against Cotton and his Puritan colleagues. Yet, again, the implications of the debate extended to England. Williams recognized this broader audience with a preface in which he pleaded with Parliament to alter the progression of English history by abandoning the persecuting policies of the past and embracing religious liberty. Williams warned that history would judge Parliament and, therefore, he encouraged its members never to let it be said that they, by supporting religious persecution, committed "a greater rape" than "if they had forced or ravished the bodies of all the women in the world."[30] Not surprisingly, members of Parliament did not appreciate Williams's advice; they responded by burning *The Bloudy Tenent.*[31]

The Bloudy Tenent had attacked Cotton and New England before Parliament and all of England. Understandably, Cotton responded with his own graphically-titled work, *The Bloudy Tenent, Washed And made white in the bloud of the Lambe,* published in 1647. Not to be outdone, Williams issued a lengthy retort, *The Bloody Tenent Yet More Bloody,* which he published in 1652 while on a return trip to England. As did its predecessor, *The Bloody Tenent Yet More Bloody* contained a preface addressed to Parliament in which Williams praised this "Long Parliament," which had met since 1640, for its good service to England during the years of war and unrest. The civil war between Parliament and King Charles was over. Charles was executed in 1649 and William

---

[29] Gaustad, *Liberty of Conscience,* 69. Modern readers should note that "tenent" is a seventeenth-century variant of "tenet."

[30] Williams, *Bloudy Tenent,* in vol. 3 of *Complete Writings,* 9.

[31] Williams, *Correspondence,* 628.

Laud was tried and beheaded in 1645. Now that these persecutors had received their just rewards, Williams believed, the time was right for Parliament to end the cycle of persecution by embracing absolute freedom of conscience for all. In proving his point, Williams illustrated his argument with an abundance of images. For instance, he reminded Parliament that "the bloody tenent of persecution" is "a murderous malefactor," similar to "a notorious and common pirate, that takes and robs, that fires and sinks (spiritual ships and vessels) the consciences of all men, of all sorts, of all religions and persuasions."[32]

In addition to his preface to Parliament, Williams included a preface to Puritan New England, his former persecutors. He reminded his Massachusetts neighbors that, while they "sat dry on" their "safe American shores," European nations and England itself had endured the ravages of war and violence. Thus he presented New England with his "discourse of blood, of the bloody tenents of persecution, oppression, and violence, in the cause and matters of conscience and religion."[33] Public chastisement of New England was clearly in order, Williams believed, because despite their arrogant profession "to draw nearer to Christ Jesus than other states and churches," New England Puritans were avid believers in the "Bloody Doctrine" of persecution.[34]

In all of these writings, Williams constantly engaged the Bible. To be sure, he saturated his writings with scripture; virtually every point on every page has an accompanying biblical reference or is part of a discussion of a biblical theme or text. Moreover, throughout Williams's various writings, there is a consistent view of scripture whereby he opposed violent persecution and endorsed religious liberty for all. The task of this book is to reveal his biblical vision, to uncover the important biblical dimensions in the thought of this pivotal radical who became the first prophet of liberty in

---

[32] Williams, *Bloody Tenent Yet More Bloody*, in vol. 4 of *Complete Writings*, 5.

[33] Ibid., 23.

[34] Ibid., 24.

America. Partially due to the scattered style of his writings and partially because many Americans have used his name to provide historical support for their ideas without actually reading his books, few appreciate the biblical dimensions of his thought. This project, therefore, will assess many views of Williams that writers and historians have expressed in modern America. As chapter one demonstrates, Williams seldom lacked admirers in the twentieth century, though most of them had difficulty agreeing about who he really was.

CHAPTER 1

THE MODERN QUEST FOR
THE ELUSIVE ROGER WILLIAMS

"Roger Williams," said Grandfather, "...[had] opinions of civil and religious matters [that] differed...from those of the rulers and clergymen of Massachusetts. Now the wise men of those days believed, that the country could not be safe, unless all the inhabitants thought and felt alike.... They had the power to deprive this good man of his home, and to send him out from the midst of them, in search of a new place to rest...so Roger Williams took his staff and traveled into the forest, and made treaties with the Indians, and began a plantation which he called Providence...."

"When he was driven from Massachusetts," said Laurence, "he must have felt as if he were burying himself forever from the sight and knowledge of men. Yet the whole country has now heard of him, and will remember him forever."

"Yes," answered Grandfather, "it often happens that the outcasts of one generation are those, who are reverenced as the wisest and best of men by the next."

Nathaniel Hawthorne[1]

---

[1] Nathaniel Hawthorne, *Grandfather's Chair*, in vol. 6 of *The Centenary Edition of the Works of Nathaniel Hawthorne*, ed. William Charvat, Roy Harvey Pearce, and Claude M. Simpson (Columbus: Ohio State University Press, 1972) 26–27. For a study that considers Hawthorne's interpretation of Williams, see Donald W. Cowart, "'A Minister I Will Not Be': Historical Ministers in the

Possibly no figure out of the American past today enjoys a greater prestige than Roger Williams—and for none is esteem based on so little familiarity with his deeds or so comprehensive an ignorance of his words.

Perry Miller[2]

Historians have never tired of pondering and praising Roger Williams. As a recent essay claims, Williams has been "a hero who has transcended time" and "a man for all eras," because nearly every generation of historians has found something to admire about him.[3] Above all, interpreters have commended Williams as an intellectual pioneer because he was among the first to advocate religious liberty and the separation of church and state in America.[4] Indeed, Williams argued for these convictions, and made them the basis of a colonial government in Rhode Island when most church and civil leaders in New England considered them theologically

---

Works of Nathaniel Hawthorne" (Ph.D. dissertation, University of South Florida, 1995) 267–304.

[2] Perry Miller, *Roger Williams: His Contribution to the American Tradition* (New York: Bobbs-Merrill, 1953) xi.

[3] Raymond D. Irwin, "A Man for All Eras: The Changing Historical Image of Roger Williams, 1630–1993," *Fides et Historia* 26/3 (1994): 7.

[4] We must distinguish between Williams's understanding of *religious freedom* and *religious toleration*. As Edwin Gaustad observes, "Williams argued passionately not for mere 'tolerance,' but for full and unqualified freedom in matters of conscience. In the seventeenth century, few would have confused the begrudging nature of tolerating dissent with the explicit assertion that error had the same rights as truth so far as any civil disability or restriction was concerned" ("Review of Hugh Spurgin's *Roger Williams and Puritan Radicalism in the English Separatist Tradition,*" *Church History* 61/4 [1992]: 453). This point was well made by an anonymous pamphleteer, who, writing one year after Williams's *Bloudy Tenent,* argued that even though "there is but one truth...this truth cannot be so easily brought forth without...liberty; and a general restraint, though intended but for errors, yet through the unskillfulness of men, may fall upon the truth; and *better many errors of some kind suffered, than one useful truth be obstructed or destroyed*" (*The Ancient Bounds* [London: Henry Overton, 1645] vi; emphasis added).

absurd and politically dangerous. In vivid contrast to modern historians' praise of Williams, most of his contemporaries did their best to avoid him. As William McLoughlin observed, "almost no one in colonial New England ever praised" Williams's experiment in Rhode Island, "sought his advice, quoted his books, or tried to imitate his practices."[5] This was an understandable reaction, for Williams challenged the intellectual foundation of the Puritan establishment in New England.[6] Yet Williams's reputation changed dramatically in succeeding generations. While most colonialists feared and shunned Williams's ideas in the seventeenth century, in the eighteenth century Thomas Jefferson and his colleagues enshrined Williams's opinions into American orthodoxy.

From that point, nearly all interpreters have considered Williams an American hero. Indeed, three prominent historians recently deemed Williams "the best exemplar of the truly positive Puritan influence in American culture."[7] He remains popular in

---

[5] William G. McLoughlin, *Soul Liberty: The Baptists' Struggle in New England, 1630–1833* (Hanover: Brown University Press, 1991) 19. McLoughlin goes on to say that "even in Rhode Island [Williams] was often assailed as unsound—and to the other New England colonies, Rhode Island was always the prime example not of the virtues but of the horrors of religious liberty.... During and after the colonial period, Rhode Island, 'the licentious Republic' and 'sinke hole of New England,' was an example to be shunned." See 19–20.

[6] Darren Staloff discusses Williams's intellectual challenge to his Puritan colleagues. Staloff emphasizes that Williams's argument that "the state-supported system of civil and ecclesiastic cultural domination was illegitimate and should be dismantled" posed "the first major challenge" to the Puritan establishment in seventeenth-century Massachusetts (*The Making of an American Thinking Class: Intellectuals and Intelligentsia in Puritan Massachusetts* [New York: Oxford University Press, 1998] 37, 20).

[7] Mark A. Noll, George M. Marsden, and Nathan O. Hatch, *The Search for Christian America* (Colorado Springs: Helmers & Howard, 1989) 37. Note also Keith Stavely's comment that Williams was "the most original mind of the founding generation" of Puritans ("Roger Williams and the Enclosed Gardens of New England," in *Puritanism: Transatlantic Perspectives on a Seventeenth-Century Anglo-American Faith*, ed. Francis J. Bremer, Massachusetts Historical Society Studies in American History and Culture, no. 3 [Boston: Massachusetts Historical Society, 1993] 274).

current scholarship not only for his ideas concerning church, state, and religious liberty, but also for his work with Native Americans because he knew more about the Narragansett tribe than perhaps any colonist in the early seventeenth century.[8]

Historians have also commended Williams's heroic fortitude. He stood faithfully by his principles despite many opposing forces in both old and New England. He believed that truth was a rare and valuable commodity and that Christ demanded struggle and sacrifice from his followers in the turbulent seventeenth century. Williams crafted his polemical writings on behalf of that truth, and in the process he expected controversy, endured strife, and deemed compromise blasphemous.[9] As Perry Miller said, "Williams was the one worldling, in the terms of his time, who would never, never

---

[8] Williams's *A Key Into the Language of America* (in vol. 1 of *The Complete Writings of Roger Williams* [Providence: Narragansett Club Publications, 1866; reprint, New York: Russell & Russell, 1963]) has received abundant attention from scholars in recent years. Leonard Vraniak views the *Key* as an example of Williams's self-presentation as an expert on the new world and, most particularly, Native American culture—a topic of much interest in English society. By tapping into such a hot topic, Williams won the renown of important people and helped to secure a charter for Rhode Island. (See Leonard J. Vraniak, Jr., "Created Works, Created Selves: Intersections of Genre and Self-Fashioning in the New World" [Ph.D. diss., Louisiana State University, 1997] 118–69). Thomas Scanlan suggests that Williams's *Key* was also a subtle polemic against the Bay Colony, which sought to block his bid for a charter. By proclaiming himself an advocate of the Native Americans, Williams placed himself in contrast to the Puritans, who failed to understand them (Scanlan, "Conversion, Suppression, or Limited Partnership: Problems in the Protestant Colonial Ethic" [Ph.D. diss., Duke University, 1992] 73; see also 70–106). In contrast, Joshua Bellin has approached the *Key* from an economic perspective, arguing that the "non-accumulative society" of the Narragansetts impressed Williams, who used it to denounce the "market economies" of the English ("The Demon of the Continent: American Literature, Indian Conversion, and the Dynamics of Cultural Exchange" [Ph.D. diss., University of Pennsylvania, 1995] 89).

[9] As Andrew Delbanco expressed it, "the tragedy of Roger Williams was his antipathy to one idea: the idea of pragmatic compromise" (*The Puritan Ordeal* [Cambridge: Harvard University Press, 1989] 100).

concede an inch to worldliness."[10] Likewise, Williams impressed Edmund Morgan with his "intellectual courage"; he was a rare individual "who had the nerve to trust his own mind."[11] Thus, Williams has intrigued historians not only with his ideas, but also with his nerve and tenacity. Although Williams "did not always speak his piece with economy or grace," Edwin Gaustad affirms that "he unfailingly spoke it with courage and passion."[12]

Not only has Roger Williams impressed historians, he also continues to puzzle them. Despite the vast number of historical treatments of Williams since the eighteenth century, he remains something of an enigma. In 1651, Roger Williams observed that he was living in "searching, disputing, and dissenting times."[13] Meanwhile, a glimpse at the interpretations of Williams over the years reveals that the searching has multiplied, and the disputing and dissenting have continued. I attempt to organize this dissension by focusing on what I believe are the two most persistent questions in Williams scholarship. The first question concerns Williams's intellectual *perspective*. What was the nature of his thought? What intellectual outlook led him to his famous convictions concerning church, state, and religious freedom? The second question regards his place within his intellectual *context* in seventeenth-century New England. To what degree can we attribute Williams's mindset to

---

[10] Perry Miller, "Roger Williams: An Essay in Interpretation," in vol. 7 of *The Complete Writings of Roger Williams* (New York: Russell & Russell, 1963) 21. This quote from Miller reveals the widespread opinion of Williams as an "extreme," even eccentric "purist." See Stephen Foster, "English Puritanism and the Progress of New England Institutions, 1630–1660," in *Saints and Revolutionaries: Essays on Early American History,* ed. David D. Hall, John M. Murrin, and Thad W. Tate (New York: W. W. Norton & Company, 1984) 18.

[11] Edmund S. Morgan, *Roger Williams: The Church and the State* (New York: Harcourt Brace, 1967) 142; idem, "Miller's Williams," *New England Quarterly* 38 (1965): 516.

[12] Edwin S. Gaustad, *Liberty of Conscience: Roger Williams in America,* ed. Mark A. Noll and Nathan O. Hatch, Library of Religious Biography (Grand Rapids: William B. Eerdmans Publishing, 1991) xi.

[13] Williams, *The Correspondence of Roger Williams,* ed. Glenn W. LaFantasie (Hanover: Brown University Press, 1988) 1:346.

the Puritan milieu in which he lived? Was he a unique thinker whose thought stood in stark contrast to that of his Puritan contemporaries? Or did his radical opinions draw from Puritan theology, differing from it only in nuances and degrees? Historians have offered various responses to these questions, prompting a longstanding debate over Williams's intellectual perspective and how he fit into his seventeenth-century world. As the following discussion of modern studies of Williams will demonstrate, at least one significant gap remains in scholarly attempts to locate Williams within the intellectual world that he inhabited. That is, historians have not taken sufficient account of Williams's biblical interpretation in its seventeenth-century context.[14]

During the first half of the twentieth century, historians did not view scripture as a primary force that shaped Williams's convictions. Many viewed Williams as a liberal prophet who pointed the way to America's future in spite of his Puritan context. While numerous interpreters espoused this liberal Williams, I will focus on the influential work of Progressive historians Vernon Louis Parrington and James Ernst.[15] Together, they clearly presented this

---

[14] I do not intend to chart the entire course of Williams's historiography from the seventeenth century to the present, for that has been done admirably elsewhere. See Irwin, "A Man for All Eras"; Edward Wallace Coyle, "From Sinner to Saint: A Study of the Critical Reputation of Roger Williams with an Annotated Bibliography of Writings about Him" (Ph.D. diss., University of Massachusetts, 1974); idem, *Roger Williams: A Reference Guide* (Boston: G. K. Hall & Co., 1977); LeRoy Moore, "Roger Williams and the Historians," *Church History* 32 (1963): 432–51; Nancy E. Peace, "Roger Williams: A Historiographical Essay," *Rhode Island History* 35/4 (1976): 103–13; and Donald Skaggs, *Roger Williams' Dream for America* (New York: Peter Lang, 1993); idem, "Roger Williams in History: His Image in the American Mind" (Ph.D. diss., University of Southern California, 1972). Instead, this study is concerned with the use historians have made of Roger Williams in the twentieth century. This focus is appropriate because it is only in this century that interpreters recognized Williams as a biblicist.

[15] The studies that interpret Williams as a liberal prophet include Samuel Hugh Brockunier, *The Irrepressible Democrat: Roger Williams* (New York: Ronald Press, 1940); Emily Easton, *Roger Williams: Prophet and Pioneer* (Boston:

liberal picture of Williams the American prophet. In the mid-twentieth century, Perry Miller disputed the Progressive historians' claim that Williams was an Enlightenment thinker before his time—a liberal who rejected the harsh Calvinist theology of his Puritan contemporaries. In contrast, Miller argued that Williams was just as theologically-minded as the Puritans, perhaps even more so. In Miller's view, Williams threatened the Puritan commonwealths because of his eccentric, fanatical obsession with biblical typology—a controversial and rare way of reading the Bible. Ironically, Miller repeated the errors of the Progressive historians in the area that he most wanted to correct—understanding Williams in his seventeenth-century context. To be sure, Miller asserted the theological nature of Williams's thought, arguing that to depict Williams as an Enlightenment thinker in the seventeenth century was anachronistic foolishness. But Miller's concentration on Williams's typological interpretation of the Bible again isolated Williams from his seventeenth-century world. Miller failed to recognize that Williams's typology was not so rare, that most of his Puritan contemporaries used typological exegesis as well. While departing from Miller's analysis on certain points, later historians have followed his basic conclusion that Williams's primary biblical argument was his typological exegesis of the Old Testament. The result is a narrow view of Williams's biblical interpretation that does not adequately represent the fullness of his biblical case for religious liberty. This book proposes to correct this interpretation by examining Williams's most critical biblical arguments and the ways in which they shaped his radical convictions.

Houghton Mifflin, 1930); and Arthur B. Strickland, *Roger Williams, Prophet and Pioneer of Soul Liberty* (Boston: Judson Press, 1919).

I. LIBERAL FREEDOM AMID THEOLOGICAL TYRANNY: ROGER WILLIAMS THE AMERICAN PROPHET, 1900–1949

In his *Main Currents in American Thought,* Vernon L. Parrington evaluated American history as a conflict between the friends and enemies of democracy.[16] He condemned the Massachusetts Bay Puritans for their theocratic government, which stood in stark contrast to the establishment of religious freedom and democracy that later dawned in America. According to Parrington, Puritans committed many errors, the greatest being their appalling relish for John Calvin's theological government. In sixteenth-century Geneva, Calvin had established a theocratic rule that ministers guided and magistrates enforced. Because Calvin combined religious and secular authority, Parrington considered him a "tyrant" who used the power of the state to enforce God's commands—with violence when necessary. As Parrington said, "a few splotches of blood on the white garments of the Church did not greatly trouble" Calvin.[17] Much to Parrington's dismay, Puritans brought Calvin's ideas concerning church and state to America. Consequently, as LeRoy Moore observed, Parrington considered the Puritans "an anomaly on the American scene, foreign to everything true, good, and beautiful in the maturing national culture."[18]

This negative reading of Puritanism naturally invited a positive assessment of Roger Williams, Massachusetts Bay's archenemy. Parrington denied the impact of theology on Williams's thought, praising him as a liberal philosopher caught in an age dominated by gloomy Calvinists. Much to his credit, Williams rejected Calvin's theology just as adamantly as later enlightened thinkers

---

[16] Richard Hofstadter, *The Progressive Historians: Turner, Beard, Parrington* (Chicago: University of Chicago Press, 1968) 414–15. See also David D. Hall, *Puritanism in Seventeenth-Century Massachusetts* (New York: Holt, Rinehart, and Winston, 1968) 49.

[17] Vernon L. Parrington, in vol. 1 of *Main Currents in American Thought* (New York: Harcourt Brace, 1927) 20–21.

[18] Moore, "Historians," 442.

would, concerning himself more "with social commonwealths than with theological dogmas."[19] Parrington judged that Williams "was primarily a political philosopher rather than a theologian."[20] Instead of a disciple of Calvin, Williams was "a forerunner of Locke and the natural-rights school, one of the notable democratic thinkers that the English race has produced."[21] Hence, Parrington judged that Williams protested against Massachusetts Bay with political, not religious, fervor. In essence, Parrington observed that "England gave her best when she sent us Roger Williams," and Parrington did not regard this as a theological contribution.[22]

Parrington, therefore, depicted Williams as a prophet of future ideals who belonged to a later and brighter America. Williams was a "transcendental mystic" years before Emerson, and a "speculative seeker" who dreamed of a liberal society based on freedom of thought and conscience. Moreover, as a political philosopher, Williams was the forerunner of Paine and the French romantic school. In Roger Williams, Parrington found an Enlightenment thinker and democrat born to a generation that did not share his progressive ideas. "The gods," Parrington reflected, "were pleased to have their jest with Roger Williams by sending him to earth before his time."[23]

When Parrington described the development of Williams's political thought, he relied partially on his student, James Ernst, who did much of the research to substantiate his teacher's thesis.[24] Ernst later published a biography of Williams that developed his and Parrington's interpretation. In this book, *Roger Williams: New*

---

[19] Parrington, *Currents*, 64.

[20] Ibid., 66.

[21] Ibid. William Haller also represented Williams in this way. Haller asserted that Williams's "*The Bloudy Tenent* was perhaps the most extreme statement of the theory of natural rights which had yet appeared" (*Tracts on Liberty in the Puritan Revolution, 1638–1647*, 3 vols., *Records of Civilization, Sources and Studies*, vol. 1:18 [New York: Columbia University Press, 1934] 60).

[22] Parrington, *Currents*, 74.

[23] Ibid., 62.

[24] Ibid., 67n.16.

England Firebrand, Ernst attempted a full-scale assessment of Williams's life and legacy.[25]

Most importantly, Ernst associated Williams's demands for religious liberty and separation of church and state with a concern for natural rights. Ernst stressed that Williams distanced himself from the Puritans, who depended on the Bible for authoritative instruction in political matters. While Ernst admitted that Williams often quoted scripture, he downplayed its impact on his thought, arguing that "Christianity, as such, made no contribution to [Williams's] political theory."[26] By this reasoning, Ernst remained faithful to Parrington, who, as LeRoy Moore said, disposed "of Williams's theological idiom as just so much gibberish—verbal camouflage for truly enlightened ideas."[27]

How, then, may we appraise V. L. Parrington's and James Ernst's evaluations according to our two interpretive questions regarding Williams's intellect and context? Clearly Parrington and Ernst focused on Williams's intellectual perspective at the expense of his historical context. They believed that Williams rejected his Puritan contemporaries' theological worldview and their "Bible commonwealths." In contrast to the Puritans, Williams was an enlightened individual who thought in social, political terms and gave little heed to the Bible or theological issues in general. Moreover, this enlightened intellect caused Williams's banishment from the Puritan oligarchy for preaching heretical political doctrines of religious freedom and separation of church and state, which later became the pillars of an emerging society. Parrington and Ernst praised Williams because he rebelled against the Puritan establishment and proclaimed the virtues of a later, enlightened America. In the end, Williams the outcast became the voice for a future nation.

---

[25] James E. Ernst, "The Political Thought of Roger Williams" (Ph.D. diss., University of Washington, 1928); idem, *Roger Williams: New England Firebrand* (New York: The Macmillan Company, 1932).

[26] Ernst, *New England Firebrand,* 422, 436.

[27] Moore, "Historians," 443.

II. PERRY MILLER: ROGER WILLIAMS
THE ISOLATED PURITAN, 1950–1967

In *The Kingdom of God in America*, H. Richard Niebuhr reprimanded Progressive historians for their failure to apprehend the impact of theological ideas on American history. Niebuhr considered it an injustice for "social interpreters" such as Parrington to conclude that "political and economic interests are alone real and the language of politics and economics is the only universal tongue."[28] This point was particularly relevant to the Progressive critics' treatment of Roger Williams. Niebuhr claimed that "despite the modern tendency to interpret Roger Williams as primarily a political thinker, it seems impossible that one should read his writings without understanding that he…was first of all a churchman."[29] Yet Niebuhr's perspective remained mostly absent from studies of Williams until the early 1950s. An important indication that the reputation of Williams was finally changing came in an essay by Mauro Calamandrei, who argued that:

> far from being a humanist Roger Williams believed in the radical depravity of man and the necessity of Grace; …far from being a rationalist Williams was a Biblicist; …far from being an optimist in history, Williams was a Millenarian; and rather than being a democratic Baptist Williams believed in the prophetic ministry free from any congregational limitations—in short, …*rather than being a man of the Renaissance and the Enlightenment Roger Williams was a Puritan.*[30]

---

[28] H. Richard Niebuhr, *The Kingdom of God in America* (New York: Harper & Row Publishers, 1937; reprint, Middletown: Wesleyan University Press, 1988) 199.

[29] Ibid., 68.

[30] Mauro Calamandrei, "Neglected Aspects of Roger Williams' Thought," *Church History* 21 (1952): 239, emphasis added. See also Calamandrei, "The Theology and Political Thought of Roger Williams" (Ph.D. diss., University of Chicago, 1953).

The majority of Williams's interpreters after 1950 echoed this statement of Williams's Puritan mindset.[31] These critics challenged the Progressive historians' interpretation of Williams, claiming that it misconstrued Williams's perspective and improperly evaluated his arguments for religious freedom. In contrast to the liberal historians before them, therefore, interpreters of Williams since the 1950s agreed with Edmund Morgan's statement that "Williams' every thought took its rise from religion."[32]

Yet dissension among historians continued because, while most admitted that Williams was a theologian well-suited to his Puritan context, they disagreed as to what it was about his religious thought that led to his radical convictions. What theological beliefs prompted Williams to advocate religious liberty when his Puritan colleagues considered the idea dangerous? Thus historians continue to debate the nature of Williams's religious thought. And, while scholarly treatments of Williams over the past forty years have multiplied, they have reached little agreement on how to characterize him. In attempting to find the "key" to Williams's thought, historians have offered a startling number of conclusions, including Separatism,[33] Calvinism,[34] church and state,[35] church and ministry,[36] the classical tradition,[37] millennialism,[38] and primi-

---

[31] In addition to those mentioned, some of the first studies to posit this theological understanding of Williams were: Winthrop Hudson, "Roger Williams, No Secularist," *Christian Century* 68 (1951): 963–64; Clarence S. Roddy, "The Religious Thought of Roger Williams" (Ph.D. diss., New York University, 1948); and Alan Simpson, "How Democratic Was Roger Williams?," *William and Mary Quarterly* 13 (1956): 53–67.

[32] Morgan, *Roger Williams*, 86.

[33] See Edwin S. Gaustad, "Roger Williams and the Principle of Separation," *Foundations* 1 (1958): 55–64; and Hugh Spurgin, *Roger Williams and Puritan Radicalism in the English Separatist Tradition*, vol. 34 of Studies in American Religion (Lewiston: Edwin Mellen Press, 1989).

[34] Leroy Moore, "Religious Liberty, Roger Williams, and the Revolutionary Era," *Church History* 34/1 (1965): 57–76.

[35] Morgan, *Roger Williams*.

[36] David L. Mueller, "Roger Williams on the Church and Ministry," *Review and Expositor* 55 (1958): 165–81.

tivism.[39] Regardless of their differing conclusions, most historians have agreed on one issue—that Williams's argument for religious freedom depended on his use of typology as his favorite method for interpreting the Bible. The stimulus for this consensus among historians came from Perry Miller.

Perry Miller changed the way historians understood Williams in the twentieth century. As he had done for New England Puritans, Miller reinterpreted Roger Williams and his importance

---

[37] Richard M. Gummere, *The American Colonial Mind and the Classical Tradition: Essays in Comparative Culture* (Cambridge: Harvard University Press, 1963); idem, "Church, State, and the Classics: The Cotton-Williams Debate," *Classical Journal* 54 (1958): 175–83.

[38] Gilpin, *The Millenarian Piety of Roger Williams* (Chicago: University of Chicago Press, 1979).

[39] Crawford Leonard Allen, "'The Restauration of Zion': Roger Williams and the Quest for the Primitive Church" (Ph.D. diss., University of Iowa, 1984); idem, "Roger Williams and 'The Restauration of Zion,'" in *The American Quest for the Primitive Church,* ed. Richard T. Hughes (Urbana and Chicago: University of Illinois Press, 1988), 33–68; Richard T. Hughes and C. Leonard Allen, *Illusions of Innocence: Protestant Primitivism in America, 1630–1875* (Chicago: University of Chicago Press, 1988); see also John J. Teunissen and Evelyn J. Hinz, "Roger Williams, St. Paul, and American Primitivism," *The Canadian Review of American Studies* 4/2 (1973): 121–36. The Puritan esteem for the primitive church was expressed well by Thomas Brightman, who asserted that for "the first hundred years the church remained a chaste virgin; in the ages next following she began to play the wanton, defiling her marriage bed somewhat" (*The Works of that Famous, Reverend and Learned Divine, Mr. Tho. Brightman* [London: n.p., 1644] 53). For a review essay that is somewhat critical of concentration on primitivism, see W. Clark Gilpin, "Recent Studies of American Protestant Primitivism," *Religious Studies Review* 19/3 (1993): 231–35. Gilpin cautions that primitivist "restorationism is nothing if not a theory to change." Further, Gilpin asserts that "appeals to the authority of the ancient time do not entail a negative attitude toward progress and modernization. Primitivism was not necessarily averse to progress; it simply sought norms to direct it into the future, to enable it to distinguish between 'true' and 'false' progress" (Ibid., 234–35). Gilpin's emphasis on primitivism as a means of moving toward the future coheres with his interpretation of Williams, whom Gilpin asserted was a future-looking millenarian although he held a primitivist focus on the early church. (See Gilpin, *Millenarian Piety,* 50).

in American history, thereby casting new light on a hero that most Americans thought they knew well. Miller first presented his reassessment of Williams in a book that he published in 1953 as part of the *Makers of the American Tradition* series. These volumes proposed to rediscover great individuals from America's past and reclaim their relevance to a time of anxiety and crisis in the middle twentieth century. As general editor Hiram Haydn explained, the goal of the collection was to help the nation to reexamine itself in light of its roots. Haydn hoped the series would reinvigorate the nation's resolve to be "a free and confident America" that would shine as a beacon of freedom for the rest of the world.[40] To that end, Miller's book on Williams accompanied books by other scholars on such national heroes as Benjamin Franklin and Andrew Jackson. Not a biography in the traditional sense, this book presented selections from Williams's writings interspersed with Miller's commentary. In 1963, Miller repeated some of the themes from this book in "Roger Williams: An Essay in Interpretation," which he published as an introduction to a new volume of Williams's *Complete Writings*.[41] The influence of these works is such that, for over forty years now, they have obliged interpreters to converse with "Miller's Williams."[42]

Miller's work on Williams cohered with his challenge to previous interpretations of American Puritanism. Miller argued that both historians' sweeping condemnations of the Puritans and their praise of Williams suffered from misunderstandings. While Miller did not deny that Williams deserved praise, he argued that Williams had received admiration for the wrong reasons. Thus Miller attempted "to cut through the fog of adulation to the much greater—although often more puzzling" Roger Williams. Miller believed that the Progressive historians had formed Williams in their own image, creating "a figure admirable by the canons of modern secular liberalism, but only distantly related to the actual

[40] Miller, *Contribution*, ix.
[41] Miller, "Essay in Interpretation," in vol. 7 of *Complete Writings*, 5–25.
[42] Morgan, "Miller's Williams," 513–23.

Williams."[43] The "actual Williams," Miller argued, shared the theological perspective of his Puritan contemporaries. Miller therefore seized the enlightened, secular figure the Progressives had designed and ushered him back to his rightful place in seventeenth-century New England. In so doing, Miller wryly remarked that John Cotton and his Puritan colleagues would not have "insulted" Williams as the Progressive historians did by claiming that he was a social rather than a theological thinker. To the contrary, Miller insisted that Williams was as good a Calvinist as any Puritan. "In all doctrinal respects," Miller argued, Williams "was as rigidly unbending as Thomas Hooker himself, and probably was more correct confessionally than John Cotton."[44] In fact, Miller contended that "even for theologians in an ultratheological era, the cast of Williams's mind was much too theological." Furthermore, Miller said that it was Williams's *theological* insights that posed "his challenge to the twentieth century as well as to the seventeenth."[45]

Despite the theological similarities between Williams and the Puritan leaders of Massachusetts Bay, Miller believed that they disagreed over how to interpret the Bible. Miller insisted that this was quite serious, because it was a society for which "the Bible was the all-encompassing rule of human existence, social or individual."[46] Indeed, Williams did not live at a time in which scripture was a secondary apparatus, used only to confirm opinions already decided by enlightened reason.[47] Rather, in the Puritan world, Miller asserted that "reason [did] not make clear the sense of scripture, but the clear sense of scripture create[d] the reason."[48]

In order to explain how Williams offended Puritan biblical interpretation, we need to clarify what Miller believed was the key

---

[43] Miller, *Contribution*, xiii.

[44] Miller, "Essay in Interpretation," in vol. 7 of *Complete Writings*, 22.

[45] Miller, *Contribution*, 27.

[46] Miller, "An Essay in Interpretation," in vol. 7 of *Complete Writings*, 10.

[47] Miller, *Contribution*, 27.

[48] Perry Miller, "General Introduction," in *The Puritans: A Sourcebook of their Writings*, ed. Perry Miller and Thomas H. Johnson (New York: Harper & Row Publishers, 1963) 55.

to Puritan thought: the idea of covenant. In his groundbreaking reinterpretation of American Puritanism, Miller stressed that the Puritans' reading of scripture led them to envision their alliance between church and state as a covenant between their society and God. Specifically, they understood their government as a continuation of God's national covenant with Israel, the chosen people of the Old Testament.[49] The Puritans believed that when Christ came he did not nullify this covenant; rather, he sealed it, blessing it as the foundation for building a Christian society. Accordingly, New England divines believed that God related to his people through a covenant that extended "from Palestine to Boston."[50] For the Puritans, this story of "an unbroken progress from Abraham through Christ," and "all the way to the Congregational churches of New England," was the foundation of all biblical knowledge; "it *was* the Bible."[51]

According to Miller, this national covenant idea was vital to the mission that led the Puritans to America—their "errand into the wilderness."[52] Miller discovered one of the earliest and best expressions of this "errand" in the famous sermon delivered by

---

[49] Perry Miller, *The New England Mind: The Seventeenth Century* (Cambridge: Belknap Press of Harvard University Press, 1939), see especially 463–91. See also Perry Miller, *Orthodoxy in Massachusetts, 1630–1650* (Cambridge: Harvard University Press, 1933) 234–39. Miller believed that the Puritans' understanding of the national covenant complemented their reliance on the covenant of grace. As Harry S. Stout has said, "One covenant—the 'covenant of grace'—referred to individuals and personal salvation in the life to come. The other covenant—the national covenant—applied to nations and governed their temporal success in this world. In early Puritanism, these two contradictory covenants—one of faith, the other of works; one unconditional, the other conditional—existed in creative tension"; see Harry S. Stout, "The Puritans and Edwards," in *Jonathan Edwards and the American Experience*, ed. Nathan O. Hatch and Harry S. Stout (New York: Oxford University Press, 1988) 143.

[50] Miller, "An Essay in Interpretation," in vol. 7 of *Complete Writings*, 11.

[51] Ibid., 16, 23.

[52] Perry Miller, "Errand Into the Wilderness," in *Errand Into the Wilderness*, (Cambridge: Belknap Press of Harvard University Press, 1956) 1–15.

John Winthrop while sailing toward New England aboard the *Arbella*. There, Winthrop called his people "new Israelites" and declared that their faithfulness to Israel's example held vital implications for the government that they would establish in Massachusetts Bay.[53] Winthrop pledged that they would seek to implement "a due form of Government, both civil and ecclesiastical."[54] In so doing, Winthrop and his colleagues hoped to be a "City upon a Hill," set apart as an example for the entire world to behold.[55] Thus, according to Miller, the Puritans were on a divine "errand" or mission. They comprised "an organized task force of Christians" who strove to live as a biblical people by organizing their society in covenant with God.[56] Consequently, Miller argued that the entire Puritan "errand" depended upon a civil government that protected their Congregational church structure. Their mission required that Puritan society be "deliberately, vigorously, and consistently intolerant" because the civil magistrate had the holy task of purging the colony of religious heretics, troublemakers, and dissenters.[57] The fact that Puritan officials banished Roger Williams from Massachusetts Bay demonstrates that they took this responsibility seriously.

In Miller's view, the Puritans banished Williams because he read the Bible in a way that jeopardized the government of Massachusetts Bay and endangered their "errand into the wilderness." Specifically, Williams introduced a subversive element into Puritanism because of his "addiction" to what Puritans considered an "irresponsibly whimsical," even "criminally insane" method of biblical interpretation: typology.[58] Puritans feared the

---

[53] Miller, *New England Mind*, 477.

[54] John Winthrop, "A Modell of Christian Charity," in *The Puritans: A Sourcebook of Their Writings*, ed. Perry Miller and Thomas H. Johnson (New York: Harper & Row Publishers, 1963) 197.

[55] Winthrop, "Modell," 199.

[56] Miller, "Errand," 11.

[57] Ibid., 5.

[58] Miller, "An Essay in Interpretation," in vol. 7 of *Complete Writings*, 15, 22.

boundlessness of typological exegesis. As Michael McGiffert argued, Puritans thought that typology was "both distasteful and dangerous because it opened the door to subjective, visionary misreadings of the Word."[59] Typology invited exegetical anarchy into Puritan New England. Miller admitted that typological exegesis was not new with Williams and that interpreters of scripture had used it throughout church history. But Miller observed that typology had lost favor in Protestant circles in the seventeenth century. Williams's recovery of typology therefore secluded him from other Puritan exegetes. As Miller said, the Puritans of Massachusetts Bay believed that Williams's "resort to typology was a relapse into a fever which the Reformation believed it had nursed to health. He was a dog returning to the vomit of a decadent scholasticism."[60]

In its most common usage, this method of interpretation views events and persons in the Old Testament as "types" that symbolize events and persons in the New Testament. For instance, one who uses typology may understand the Old Testament story of Jonah being swallowed by a fish as a prefiguration of Christ's descent into hell. In this example, Jonah is a type or figure and Christ is the fulfilling antitype.[61] Without its New Testament antitype, the story of Jonah and the great fish lacks its full spiritual meaning. The typologist, therefore, interprets events and persons in the Old Testament as symbols that gain true meaning only when enlightened by New Testament antitypes that reveal their spiritual significance for the church.

Miller contended that Williams's typology was dangerous because it denied the continuity of a national covenant from the Old Testament times to seventeenth-century Boston, and thereby undermined the foundation of Puritan government. Much to the Puritans' consternation, Williams used typological exegesis to deny

---

[59] Michael McGiffert, "American Puritan Studies in the 1960s," *The William and Mary Quarterly* 27/1 (1970): 55.

[60] Miller, "An Essay in Interpretation," in vol. 7 of *Complete Writings*, 23.

[61] Morgan, "Miller's Williams," 514.

their use of Israel as a model for their alliance between church and state. Williams asserted that Israel was a type of Christ's church, not the secular state. Thus, after Christ's coming, Israel no longer stood as a government that could enforce religious belief. As its antitype, the church superseded Israel, transforming its former civil authority into the spiritual power of the church. Consequently, Miller surmised that Williams's typology destroyed the "organic descent from the state church of Jerusalem to the political bodies of church and state in Massachusetts."[62] According to Williams, Christ superseded the Old Testament and broke the continuity by which Puritans viewed Israel as a model for government. Since the coming of Christ, no "national church" could "claim to be in covenant with God," and no government had any authority over the religious conscience.[63] As Miller asserted, Williams believed that the Puritan use of Israel to justify their government in New England was "a prostitution of theology to social expediency."[64]

Given the typological attack on Puritan government, Miller thought it was no wonder that the Puritans banished Williams from their sight. Yet Miller concluded that Williams's typological radicalism did not end in the seventeenth century; rather, it secured his legacy for later American history. For Miller, Roger Williams remained relevant to the twentieth century not because he was a liberal prophet, but because he was a subversive biblicist who remains "today, if he be listened to, as serious a threat to any sort of 'establishment' as he was visibly to that constructed by the Puritans of Massachusetts Bay."[65]

Miller actually agreed with the liberal historians that Williams was a prophet, but in a different sense. That is, Williams was not a herald of the enlightened future, but he was a seventeenth-century Jeremiah who proclaimed divine judgment on what others saw as a

---

[62] Miller, "An Essay in Interpretation," in vol. 7 of *Complete Writings,* 17.

[63] Ibid., 18.

[64] Miller, *Contribution,* 28.

[65] Miller, "An Essay in Interpretation," in vol. 7 of *Complete Writings,* 6.

"righteous community."[66] As Edmund Morgan observed, Miller's Williams would have denied the sense of a "divine mission" that continued in the American mind long after Winthrop attributed it to New England.[67] His typological reasoning would have rejected an understanding of America in terms of Manifest Destiny or God's new Israel. As Morgan concluded, Williams's thought was "thrilling, noble, and seditious"; certainly, "Perry Miller and John Winthrop were both right in considering him a dangerous man."[68] Williams insisted that God had covenanted with only one nation in history: ancient Israel. Thus, Christ's appearance invalidated any nation's claims to be a chosen people in covenant with God. Only the church had fulfilled Israel's type, not any nation. Henceforth, no nation has received divine authorization to intervene in spiritual matters.[69]

Despite Miller's efforts to place Williams in his historical context, "Miller's Williams" was as isolated as the liberal Williams of Parrington and Ernst. While he demonstrated that Williams was a biblically-minded Puritan and not a secular liberal, Miller misunderstood Williams's thought in its seventeenth-century context. In Miller's view, typology dominated Williams's view of the Bible and made Williams a lone radical, separated from his Puritan contemporaries who disdained typology. Thus, similar to the image of the liberal prophet designed by Parrington and Ernst, Miller's Williams was an eccentric whose radical thought dramatically separated him from his intellectual milieu. Miller alleged that "Williams was so intense a Biblicist that he made little use, in his writings, of secondary sources, of the works of the Fathers, or of Protestant theologians."[70] Essentially, "Miller's Williams" was an individualist who "fought the fight for freedom by his own lights

---

[66] Miller, *Contribution*, 30.
[67] Morgan, "Miller's Williams," 522.
[68] Ibid., 523.
[69] Miller, *Contribution*, 54.
[70] Miller, "An Essay in Interpretation," in vol. 7 of *Complete Writings*, 14.

and not by anyone else's."[71] For Miller, Williams was an isolated radical who did not glean his unorthodox typological reading of scripture from predecessors or contemporaries. Instead, Miller attributed Williams's typological "addiction" to his "personality," claiming that Williams was a gentle soul whose personal "sweetness" forced him to resist "the notion of a brutal uniformity forced upon the church, and a dogmatic" method of biblical interpretation.[72]

III. WILLIAMS AND THE TYPOLOGICAL "ERRAND"

Perry Miller's assessment of Williams generated a significant conversation among Puritan scholars in the 1960s. While the majority of these historians did not focus exclusively on Roger Williams, they did seek to explore Miller's views on typology in Puritan New England. And, since Miller's description of typology pivoted on Williams, any reassessment of Puritan typology required a foray into this radical's controversial writings.[73] Perhaps the most important critic of Miller's understanding of Puritan typology was Sacvan Bercovitch. One of Bercovitch's primary concerns was to reassess Miller's errand thesis, recasting it into a typological framework.[74] Bercovitch agreed with Miller's thesis that

---

[71] Miller, *Contribution*, xiii.

[72] Miller, "An Essay in Interpretation," in vol. 7 of *Complete Writings*, 15.

[73] McGiffert, "American Puritan Studies," 55.

[74] Sacvan Bercovitch, "New England's Errand Reappraised," in *New Directions in American Intellectual History*, ed. John Higham and Paul K. Conkin (Baltimore: Johns Hopkins University Press, 1979) 85–104. Many scholars have attempted to probe the relationship between the works of Miller and Bercovitch. While several studies have described Bercovitch as an antagonist of Miller, a recent essay by Arne Delfs argues that Bercovitch's work was "not one more attack on, but rather a sophisticated defense of, Miller's coherent view of Puritanism." Delfs states that Bercovitch's typological critique of Miller "was an attempt to counter the mounting criticism of social historians" and others on Miller's work ("Anxieties of Influence: Perry Miller and Sacvan Bercovitch," *New England Quarterly* 70/4 [1997]: 602). Above all, Delfs contends that Bercovitch's typological reconstruction of Miller's errand thesis "has served to reconstruct

the Puritans came to America on a mission or "errand," seeking to form a society that would be a model for godly nations everywhere. Yet Bercovitch argued that Miller neglected the importance of biblical typology to the Puritan's mission in America. Accordingly, Bercovitch sought to recapture the importance of typology in Puritan thought, and this goal led him to reinterpret Miller's view of Roger Williams. Bercovitch pursued this reassessment of Williams in one of his earliest essays, "Typology in Puritan New England: The Williams-Cotton Controversy Reassessed."[75] In this essay, Bercovitch denied Miller's claim that typological exegesis necessarily conflicted with Puritan covenant theology. In addition, Bercovitch disagreed with Miller's belief that typology was an eccentric method of biblical interpretation that was mysteriously present in Williams's thought. In opposition to Miller, Bercovitch argued that typology was hardly an exegetical perversion that only radicals such as Williams used. To the contrary, typology pervaded "all branches of early American writing" and made a great

---

and defend Miller's Puritan work against the growing dissensus in American Studies and culture" (615). For other studies of the relation between the work of Miller and that of Bercovitch, see: David Harlan, "A People Blinded from Birth: American History According to Sacvan Bercovitch," *Journal of American History* 78/3 (December 1991): 949–71. Harlan argued that "Bercovitch has come not to honor Miller but to bury him; Bercovitch's interpretation of American Puritanism is not an extension and completion of Miller's work, but its denial and negation" (ibid., 952). See also Francis T. Butts, "The Myth of Perry Miller," *American Historical Review* 87/3 (1982): 665–94 (see especially 686–88); Philip Gura, "The Study of Colonial American Literature, 1966–1987: A Vade Mecum," *William and Mary Quarterly* 45/2 (1988): 305–41 (see especially 310–14); James Hoopes, "Art as History: Perry Miller's *New England Mind*," *American Quarterly* 34 (1982): 3–25 (see especially 16–20); Daniel Howe, "Descendants of Perry Miller," *American Quarterly* 34 (1982): 88–94; Ormond Seavey, "Sacvan Bercovitch and Perry Miller: Perricide Regained," *Studies in Puritan American Spirituality* 3 (1992): 149–64.

[75] Sacvan Bercovitch, "Typology in Puritan New England: The Williams-Cotton Controversy Reassessed," *American Quarterly* 19 (1967): 163–91. For a good, succinct summary of the correspondence between Williams and Cotton, see Larzer Ziff, *The Career of John Cotton: Puritanism and the American Experience* (Princeton: Princeton University Press, 1962) 266–68.

impression on Puritan culture.[76] Typology did not belong exclusively to the lunatic fringe; it was an essential part of the mainstream. In contrast to Miller, Bercovitch believed that typological exegesis contributed much to the "New England Mind," and that it even provided a crucial element in Puritans' understanding of themselves in a national covenant with God.

Regarding Williams, Bercovitch corrected Miller's conclusion that Williams's radicalism was due solely to his typological exegesis. Bercovitch argued that the debate between Williams and Cotton was "not a clash between a typologist and a Puritan, but an opposition between two different typological approaches."[77] By using their own brand of typology, Cotton and his colleagues asserted that God's Israel of the Old Testament was a type that found fulfillment in New England's Bible Commonwealth. Thus the Bay Colonists understood themselves as "the remnant that would inaugurate the millennium" by establishing a society that would be "a preview of the New Jerusalem" that would dawn in America.[78] Hence, Bercovitch argued that typology was an essential element of the Puritans' vision of their place in history, their "errand into the wilderness." Indeed, it was because of typology, not in spite of it, that Bay Puritans saw their Bible Commonwealth as God's new Israel. Typology provided the basis for the Puritans' sense of association with Israel. In Bercovitch's view, the Puritans used typology to envision their role in bringing God's kingdom to its historical climax in America. Bercovitch expanded his conception of typology in the Puritan mind and beyond in his book, *The American Jeremiad*. Here, Bercovitch reiterated that this typological errand was crucial to the American Puritans' uniqueness because it made it possible for them "to give the kingdom of God a local habitation and a name."[79] Furthermore,

---

[76] Bercovitch, "Typology in Puritan New England," 167–70.

[77] Ibid., 167.

[78] Sacvan Bercovitch, *The American Jeremiad* (Madison: University of Wisconsin Press, 1978) 42; idem, "Typology," 176.

[79] Bercovitch, *Jeremiad*, 40.

Bercovitch argued that this Puritan typological vision evolved into secular ideas of American exceptionalism and Manifest Destiny in the eighteenth and nineteenth centuries.

Bercovitch emphasized that the Puritans' typological understanding of themselves as God's "new Israel" in America was essential to their distinctiveness in the seventeenth century. Not surprisingly, European Protestants rejected the Puritans' fantastic claims to be the forerunners of the millennium on American shores. Such an idea was blasphemous to Protestants who stood outside the confines of Puritan New England. In this schema, Bercovitch claimed that Roger Williams was not the dangerous radical that Miller had described, but he was the voice of reason—a thoughtful Calvinist who "tried to argue the orthodoxy out of its strange, unique folly."[80] Thus, Miller and Bercovitch reached opposite conclusions regarding Williams's typology. Miller regarded it as radical and dangerous; Bercovitch called it conservative. In Bercovitch's view, the Puritans' typological errand was radical and strange while Williams spoke for the rest of Protestant Europe. He used his more conventional typological exegesis in an attempt to return Cotton and his colleagues to an orthodox understanding of scripture and a realistic understanding of themselves.[81] That is, Williams opposed the Bay Puritans' claims to be God's "new Israel." He reminded them that the Israelite nation was part of the Old Testament—a unique history relevant to the seventeenth century only as a spiritual guide and not as a model for civil governments. Thus New England's Puritan commonwealth was not Israel's antitype; Christ's spiritual kingdom was. Bercovitch concluded that, far from being radical, Williams's typological interpretation of scripture was conservative, traditional, and even traceable to such heralded Christian classics as Augustine's *Confessions*.[82]

---

[80] Ibid.
[81] Ibid.
[82] Ibid., 41.

Throughout the 1960s and 1970s, numerous scholars followed Bercovitch's attempt to reveal typology's importance to the Puritans' belief that they were God's chosen people in America.[83] This interest in Puritan typology influenced the way most interpreters came to view Roger Williams. Since Miller and Bercovitch, most studies of Williams have emphasized his typological interpretation of the Bible, arguing that typology provided Williams with his biblical defense of religious liberty. This emphasis on Williams's typology has remained, despite continuing disagreements concerning his intellectual background, personality, and the key to his overall thought. Yet, while most interpreters of Williams admitted that his typological exegesis was critical, they disagreed over how to characterize his typology. For instance, Jesper Rosenmeier argued that the dispute between Williams and Cotton stemmed from their fundamental disagreement about how to use typology in discerning the nature of Christ's incarnation.[84] In contrast, Richard Reinitz argued Williams's use of typology emerged from his understanding of the conscience.[85] In 1979, Clark

---

[83] The scholarly works that have made such claims for typology's legacy include: Sacvan Bercovitch, *The Puritan Origins of the American Self* (New Haven: Yale University Press, 1975); Ursula Brumm, *American Thought and Religious Typology*, trans. John Hoaglund (New Brunswick: Rutgers University Press, 1970); Mason I. Lowance, Jr., *The Language of Canaan: Metaphor and Symbol in New England from the Puritans to the Transcendentalists* (Cambridge: Harvard University Press, 1980); idem, "Typology and the New England Way: Cotton Mather and the Exegesis of Biblical Types," *Early American Literature* 4 (1969): 15–37; and Jesper Rosenmeier, "Veritas: The Sealing of the Promise," *Harvard Library Bulletin* 16 (1968): 26–37. For an important criticism of this viewpoint and a helpful bibliography, see Reiner Smolinski, "Israel Redivius: The Eschatological Limits of Puritan Typology in New England," *New England Quarterly* 63 (1990): 357–95.

[84] Jesper Rosenmeier, "The Image of Christ: The Typology of John Cotton" (Ph.D. diss., Harvard University, 1965); idem, "The Teacher and the Witness: John Cotton and Roger Williams," *William and Mary Quarterly* 25 (1968): 408–31.

[85] Richard Reinitz, "The Separatist Background of Roger Williams' Argument for Religious Toleration," in *Typology and Early American Literature*, ed.

Gilpin joined the fray, arguing that Williams's typological argument for religious freedom depended upon his "millenarian piety," his forward-looking anticipation of Christ's future kingdom.[86] Arguing in opposition to Gilpin, Crawford Leonard Allen asserted that Williams was primarily a backward-looking primitivist, not a millenarian, and that Williams's use of typology was part of this zeal to recover the purity of the New Testament church.[87] These studies demonstrate that, while many historians have regarded typology as Williams's most important biblical argument for religious freedom, they have reached conflicting conclusions on how to characterize his typology and its place in his thought.[88]

How may we assess these typological portraits of Williams's thought? I contend that the emphasis on Williams's typology has made a great contribution to our understanding of him in his Puritan context. Beginning with Miller, scholars showed that the Progressive historians had misunderstood Williams by neglecting the biblical character of his thought. But preoccupation with typological exegesis in early New England has its drawbacks. In recent years, studies have questioned the impact of typology on New England Puritanism, casting doubts on the view that the Puritans understood their migration to America in terms of a typologically motivated errand or mission.[89] Among the detractors,

---

Sacvan Bercovitch (Amherst: University of Massachusetts Press, 1972) 107–37; idem, "Symbolism and Freedom: The Use of Biblical Typology as an Argument for Religious Toleration in Seventeenth Century England and America" (Ph.D. diss., University of Rochester, 1967).

[86] Gilpin, *Millenarian Piety*, 107–108.

[87] Allen, "The Restauration of Zion," 7, 155–65.

[88] For instance, see Richard Reinitz, "The Typological Argument for Religious Toleration: The Separatist Tradition and Roger Williams," *Early American Literature* 5/4 (1970): 75; and Gilpin, *Millenarian Piety*, 108. Some major historians still consider typology not only central to Williams's biblicism, but to his thought as a whole. For example, see Noll et al., *Search for Christian America*, 36–37.

[89] Andrew Delbanco, "The Puritan Errand Re-Viewed," *Journal of American Studies* 18 (1984): 343–60. Theodore Dwight Bozeman, *To Live Ancient Lives: The Primitivist Dimension in Puritanism* (Chapel Hill: University of North

Andrew Delbanco suspects that scholars' attraction to typology in the 1960s and 1970s arose from the fact that scholarship during those years continually asked why America was in Vietnam. He suggests that interpreters such as Bercovitch had discovered in typology a "preposterous symbolism" upon which the Puritans constructed a national myth that evolved into the idea of American Manifest Destiny in the nineteenth century. Thus Delbanco argues that the scholarly preoccupation with Puritan typology was actually an effort to provide "a genealogical explanation for American arrogance."[90] Similarly, David Harlan argued that Bercovitch's typological studies rendered Puritanism as "a system of deception" that misled America about its exceptional place in the world. Harlan surmised that Bercovitch had worked "to counter the empty glare of Puritan mythology—a mythology that…had left America blinded from birth."[91] Furthermore, in his recent study of Puritan eschatological writings, Reiner Smolinski also has taken a skeptical view of Puritan typology, arguing that seventeenth-century Puritan texts did not substantiate the lofty claims of many critics for a typological errand.[92] While these scholars did not deny that the Puritans were typologists, they argued that historians since the 1960s have greatly exaggerated typology's importance to the New England Puritans' self-understanding.

If these reappraisals of Puritan typology have merit, what are the implications for our understanding of Williams? To be sure, some reassessment of Williams is needed because historians have continually explained Williams's arguments for religious liberty and the separation of church and state by attributing them to

---

Carolina Press, 1988); see especially chapter 3, "The Errand into the Wilderness Reconsidered," 81–119; see also idem, "Biblical Primitivism: An Approach to New England Puritanism," in *The American Quest for the Primitive Church*, ed. Richard T. Hughes (Urbana and Chicago: University of Illinois Press, 1988) 19–32.

[90] Delbanco, "Errand Re-Viewed," 352; see also idem, *The Puritan Ordeal*, 217.

[91] Harlan, "Blinded from Birth," 692.

[92] Smolinski, "Israel Redivius," 358ff.

typological exegesis. In what remains of this chapter, I argue that typology was only one dimension of his biblical interpretation. By focusing exclusively on typology, historians have overlooked the depth and breadth of his biblical conception of religious liberty.

IV. BEYOND TYPOLOGY:
THE PERSUASIVENESS OF BIBLICAL MODELS

By concentrating on Williams's typological interpretation, recent scholars have neglected some of his most crucial exegetical insights. The problem is that, while Williams certainly used typological exegesis, his most important biblical arguments were not typological. Instead, Williams often used a common interpretive method that E. Brooks Holifield calls "exemplary exegesis," or the literal application of biblical examples. According to this strategy, Puritans understood certain biblical episodes, persons, and actions as authoritative models that exemplified proper beliefs and practices in the seventeenth century. Types and biblical examples differed because "types pointed beyond themselves" to future spiritual truths, but "examples bore their meanings on the surface." Also, "the visible types were abolished when they found fulfillment in their Christian antitypes," while "examples endured as perpetual models for Christian behavior."[93] As did most of his Puritan contemporaries, Williams greatly depended on realistic models that he drew from scripture and applied to life in the seventeenth century.

Scholars have only recently begun to appreciate the importance of biblical models to Puritan New England. Despite the fact that historians have credited the Puritans with forming a Bible

---

[93] E. Brooks Holifield, *Era of Persuasion: American Thought and Culture 1521–1680*, ed. Lewis Perry, Twayne's American Thought and Culture (Boston: Twayne Publishers, 1989): 46. On the distinction between biblical examples and types, see also Gerald T. Sheppard, "Christian Interpretation of the Old Testament between Reformation and Modernity," in William Perkins, *A Commentary on Hebrews 11 (1609 Edition)*, ed. John H. Augustine, *Pilgrim Classic Commentaries* (New York: The Pilgrim Press, 1991) 62.

Commonwealth, few studies have focused on Puritan biblical interpretation.[94] Harry Stout recognizes the irony that even though "the Puritan experiment depended on the Bible," most Puritan scholarship "skims over the Bible generally in accounting for the rise of Puritanism and moves directly to landmark theological statements circulated among the civil and ecclesiastical hierarchy."[95] The exception to this neglect has been the great attention interpreters have given to Puritan typology. This emphasis on typology is debatable in light of recent questions about typology's importance as part of the Puritan "errand into the wilderness" and the belief in America's "manifest destiny."[96] Historians have begun to realize that biblical typology was only one facet of Puritan biblical interpretation and that Puritans were also captivated by biblical rules and models as authoritative guides in every aspect of their social and individual lives. As T. D. Bozeman demonstrated, the Puritans believed that post-apostolic history was mostly a time of "darkness and loss"—a period of continuing decline from the purity of the biblical age. The Puritans' desire to escape from the decline and return to the purity of biblical times motivated their attempt "to live ancient lives," adhering faithfully to the biblical

---

[94] Bozeman, *Ancient Lives*, 13.

[95] Stout, "Word and Order in Colonial New England," in *The Bible in America, Essays in Cultural History*, ed. Nathan O. Hatch and Mark A. Noll (New York/Oxford: Oxford University Press, 1986) 19. George Marsden has made a similar point about the work of Perry Miller, criticizing him for his lack of emphasis on Puritan exegesis. Marsden argued that "Miller almost never acknowledges the direct scriptural antecedents of specific Puritan concepts. The biblical arguments which were at the heart of nearly every Puritan statement are simply ignored." George M. Marsden, "Perry Miller's Rehabilitation of the Puritans: A Critique," *Church History* 39/1 (1970): 93. The few studies that do concentrate on some aspect of Puritan exegesis include John R. Knott, Jr., *The Sword of the Spirit: Puritan Responses to the Bible* (Chicago: University of Chicago Press, 1980); and John S. Coolidge, *The Pauline Renaissance in England: Puritanism and the Bible* (London: Clarendon Press, 1970).

[96] For example, see Smolinski, "Israel Redivius."

narrative.[97] In this Puritan intellectual milieu, "the biblical example" was "a pervasive tool of thought." Puritans sought biblical models to justify everything from the structure of proper worship "to precise employments of eyes, feet, and speech."[98]

The preeminence of biblical models in even the smallest details of life was well illustrated by English divine William Perkins, who exerted a tremendous influence on New England Puritanism. Perkins taught that a Christian should do nothing without some rule or model from scripture to justify the action. He described the Bible as a constant source of direction, cautioning that "we must therefore in all the actions of our lives and callings, take consultation with the word of God," constantly searching "for either general or particular rules, or at least for examples" to justify all of life's activities. Perkins even argued that anything done in life without some "warrant in the word for...direction" is sinful.[99]

---

[97] Bozeman, *Ancient Lives*, 15. See also Charles Hambrick-Stowe's claim that "the Puritans believed that since the close of the apostolic age God had ceased to work in 'extraordinary' ways" (*The Practice of Piety: Puritan Devotional Disciplines in Seventeenth-Century New England* [Chapel Hill: University of North Carolina Press, 1982] 95).

[98] Bozeman, *Ancient Lives*, 153. See also Stout, *The New England Soul, Preaching and Religious Culture in Colonial New England* (New York/Oxford: Oxford University Press, 1986) 8. Describing the centrality of scripture in seventeenth-century England, Christopher Hill pointed out that scripture was "accepted as the ultimate authority on economics and politics no less than on religion and morals" (Hill, *The English Bible and the Seventeenth-Century Revolution* [London: Penguin Press, 1993] 31). Similarly, Charles Cohen observes that "American Puritanism has undergone a historiographic makeover" in recent years. As part of this reassessment, American Puritanism is seen as "more biblically rooted" than historians once surmised. Cohen emphasizes the political importance of this biblical vision, commenting that "Puritans insisted that Scripture contained the first principles for morally organizing society" (Cohen, "The Post-Puritan Paradigm of Early American Religious History," *The William and Mary Quarterly* 54/4 [1997]: 701, 703).

[99] William Perkins, *A Commentary on Hebrews 11*, 29. For a further discussion of Perkins's use of biblical examples, see John H. Augustine, "'Notable Precedents': The Vocational Rhetoric of Exemplary Figures," in William Perkins's *A Commentary on Hebrews 11*, especially 11–16.

Roger Williams shared this desire to live according to biblical models. In his famous argument for religious liberty, types and figures did not obsess him; he also sought biblical models that exemplified scripture's condemnation of persecution and its advocacy of religious liberty for all. This book reveals important biblical models that comprised Williams's scriptural worldview. His struggle for religious liberty became a battle in which he and his opponents clashed over which biblical models were appropriate guides for contemporary politics and how to interpret them properly. The following chapters highlight Williams's use of models from the Old Testament, the Gospels, the life and letters of Paul, and the Revelation. Unlike that of orthodox Puritans, Williams's reading of biblical models revealed that Christendom was a violent, anti-Christian system of government and that political power should remain separate from spiritual issues, because any alliance between these two authorities always violated the conscience, resulting in strife and persecution. Consequently, Williams's Puritan contemporaries considered him radical not only because of his typological, figurative exegesis, but also because of his interpretation of relevant biblical models.

My examination of Williams's biblical interpretation, including his struggles with other important interpreters from the Reformation through the seventeenth century, contributes to our understanding of Williams's intellectual perspective. If we are finally to understand Williams's thought in its seventeenth-century context, we must realize the importance of his biblical interpretation and how his view of scripture conflicted with that of some interpreters while adopting and shaping that of others. To be sure, Williams did not formulate his radical arguments in exegetical isolation. It is romantic to picture Williams as an outcast, alone in an American wilderness, crafting his convictions using only the Bible, but a closer look at his writings yields a more realistic perspective. He was an educated and skillful interpreter of scripture. This picture of an educated Williams is beginning to emerge in the historiography. For instance, Staloff recently pointed out that New England ministers and magistrates were initially tolerant of Williams's opinions because he was one of them—a member of the "inner party" made up of "the Puritan thinking class." Therefore, because Williams was "a Puritan intellectual," the court's "public action against him would only further advertise divisions within the thinking class." As Williams's eventual banishment made clear, however, such toleration, even of intellectuals, had its limits.[100] As such, he was aware of the interpretive traditions that preceded and surrounded him, and he referenced various interpreters of the Bible and their biblical commentaries in his writings. The chapters that follow locate Williams's place on the exegetical map of the post-Reformation world. My focus is on the biblical passages that were most crucial to his arguments and how his interpretation of these texts compared with that of his important predecessors and contemporaries, including Protestant Reformers, Anabaptists, Baptists, Separatists, and Puritans. In assessing Williams's exegesis in context, I am seeking to discover the interpretive conclusions that were original with him, as well as the areas in which he adopted the biblical interpretation of others. The effort should yield a renewed appreciation for Williams's biblical acumen and a reassessment of the nature of his thought.

---

[100] Staloff, *American Thinking Class*, 20, 22. The most palpable way in which Massachusetts Puritans recognized Williams's scholarship was their publication of his polemic against the Quakers. See Williams, *George Fox Digg'd Out of His Burrowes*, in vol. 5 of *The Complete Writings of Roger Williams* (Providence: Narragansett Club Publications, 1872; reprint, New York: Russell & Russell, 1963). For treatments of Williams's orthodox argument against "enthusiasm," see: David S. Lovejoy, *Religious Enthusiasm in the New World: Heresy to Revolution* (Cambridge: Harvard University Press, 1985) 118–19. Idem, "Roger Williams and George Fox: The Arrogance of Self-Righteousness," *New England Quarterly* 66/2 (1993): 199–225.

CHAPTER 2

THE POLITICS OF THE
OLD TESTAMENT IN NEW ENGLAND

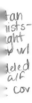

In colonial New England, a persuasive argument for religious liberty required a convincing interpretation of the Old Testament. Puritan colonists believed that they were in covenant with God, and modeled their political lives on the covenant between God and Israel in the Hebrew scriptures. Civil magistrates in Puritan New England drew upon the examples of God's chosen leaders such as Moses, David, and Josiah—rulers who guided Israel in religious purity and civil government in obedience to God's commands. In ancient Israel, those who rejected the religion were threats to the civil state. The Hebrew scriptures evaluated Israel's kings according to their ability to eliminate foreign religions from the state because religious difference was a civil crime, punishable by death. Israel waged war against foreign enemies—including the dreaded Philistines—in large part because they worshipped false gods.[1]

---

[1] Theodore Dwight Bozeman, *To Live Ancient Lives: The Primitivist Dimension in Puritanism* (Chapel Hill: University of North Carolina Press, 1988) 157. For the standard treatment of the Puritan idea of a national covenant, see Perry Miller, *The New England Mind: The Seventeenth Century* (Cambridge: Belknap Press of Harvard University Press, 1939) 463–91. As Harry Stout put it, "Israel's experience as recounted in the Old Testament" was a "model for [the Puritans'] own experience as God's 'New Israel'" in Massachusetts (*The New England Soul, Preaching and Religious Culture in Colonial New England* [New York/Oxford: Oxford University Press, 1986] 8). Many Puritans believed that the national covenant between God and Israel was transferred to New England due to England's disobedience. For instance, Thomas Hooker preached that "we may

Thus it is not surprising that the Puritans' imitation of Israel formed a society in which religious liberty was a threat to civil peace and spiritual purity. As did the kings of Israel, Puritan leaders used civil power to enforce religious observance because the success of the covenant depended upon the peoples' adherence to the national religion. Roger Williams thrust his argument for religious liberty in the face of the Puritans' lofty attempts to duplicate Israel's government in the New World. In the process of challenging the Puritans' New Israel, Williams rejected their interpretation of the Old Testament and asserted a radical vision of the Hebrew scriptures' importance to the political world.

Williams was just as serious as his Puritan foes were about upholding biblical authority and interpreting the Bible properly. To be sure, Williams was a radical, but he was a biblical radical, and that made him even more dangerous to the Puritan settlements than he would have been if he had rejected the Bible altogether. Williams's attacks on the Puritans' alliance of church and state were biblical assaults. He challenged the Puritans' political organization in the biblical arena, striking at the heart of their most sacred authority. Williams's biblical attack on the Puritan "Bible Commonwealths" was multifaceted, encompassing a variety of biblical texts and themes. His challenge to the Puritan interpretation of the Old Testament deserves particular scrutiny because it held immense implications for politics in colonial New England. My purpose in this chapter is to assess Williams's radical

---

say with Phineha's wife, I Sam. 4.22: '[The] glory is departed from Israel.' So glory is departed from England; for England hath seen her best days, and the reward of sin is coming on apace; for God is packing up of his gospel.... God begins to ship away his Noahs, which prophesied and foretold that destruction was near; and God makes account that New England shall be a refuge for his Noahs and his Lots, a rock and a shelter for his righteous ones to run unto" (*The Danger of Desertion*, in *Thomas Hooker: Writings in England and Holland, 1626–1633*, ed. George H. Williams et al. [Cambridge: Harvard University Press, 1975] 245–46). See also Alan Heimert and Andrew Delbanco, eds., *The Puritans in America: A Narrative Anthology* (Cambridge: Harvard University Press, 1985) 62, 64; Bozeman, *Ancient Lives*, 194.

view of the Old Testament's relationship to seventeenth-century politics. As did his Puritan opponents, Williams believed that God's revelation in the Hebrew scriptures encompassed all of life, including the proper ordering of the political sphere. The problem, as Williams saw it, was that his adversaries' misreading of the Old Testament led to an alliance of church and state that promoted violence against religious outsiders who did not accept the state's official religion.

This chapter will surprise many who have assumed that Williams had little use for the Old Testament—especially when discussing political issues such as the relationship between church and state. In their concentration on Williams's typology, many scholars concluded that Williams's view of the Old Testament was primarily (or even exclusively) typological—that he saw the Old Testament as a book of figures that had only spiritual, not political, relevance for contemporary life. These studies provide a misleadingly narrow view of Williams's thought. Critics argue that, while the Puritan experiment rested on a broad overview of scripture that included both the Hebrew Bible and the early Christian scriptures, Williams was an eccentric, narrow-minded radical who dismissed the Old Testament's political relevance altogether. Since Perry Miller, these interpreters have assumed that Williams drew a strong distinction between the authority of the two Testaments, accepting the New and relegating the Old to a collection of spiritual types and outdated history.[2] A clear statement of this view comes from C. L. Allen, who argued that Williams differed from the Puritans in his biblical interpretation

---

[2] Before Perry Miller, A. S. P. Woodhouse had briefly interpreted Williams along these lines in 1938. See A. S. P. Woodhouse, ed., *Puritanism and Liberty*, 2nd ed. (Chicago: University of Chicago Press, 1974) 67. However, Miller expanded and popularized this interpretation. (See Miller, "Roger Williams: An Essay in Interpretation," in vol. 7 of *The Complete Writings of Roger Williams* [New York: Russell & Russell, 1963] 11). Edmund Morgan repeated Miller's assessment of Williams's typology. (See Morgan, *Roger Williams: The Church and the State* [New York: Harcourt Brace, 1967] 91–92).

because, unlike them, he was "insistent on confining every appeal for scriptural authority or precedent to the New Testament."[3]

Such judgments of Williams's thought neglect the depth and breadth of his biblical interpretation. Most interpretations of Williams suggest that his arguments for religious liberty rested on more narrow biblical foundations than those of his Puritan opponents. By assuming that Williams avoided the Old Testament and sought to downplay its authority, many studies imply that the Old Testament was a problem for Williams that he attempted to explain away as a collection of symbols and figures that had lost all political relevance. In challenging this influential view of Williams's thought, I argue that Williams made ample use of the Old Testament in making his case for religious liberty. By questioning Williams's respect for the Old Testament's relevance to political realities, scholars have overlooked Williams's biblical acumen, leaving the impression that his biblically constructed foundations for religious liberty were unsteady and one-dimensional. This

---

[3] Crawford Leonard Allen, "'The Restauration of Zion': Roger Williams and the Quest for the Primitive Church" (Ph.D. diss., University of Iowa, 1984) 169; see also idem, "Roger Williams and 'The Restauration of Zion,'" in *The American Quest for the Primitive Church,* ed. Richard T. Hughes (Urbana and Chicago: University of Illinois Press, 1988) 33–68. For a further discussion of the issue of New Testament primitivism as it regards Williams, see E. Brooks Holifield's response to Allen and Bozeman in E. Brooks Holifield and Sidney E. Mead, "Puritan and Enlightenment Primitivism: A Response," in *The American Quest for the Primitive Church,* ed. Richard T. Hughes (Urbana and Chicago: University of Illinois Press, 1988) 69–73. Alan Heimert put the most emphasis on Williams's neglect of the Old Testament. Heimert argued that "the most significant of Williams' arguments...was that any and *all relevance* of the Old Testament, its forms, ceremonies, and institutions, was abrogated with the coming of Christ." Heimert argued that, "in Williams' mind *the whole of* the Old Testament was to be read as 'types,' and *none of its exemplary character persisted into the Christian era*" (Heimert and Delbanco, eds., *The Puritans in America,* 197, 199, emphasis added.) See also Christopher Hill's comment that "Williams saw the Old Testament as a historical document, to be expounded 'typologically'" (*The English Bible and the Seventeenth-Century Revolution* [London: Penguin Press, 1993], 31) 75.

chapter contends that Williams embraced the political importance of the Old Testament. Arguing against Puritans who lived by biblical precedent, Williams sought to realign their view of scripture with his contention that religious liberty had stronger biblical foundations than did religious persecution, and that these foundations encompassed all of scripture—the Old Testament no less than the New.

Unlike his adversaries, however, Williams did not focus on the passages in which the ancient Hebrews governed themselves through national covenants with God. As Williams recognized, the Old Testament is not exclusively a narrative of conquest that depicts the dominance of Israel's kings over pagan nations and the victories of David, Solomon, and Josiah. Much of the Old Testament describes eras of defeat and exile when God's people were in bondage to foreign rulers and Israel's national covenant was violated and powerless. Williams argued that these passages closely resembled the situation of the people of God since the coming of Christ. Williams recognized that the New Testament described God's people in control of churches, not civil states. In contrast to God's rule through kings in the Old Testament, God's great leaders in the New Testament were humble disciples, leaders in the church, not worldly kings and emperors. Indeed, Williams pointed out that, in the New Testament, God's people were often enemies of the state. The supreme example was Jesus, who was prosecuted as a criminal and executed by the Roman Empire. In Williams's view, from the New Testament forward, civil states were secular, even pagan institutions that had no divine covenants to guide them. In these new circumstances, the Old Testament's relevance to politics was limited to passages that concerned the people of God in bondage to pagan governments.

Concentrating on Old Testament narratives that depicted God's people in servitude to pagan rulers, Williams discovered some surprising biblical examples that were relevant to the political scene of his day. First, Williams praised pagan rulers who provided good examples of how civil governments ought to deal with religion in their domains. One such ruler was the Persian King

Artaxerxes (Ezra 7), whom Williams exalted as a model king. In the face of the so-called Christian rulers of the seventeenth century, Williams praised Artaxerxes, arguing that this pagan king exemplified a commitment to religious liberty that the contemporary governments of Christendom sorely needed to emulate. Second, Williams drew narratives from the Old Testament that exemplified the evils of persecuting states, including the account of Nebuchadnezzar and God's three faithful witnesses in the fiery furnace (Daniel 3) and the story of Ahab, Jezebel, and Naboth's vineyard (1 Kings 21). In his interpretation of these texts, Williams demonstrated that the Old Testament joined the New in advocating religious freedom in the state and in condemning the persecution that resulted when nations interfered with religious matters.

I. OLD TESTAMENT ISRAEL AND NEW ENGLAND POLITICS

Williams contested Puritan politics in his opposition to the "Modell of Church and Civil Power," one of the earliest statements on the relationship between church and state in Massachusetts. The "Modell" was written by a group of ministers who were concerned about Williams's influence in the Massachusetts Bay Colony in the 1630s.[4] These authors justified the government of the Colony by using terms drawn from the "national covenant" between God and Israel in the Old Testament. They gave particular attention to the "kings of Israel," carefully stipulating that these ancient figures were not symbolic "types of Christ," but were realistic models for "civil magistrates" that remained "exemplary to all Christians."[5] As such, the leaders of Israel in the Old Testament became

---

[4] Robert Francis Scholz, "'The Reverend Elders': Faith, Fellowship and Politics in the Ministerial Community of Massachusetts Bay, 1630–1710" (Ph.D. diss., University of Minnesota, 1966) 38–64. See also Bozeman, *Ancient Lives,* 169, 172.

[5] "A Modell of Church and Civil Power," in vol. 3 of *The Complete Writings of Roger Williams* (New York: Russell & Russell, 1963) 312; Bozeman, *Ancient Lives,* 157.

authoritative guides for the leaders of the Bay Colony. This biblical guideline for civil officers extended to legislative tasks, where Massachusetts's magistrates could support only those "civil laws" that "either are expressed in the word of God in Moses' Judicialls" or could be deduced "from the Word of God."[6]

In the Puritans' view, the dreaded alternative to godly rule in the state was political anarchy and religious chaos. To make this point, the "Modell" referred to the Old Testament prophet Azariah, who advised King Asa to cleanse the land of false religions and thereby avoid the perils that Israel had suffered in the past. Azariah reminded King Asa that:

> For a long time Israel was without the true God, and without a teaching priest, and without law; but when in their distress they turned to the LORD, the God of Israel, and sought him, he was found by them. In those times it was not safe for anyone to go or come, for great disturbances afflicted all the inhabitants of the lands. They were broken in pieces, nation against nation and city against city (2 Chr 15:3–6, NRSV).[7]

The prophet Azariah's warning that the lack of proper worship had led to civil chaos in the past aroused King Asa to prevent this tragic situation from recurring. Encouraged by Azariah's inspired words, Asa destroyed the idols of the land and strictly enforced compliance to Yahweh worship in the nation. Because Asa enacted these religious reforms, the Chronicler praised him as a king in the Davidic line who "did what was good and right in the sight of the Lord his God" (2 Chr 14:2, NRSV).

---

[6] "Modell of Church," in vol. 3 of *Complete Writings*, 254. The authors of the "Modell" used the example of Artaxerxes in Ezra 7 to make this claim. Their full use of this passage follows in this chapter.

[7] See "Modell of Church," in vol. 3 of *Complete Writings*, 247.

The Puritans of Massachusetts Bay shared this admiration of King Asa. Because he enforced compliance to true religion in the civil sphere, refusing to tolerate religious error in his domain, Asa became one of many examples of a good ruler that the Puritans took from the Old Testament. Impressed by biblical leaders such as Asa, the authors of the "Modell" held magistrates responsible "to forbid all idolatrous and corrupt assemblies" in Massachusetts.[8] As the prophet Azariah had warned Asa, the authors of the "Modell" warned their magistrates that "tolerating many religions in a state" would not only corrupt the churches, it would also "dissolve the continuity of the state."[9] In the seventeenth century, most people assumed that an official, state-supported church provided the uniform religious and moral foundation that ensured the peace and order of society. To such a political theory, the permission of diverse religions in the state was sheer madness because religious diversity would lead to political and moral divisions and civil peace would degenerate into chaos. These Puritan divines emphasized that religious diversity would be especially detrimental to the New England Way because, to a greater extent than any other commonwealth, the Bay Colony's "walls are made of the stones of the churches." Religious diversity would also detract from a primary reason that they had left England to travel to America, which was "to enjoy the pure ordinances" of the church.[10] Puritans feared that the presence of "false" religions in the commonwealth would lead many astray and disrupt the purity of worship in the Bay Colony. Thus, drawing from many examples of kings from the Old Testament, the "Modell" warned that, like Israel, Massachusetts Bay must enforce religious purity, for spiritual diversity caused civil disruption.[11]

---

[8] Ibid., 278.

[9] Ibid., 279.

[10] Ibid.

[11] The example of Asa is but one illustration of New England Puritans' uses of Old Testament leaders to exemplify the magistrate's duty to suppress false religion. In another vivid example, John Cotton cited the passage in which Moses and the sons of Levi massacred three thousand Israelites in one day

Roger Williams took the Puritan "Modell of Church and Civil Power" so seriously that he devoted 204 pages to printing and refuting it in his *Bloudy Tenent*.[12] The "Modell" provided Williams with much to dispute, including the idea that he found most dangerous: that magistrates have the authority "to reform things in the worship of God in a Church corrupted, and to establish the pure worship of God, defending the same by the power of the sword."[13] Much to Williams's dismay, the "Modell" argued that religious uniformity was a vital element of public life, for the "civil peace cannot stand...where religion is corrupted."[14] Because of these claims, Williams believed that the "Modell" was a violent document—a clear articulation of "the bloody doctrine of persecution for cause of conscience."[15] In his typically explicit imagery, Williams remarked that the biblical arguments of the "Modell" were "poisoned daggers" that stabbed at the "tender heart" of peace.[16] He also recognized that, in most cases, the "Modell" drew its biblical daggers from the Old Testament. In their attempts to imitate Israel, the Bay Colony's ministers were not satisfied with spiritual power. They demanded a civil "arm of flesh" that would enforce religious laws in the commonwealth.[17] But New England

---

because of their idolatrous worship (see Exodus 32:25–28). (John Cotton, *An Abstract of the Lawes of New England*, in *John Cotton: The New England Way*, ed. Sacvan Bercovitch [New York: AMS Press, 1983] 3). In keeping with Moses' example, Cotton favored the death penalty for blasphemy, atheism, idolatry, witchcraft, heresy, and other religious violations (12).

[12] "Modell of Church," in vol. 3 of *Complete Writings*, 221–425.

[13] Ibid., 311–12.

[14] Ibid., 247.

[15] Williams, *The Bloudy Tenent, of Persecution, for Cause of Conscience, discussed, in A Conference Betweene Truth and Peace*, in vol. 3 of *Complete Writings*, 221.

[16] Ibid.

[17] Williams linked this Puritan desire for civil power with the example of the Israelites, who rejected God's rule through the prophetic word and demanded that God give them a king like the other nations. Williams pointed out that God, motivated by "his anger" at the Israelites, conceded and gave them King Saul (1 Samuel 8) (Williams, *Bloudy Tenent*, in vol. 3 of *Complete Writings*,

was not ancient Israel, and Williams used his typological argument to clarify this point.

Williams rejected the Puritans' grandiose claims for Israel's centrality in their political theory. In response, he argued that Israel was a symbolic type, not a realistic example.[18] Since Israel was a type, it found its fulfillment not in political structures in seventeenth-century Massachusetts or England, but in the advent of Jesus Christ. As a type, Israel's national covenant with God in the Old Testament pointed toward the spiritual government of the church through Christ.[19] Williams contended that to neglect the typological status of Israel was to deny Christ. As Williams expressed it, the "Modell" awakens "Moses from his unknown grave, and denies Jesus yet to have seen the earth."[20] By labeling Israel and its kings as types rather than examples, Williams dismissed their relevance to seventeenth-century politics.

The basis for Williams's typological interpretation of Israel and its kings was his conviction that God's covenant with Israel was a unique phenomenon in world history. Williams repeatedly pointed out "the difference of the people of Israel and all other peoples." He believed that the Israel of the Old Testament was "unparalleled and

---

262). Williams's insertion of this passage indicates that he doubted that God ever truly advocated the use of civil power to enforce religious orthodoxy. That is, even in the case of Israel, perhaps the addition of a political state to the Israelite nation originated in God's acting out in anger against the Israelites for their disbelief. But Williams did not develop this position thoroughly. Like Williams, John Goodwin pointed out that it was not "the order or command of God, that there should be any King over Israel, but he was highly offended with the People for desiring it" (*Anti-Cavalierisme*, in vol. 2 of *Tracts on Liberty in the Puritan Revolution, 1638–1647*, ed. William Haller [New York: Columbia University Press, 1934] 225.

[18] For a good explanation of the Puritan distinction between biblical types and biblical examples, see E. Brooks Holifield, *Era of Persuasion: American Thought and Culture, 1521–1680*, ed. Lewis Perry, Twayne's American Thought and Culture (Boston: Twayne Publishers, 1989) 46.

[19] Williams, *Bloudy Tenent*, in vol. 3 of *Complete Writings*, 322; see also 328.

[20] Ibid., 221.

No evidence of biblical cov b/t God and states → claiming favor is done illegit. → Israel unmatched

unmatchable."[21] After Israel, God had no chosen nations because scripture contained no evidence that God made any other covenants with subsequent governments.[22] In the absence of biblical evidence for national covenants after Israel, Williams concluded that nations claiming God's favor did so illegitimately and arrogantly.

The nations that proclaimed themselves chosen by God were, in Williams's view, the chief perpetrators of religious violence in the seventeenth century. Williams's concern was that alliances of church and state departed from Christianity to form empires of Christendom, bearing the tragic fruits of persecution and hypocrisy. Persecution was the means whereby Christendom forcibly "converted" its citizens and hypocrisy was the result. "Converts" therefore entered Christendom's established churches because they feared prosecution by the magistrates, not because they responded to the spiritual conviction of Christ in their hearts.[23] Williams believed that these forced conversions of "profane, impenitent, and unregenerate persons" were a "profanation of the holy name and holy ordinances of the Lord." Moreover, for those who refused to feign allegiance to the established religion, a sentence of banishment or death awaited. Based on these observations, Williams argued that the dreaded results of this improper imitation of Israel in the civil state were the "slaughters of both men and women"

---

[21] Ibid., 323. For a Separatist thinker who agreed with Williams on this point, see Robert Cushman, *Reasons & Considerations Touching the Lawfulness of Removing out of England into the Parts of America*, in *Mourt's Relation or Journal of the Plantation at Plymouth by William Bradford and Edward Winslow*, ed. Henry Martyn Dexter (New York: Garrett Press, 1969) 145. See also Heimert and Delbanco, eds., *The Puritans in America*, 42. However, Separatists were not agreed on this interpretation. For a Separatist interpretation of the Pilgrim migration in parallel with the experiences of ancient Israel, see William Bradford, *Of Plymouth Plantation, 1620–1647*, ed. Samuel Eliot Morison (New York: Alfred A. Knopf, 1953) 62–63.

[22] *Bloudy Tenent*, in vol. 3 of *Copmlete Writings*, 324.

[23] Ibid., 329.

through "the insurrections and civil wars about religion and conscience."[24]

II. ARTAXERXES OF PERSIA:
EXEMPLAR OF RELIGIOUS LIBERTY IN THE OLD TESTAMENT

Many have concluded that Williams denied the Old Testament any political relevance. That is a mistake. While Williams argued that Israel and its kings were not fit for political imitation, he believed that other Old Testament figures served as admirable models for civil rulers, especially amid the chaos of religious violence that plagued the seventeenth century. He found one such example in the Persian king, Artaxerxes, who occupied a seemingly minor place in the Old Testament. Williams discussed this king in two of his writings, and Artaxerxes' relevance to politics became a significant point of contention between Williams and his opponents on issues of religious liberty and the proper relationship between church and state.

Williams first discussed this Persian ruler in *The Bloudy Tenent of Persecution* (1644), where he refuted an argument in the "Modell of Church and Civil Power." Williams later considered Artaxerxes in his *Examiner Defended* (1652), which he published in defense of a treatise titled *Zeal Examined*.[25] An anonymous English pamphleteer had published *Zeal Examined* to proclaim that those who advocated religious liberty were sane, thoughtful, and courageous individuals—not the zealous and irrational fanatics that their accusers made them out to be.[26] In both *The Bloudy Tenent* and *The*

---

[24] Ibid., 330.

[25] *Zeal Examined: or, A Discourse for Liberty of Conscience in Matters of Religion* (London: G. D. for Giles Calvert, 1652).

[26] When *Zeal Examined* faced opposition from another anonymous tract titled *The Examiner Examined,* which advocated church establishment and the authority of the magistrate in religious affairs, Williams responded with *The Examiner Defended in a Fair and Sober Answer* (in vol. 7 of *Complete Writings*). For additional background information on *The Examiner Defended,* see Perry Miller's introduction in Williams, *The Examiner Defended,* 192–94. See also

Examiner Defended, Williams's interpretation of Artaxerxes expressed his conviction that the Old Testament rejected the state persecution of religious outsiders.

Williams's disagreement with his opponents over how to interpret Artaxerxes took its point of departure from Ezra 7. This text concerns the period following Persia's defeat of Babylon, which ended Israelite captivity in Babylonian territories. Chapter seven contains a letter that the Persian king Artaxerxes wrote to Ezra, the priest and scribe of the Lord. This letter commissioned Ezra to Jerusalem and proclaimed that any Israelites who wanted to return with him could do so. King Artaxerxes even supported Ezra and his fellow travelers by sending money to buy offerings for their worship in the temple. In a further attempt to appease Ezra's God, the Persian king declared that whatever the Lord decreed should "be done with zeal" so that punishment would not "come upon the realm of the king and his heirs" (Ezra 7:23, NRSV). In response to Artaxerxes' blessings, Ezra praised God for motivating the king to act so graciously on behalf of the Israelites.

This biblical ruler who proclaimed that God's will should be done in the civil sphere fit well with the Puritan agenda in Massachusetts Bay. Accordingly, in the "Modell of Church and Civil Power," Puritan ministers seized the example of Artaxerxes, using his decree to support their argument that magistrates should supervise religion in their territories.[27] In obedience to what they called the "Law of Artaxerxes," Puritan divines ruled that civil officers were "to publish and declare, establish and ratify such Laws and Ordinances as Christ hath appointed in his Word for the well ordering of Church affairs."[28]

Gaustad, *Liberty of Conscience: Roger Williams in America,* ed. Mark A. Noll and Nathan O. Hatch, Library of Religious Biography (Grand Rapids: William B. Eerdmans Publishing, 1991) 110–12.

[27] "Modell of Church," in vol. 3 of *Complete Writings,* 261.

[28] Ibid. The use of Artaxerxes to support the argument for a national church was not unique to the "Modell." For instance, see the complaint of Henry Robinson, *Liberty of Conscience,* in Haller, vol. 3 of *Tracts on Liberty,* 143–44.

In interpreting Artaxerxes as a model for magistrates, Puritans placed this Persian king alongside great rulers of Israel who were models for contemporary magistrates because they enforced Yahweh worship while outlawing paganism. In comparison, Artaxerxes was a good model because he proclaimed that God's will be accomplished in his kingdom (Ezra 7:23). The authors of the "Modell" did not mind that Artaxerxes was a foreign ruler whose authority did not derive from God's national covenant with Israel. He enforced the worship of the Lord in the civil realm, just as the Puritans attempted to do in Massachusetts Bay, and therefore Artaxerxes fit the Puritan agenda too well for the authors of the "Modell" to ignore him, regardless of his foreign and pagan lineage. The authors of the "Modell" praised any Old Testament king, either pagan or godly, who commanded his subjects to obey the Lord. Thus, when he enforced God's decrees in the civil sphere, the pagan Artaxerxes provided just as useful a model for Puritans as the godly Asa.

Williams objected to this use of Artaxerxes. Unlike his opponents, Williams believed that it was essential to maintain the distinction between these two kinds of rulers. He emphasized that Artaxerxes was not one of God's chosen kings of Israel. Artaxerxes was no Asa. On the contrary, Artaxerxes was a Persian king who ruled God's people after the exile. No longer did the Israelites control their own government as they had during the days of the Davidic theocracy. Instead, they "were as lambs and sheep in the jaws of the lion" who took orders from "devouring tyrants of the world" such as Artaxerxes, "a stranger" to the Lord and "a Gentile idolater" who "held the people of God in slavery."[29] Williams refused to equate such a ruler with God's chosen rulers of Israel, who had a unique authority to rule in both civil and religious jurisdictions. Pagan rulers such as Artaxerxes did not have religious

---

[29] Williams, *Bloudy Tenent*, in vol. 3 of *Complete Writings*, 265; idem, *Examiner Defended*, in vol. 7 of *Complete Writings*, 227.

authority because they did not share in God's national covenant with Israel.[30]

While he insisted that pagan rulers set poor spiritual examples, Williams acknowledged that they could still be good political models. He agreed with the Puritans that Artaxerxes was a good political example. Yet, while the Puritans praised Artaxerxes despite his paganism, Williams recommended him because of it. That is, Williams believed that Artaxerxes was a relevant model for political rulers precisely because he was *not* a godly king who shared in God's national covenant with Israel. As Williams had explained, God's chosen rulers in Israel were types that found fulfillment in Christ, and thus were not patterns for political rule in succeeding eras. Since Artaxerxes was not one of Israel's anointed rulers, he was not a type of Christ.[31] He was simply a pagan king, similar to countless others who ruled from the Old Testament era to the seventeenth century. This meant that Artaxerxes, if he ruled justly, could serve as a biblical model to guide political rulers throughout history. Williams determined that Artaxerxes did rule justly, exemplifying traits that political rulers of all eras should imitate. Thus, in opposition to the Puritan imitation of Israel, Williams made the ironic point that the pagan king Artaxerxes was more politically relevant to the seventeenth century than were any of Israel's great rulers.

Williams admired Artaxerxes because he did not command his subjects to follow the state's official religion. Here Williams disagreed with the Puritan exegesis of Ezra 7. In their "Modell of Church and Civil Power," Puritan divines emphasized Artaxerxes' declaration that whatever God commands should "be done with zeal." Puritans read this command as an endorsement of the magistrate's responsibility to see that God's will is accomplished (see Ezra 7:23).[32] Williams opposed this interpretation by referring to the overall context of this statement. Earlier in the narrative,

---

[30] Williams, *Bloudy Tenent,* in vol. 3 of *Complete Writings,* 265.

[31] Ibid.

[32] "Modell of Church," in vol. 3 of *Complete Writings,* 261.

Artaxerxes had declared that all Jews were free to return to Jerusalem with Ezra (cf. Ezra 7:13). Williams noted that this was not "a positive command that any of the Jews *should* go" to Jerusalem, nor did Artaxerxes command that each Jew "*should* practice his own worship" by following the Lord's guidelines.[33] Artaxerxes did not force the Jews to worship God in Jerusalem. He only granted religious freedom to the Jews, allowing them to worship their Lord and to return home with Ezra *if* they wished to do so. From this perspective, Williams argued that "the law of Artaxerxes was an absolute Law of Toleration of the Jews' conscience," and not a biblical command for magistrates to enforce religious conformity.[34]

Artaxerxes' advocacy of religious liberty was even more amazing because, in allowing the Jews to worship as they chose, this Persian king extended liberty to a religion that was "vastly differing from and opposite to his" own.[35] Williams contrasted this liberating attitude of Artaxerxes with the civil enforcers of orthodoxy in England and New England. Unlike the so-called Christian rulers in the seventeenth century, Artaxerxes did not force his own religion on his citizens even though he believed it "to be the only true one."[36]

Williams attributed Artaxerxes' liberating decree not to the goodness of this Persian ruler, but to the providence of God. Although he rejoiced that Artaxerxes exemplified what a good king should be, Williams did not lose sight of Artaxerxes' paganism. Artaxerxes was a just king, but he was not a godly king. His remarkable proclamation of religious liberty demonstrated that God occasionally opened "the hearts of tyrants," prompting them "greatly to favor and further" God's people.[37] Because he allowed

---

[33] Williams, *Bloudy Tenent,* in vol. 3 of *Complete Writings,* 265; emphasis added.

[34] Williams, *Examiner Defended,* in vol. 7 of *Complete Writings,* 276.

[35] Ibid.

[36] Ibid., 227.

[37] Williams, *Bloudy Tenent,* in vol. 3 of *Complete Writings,* 265.

the Jews their religious freedom, Artaxerxes joined the chorus of other hostile rulers in the Old Testament who extended some mercy to the Israelites. Williams believed that such gracious acts issued not from piety, but from fear. Pagan kings acted mercifully toward God's people not because they wanted to please God, but because they feared the calamities that might result from displeasing him. A survey of the Old Testament proved to Williams that the "terrors and convictions of an affrighted conscience" occasionally motivated rulers such as Pharaoh, Nebuchadnezzar, Cyrus, Darius, and Artaxerxes to issue "wonderful decrees" on behalf of the Jews and their God.[38] Nevertheless, Williams did not quibble over motivations. Even if these Old Testament tyrants acted out of fear, Williams praised them for their occasional acts of mercy, declaring that they provided great examples for rulers in the seventeenth century.

This scenario supported Williams's conviction that the biblical God took the side of the persecuted against their persecutors. Artaxerxes advocated religious freedom not because of any sense of charity, but because he feared a God who demanded the freedom of his people. Williams believed that this was not an isolated case, but a consistent biblical principle that he found in both Testaments. In the Old Testament, God opposed religious persecution through rulers such as Artaxerxes. Similarly, in the New Testament, Williams found that the "doctrine of Christ" was "lamentably contrary" to "the doctrine of persecution for cause of conscience."[39]

In sum, through his exegesis of Artaxerxes, Williams defined an important example of the political applicability of the Old Testament to the seventeenth century. As a pagan king who ruled justly, Artaxerxes was relevant to the period after the extinction of Israel's national covenant—a time when all governments were

---

[38] Nevertheless, Williams repeatedly noted that this did not grant to these tyrants "the spiritual crown of governing the worship of God, and the conscience of [their] people." Williams, *Bloudy Tenent*, in vol. 3 of *Complete Writings*, 266; idem, *Examiner Defended*, in vol. 7 of *Complete Writings*, 227.

[39] Williams, *Bloudy Tenent*, in vol. 3 of *Complete Writings*, 425.

pagan. After the national covenant of the Old Testament, no political entities could rightly claim divine sanction. In the new situation in which all political institutions were secular, Williams selected Old Testament narratives that described the existence of the people of God under hostile rule. Williams believed that these passages better reflected the political situation of the post-biblical era than did the narratives of the Israelite covenant, which depicted God's people in control of their civil governments. In this political context in which all governments were worldly rather than godly, Williams found much to admire in the merciful acts of pagan kings such as Artaxerxes, who did not persecute differing religions but allowed them the freedom to exist in his empire.

Williams charged the governments of his day to abandon their adherence to the national covenant of Israel and to explore alternate passages from the Old Testament that represented pagan rulers who acted mercifully to God's people. In his preference for such passages, Williams argued that the Puritan reading of the Old Testament was not only violent; it was also obsolete. In adhering to the models of such political rulers as Asa, Massachusetts Bay clung to an outdated reading of the Old Testament. Asa was no longer relevant to politics, but Artaxerxes was. Because this Persian king "gave free liberty of conscience to" his subjects, he had much to teach the Winthrops, Cottons, and Parliaments of the world.[40] Williams hoped that all civil leaders would reread the Old Testament, looking past Israelite kings such as Asa and David to follow Artaxerxes and "take off the yokes of violence, and permit

---

[40] Williams, *Examiner Defended*, in vol. 7 of *Complete Writings*, 227. An anonymous work, probably written by Williams, cited Artaxerxes as a "Scripture example" that Parliament would do well to follow. Here, the author described Artaxerxes as a figure that God used to protect his people in the context of a hostile political situation, thus demonstrating "the Lord's jealousy over his peoples' liberties" (*A Paraenetick, or, Humble Addresse to the Parliament and Assembly for (Not Loose, But) Christian Libertie* [London: Matthew Simmons for Henry Overton, 1644] 4).

(at least) the consciences of their subjects" to worship as they pleased.[41]

III. THE OLD TESTAMENT WITNESS
AGAINST THE POLITICS OF PERSECUTION

Despite the example of Artaxerxes, Williams recognized that pagan rulers in the Old Testament were not always so tolerant. Sometimes they were models of religious persecution. In those cases, Williams focused on narratives that described the plight of God's faithful who endured hostile political circumstances. In emphasizing these passages, Williams pointed out that the Old Testament joined the New Testament in condemning nations that advocated the "bloody tenent of persecution." Indeed, the Old Testament perhaps was even more striking than the New in describing the persecution of God's people. Throughout the Old Testament, foreign nations such as Assyria, Babylonia, and Persia conquered and captured Israel. Always the advocate of the persecuted, Williams seized upon narratives from the Old Testament that described the courageous responses of God's people to such hostile circumstances. In these stories of exile and persecution, Williams found vivid models for God's embattled saints in the seventeenth century.

Two particular narratives were especially important to Williams. First, in the book of Daniel (chapter 3), he found a clear exemplification of a pagan state's attempt to force its subjects to adopt the official religion of the empire. Williams believed that the empires of Christendom in the seventeenth century resembled that of King Nebuchadnezzar, who threw God's three faithful witnesses into a furnace because they refused to worship the golden image that represented the state's religion. In this narrative, Williams discovered that the essence of Christendom's evil was its idolatry. Through this image of forced idol worship, Williams portrayed the idolatrous character of any political state that forced its citizens to

---

[41] Williams, *Bloudy Tenent,* in vol. 3 of *Complete Writings,* 267; see also 397. *Examiner Defended,* in vol. 7 of *Complete Writings,* 228.

honor the state's "official" religion. Second, Williams argued that the story of Naboth's vineyard (1 Kgs 21) exemplified another aspect of Christendom's character: its hypocrisy. In this story, Williams found an Old Testament example that condemned Christendom's attempt to hide its practice of persecution behind a veil of religious piety. Through these narratives, Williams criticized the state's control of religion as an idolatrous and hypocritical form of politics that had bloody consequences, whether in ancient times or in the seventeenth century.

A. Nebuchadnezzar and the Three Witnesses: Christendom as Political Idolatry

If Artaxerxes was Williams's dream of how a civil ruler should relate to religion, Nebuchadnezzar was his nightmare. In Daniel 3, Nebuchadnezzar was a Babylonian king who set up a golden statue and commanded all of his subjects to worship it. Failure to do so was punishable by death in a fiery furnace. The heroes of the story were three devout Jews: Shadrach, Meshach, and Abednego. Because of their uncompromising loyalty to the Lord, they refused to worship Nebuchadnezzar's golden image. Infuriated, Nebuchadnezzar had them thrown into the furnace. But the three Jews did not die. Miraculously, God preserved them from the fire because they had "disobeyed the king's command and yielded up their bodies rather than serve and worship any god except their own" (Dan 3:38, NRSV).

Williams lamented that Nebuchadnezzar's practice of forced religious uniformity was thriving in both England and New England. Williams found a striking similarity between Nebuchadnezzar's forced idol worship and the religious persecution of the sixteenth and seventeenth centuries:

The three famous Jews were cast into the fiery furnace for refusing to fall down (in a non-conformity to the whole conforming world) before the golden Image, Dan. 3.21. So thousands of Christ's witnesses (and of late in those bloody

Marian days) have rather chose to yield their bodies to all sorts of torments, than to subscribe to doctrines, or practice worships, unto which the States and Times (as Nebuchadnezzar to his golden Image) have compelled and urged them.[42]

Despite the claims of his Puritan rivals that they imitated Israelite rulers such as Asa, Williams believed that they were actually disciples of the Babylonian King Nebuchadnezzar. As did this notorious pagan king, Puritan governors claimed divine approval to establish religious laws and to force their subjects to obey them, even though God had granted no such permission.[43] And Williams was living proof that, like Nebuchadnezzar, Massachusetts Bay inflicted civil punishments on those who refused to bow to the government's "idols" of religious uniformity. Similar to the cruel practices of ancient Babylon, rulers in England and New England enforced religious obedience with the threat of violence.

England's recent history provided Williams with more evidence for Nebuchadnezzar's policies in the seventeenth century. Pointing to the multiple shifts in religious observance in England, Williams found it shameful that the nation had changed its official

---

[42] Williams, *Bloudy Tenent*, in vol. 3 of *Complete Writings*, 63.

[43] Puritans agreed with Williams that Nebuchadnezzar enforced a religious command that was of human and not divine origin. However, they disagreed with Williams's conclusion that any religious laws enforced by a magistrate were illegitimate. For instance, William Perkins cited this passage in the context of his distinction between human and divine laws. He argued that some laws commanded by the magistrate were of divine, not human, origin. These included religious duties concerning morality and proper worship. While magistrates commanded obedience to them, these were not their laws, but God's laws. Therefore, all citizens owed their obedience to them. However, Perkins acknowledged that some religious laws commanded by magistrates were not ordained by God. In these cases, citizens were "bound in conscience not to obey" these commands. Perkins put the commands of Nebuchadnezzar in this latter category. (See William Perkins, *A Discourse of Conscience*, in *William Perkins, 1558–1602*, ed. Thomas F. Merrill [Nieuwkoop: B. De Graaf, 1966] 33–34.)

religion "with wondrous ease" every time "a stronger sword" took the throne and commanded obedience to the ruler's religious faith. In his view, this political enforcement of religion duplicated "the ancient pattern of Nebuchadnezzar's bowing the whole world in one most solemn uniformity of worship to his golden image."[44]

Williams also found Nebuchadnezzar's pattern of forced worship in Christendom's attempts to convert the Native Americans to Christianity. In his 1645 book, *Christenings Make Not Christians*, Williams objected to these drives to convert the Native Americans, arguing that such movements better resembled military conquests than Christian conversions. This was a distinguishing mark of Christendom—disregarding the work of God's Spirit to convict souls peacefully, national churches used corporeal punishments to force "conversion." Williams found an example of Christendom's persecution of native peoples in the Catholic missionary efforts of the recent past. He determined that Catholic missionaries had pursued "monstrous and most inhumane conversions" in baptizing "thousands, yea ten thousands of the poor Natives, sometimes by wiles and subtle devices, sometimes by force compelling them to submit to that which they understood not, neither before nor after their monstrous Christening of them."[45] Again, Williams identified Christendom with the example of Nebuchadnezzar. As this Babylonian ruler forced the world to bow to his religion, Christendom's missionaries practiced "a conversion of people to the worship of the Lord Jesus by force of arms and swords of steel."[46]

---

[44] Williams, *Bloudy Tenent*, in vol. 3 of *Complete Writings*, 137.

[45] Williams, *Christenings Make Not Christians*, in vol. 7 of *Complete Writings*, 36.

[46] Ibid., 38. See also Gaustad's discussion in *Liberty of Conscience*, 30–31. As Gaustad put it, Williams believed that "Native Americans deserved better than persecution disguised as evangelism" (31). Williams found no use for the imperialism of the English who based their cultural superiority on an assumed theological correctness or moral righteousness. His writings abound with respect for Narragansett culture. An instance is found in one 1654 letter in which he wrote the General Court that had banished him: "I humbly pray your

Because the empires of Christendom, including the Massachusetts Bay Colony, followed the example of Nebuchadnezzar, Williams believed that texts such as this one from Daniel 3 bêtter illustrated the political situation of his day than passages that described Israel's national covenant with God. Israel's national covenant was dead; but Nebuchadnezzar's evil empire of Christendom unfortunately prospered, with "Nebuchadnezzar's golden images" providing the example for "the state worships of after ages."[47] While the example of Asa as a godly king ruling his empire in civil and religious matters was extinct, the example of Nebuchadnezzar as a persecuting ruler continued to plague political history from biblical times to the seventeenth century.[48] In imitation of Nebuchadnezzar, nations of Christendom in the seventeenth century preached a bloody doctrine of persecution, violently disposing of any who dared to transgress their official religion.[49]

---

consideration whether it be...not only possible but very easy for the English to live and die in peace with all the Natives" (*The Correspondence of Roger Williams*, ed. Glenn W. LaFantasie, vol. 2 [Hanover: Brown University Press, 1988] 409). Also notable is a major theme of his *A Key Into the Language of America* (in vol. 1 of *The Complete Writings of Roger Williams* [Providence: Narragansett Club Publications, 1866; reprint, New York: Russell & Russell, 1963]) in which he rejects assumed European superiority by emphasizing that the Natives were "more 'civil'" than the Europeans. (See Jack L. Davis, "Roger Williams Among the Narragansett Indians," *New England Quarterly* 43 [1970]: 595–96.) Williams even used the point of freedom of conscience to illustrate one of the ways in which Native Americans were superior to Europeans. He observed that the Narragansetts "have a modest religious persuasion not to disturb any man, either themselves, English, Dutch, or any in their conscience and worship" (*Key*, in vol. 1 of *Complete Writings*, 193). See also John J. Teunissen and Evelyn J. Hinz, "Roger Williams, St. Paul, and American Primitivism," *The Canadian Review of American Studies* 4/2 (1973) 131.

[47] Williams, *The Bloody Tenent Yet More Bloody*, in vol. 4 of *The Complete Writings of Roger Williams* (Providence: Narragansett Club Publications, 1870; reprint, New York: Russell & Russell, 1963) 59 and 358.

[48] Ibid., 358.

[49] See also other quotes from Williams in *Queries of Highest Consideration*, in vol. 2 of *The Complete Writings of Roger Williams* (Providence: Narragansett

In describing Nebuchadnezzar as a model for later governments that united church and state, Williams exposed the
idolatrous character of Christendom.[50] Williams repeated his claim
that, aside from ancient Israel, "all commonwealths that ever have
been, are, or shall be in the world" are "merely civil" authorities,

---

Club Publications, 1867; reprint, New York: Russell & Russell, 1963) 258;
Christenings, in vol. 7 of *Complete Writings*, 38; *Bloudy Tenent*, in vol. 3 of
Complete Writings, 157; and *Bloody Tenent Yet More Bloody*, in vol. 4 of *Complete
Writings*, 283. Anabaptist writers of the sixteenth century also used
Nebuchadnezzar as an example of religious persecution that provided a measure
for persecuting rulers in later times. For instance, Dirk Philips cited
Nebuchadnezzar's persecution in comparison with the persecuting "tyrants" of
the sixteenth century (*Enchiridion or Handbook of Christian Doctrine and
Religion*, in *The Writings of Dirk Philips*, ed. Cornelius J. Dyck, William E.
Keeney, and Alvin J. Beachy [Scottdale: Herald Press, 1992] 404; see also 181–82,
186).

[50] Separatist interpreters read this passage as it pertained to idolatry. For
instance, Ainsworth interpreted Daniel 3 in the context of his Separatist
argument that the saints should have no communion with impurity. He
emphasized the resistance of the three witnesses to Nebuchadnezzar's idolatry.
Like these witnesses, Christians were to flee "all idolatry which is Satan's
worship, and outward communion therewith" (Ainsworth, *Communion of Saints*
[London: John Bellamie and Ralph Smith, 1641] 103, 193, 244). Ainsworth also
used the passage to argue that Christians should avoid idolatry even when idol
worship is commanded by the civil magistrate. However, unlike Williams,
Ainsworth did not make any particular application of the passage to
contemporary governments (108). Henry Barrow's interpretation was similar to
that of Ainsworth. Barrow understood Daniel chapters 3 and 6 as examples that
justified Christians' disobedience to magistrates who either establish a "false
religion, or neglect their duty" to condemn false religion. Therefore, in contrast
to Williams's use of Daniel 3 as a condemnation of any form of Christendom,
Barrow used the passage as a safeguard against magistrates who abdicate their
responsibility to establish true religion and "compel all their subjects to the
hearing of God's word" (*Reply to Dr. Some's A Godly Treatise*, in *The Writings of
Henry Barrow, 1587–1590*, ed. Leland H. Carlson [London: Allen and Unwin,
1962] 159; see also 166). In the same volume, see also Barrow's *The First Part of
the Platforme*, 229, and *A Brief Discoverie of the False Church*, 406. See also the
citation of John Tombes, an English Baptist: *Jehova-Jireh; or, God's Providence in
Delivering the Godly* (London: Michael Sparkes, Sr., 1643) 23.

with no religious jurisdiction.[51] Any civil government, other than ancient Israel, that claimed religious authority was illicit. Williams reasoned that governments derived their power from the people, and that the people had no spiritual authority to entrust to their governments, since spiritual power came only from God. This meant that political bodies had no power to police the conscience, nor did they have the capability to distinguish religious truth from error. In governing religious matters, therefore, Christendom exercised a power that it did not rightly possess. Christendom coerced the people who gave it power, using spiritual authority that the people could not entrust to it. Williams called this a "policy of Satan" and a governmentally-endorsed "soul rape." In associating this policy with Nebuchadnezzar's golden image, Williams depicted Christendom as political idolatry, for the states of Christendom claimed divine sanction and status that God had never bequeathed to them.[52] Williams argued that, in Christendom, "kings and queens, parliaments and princes" set themselves up as "gods of the nations" by establishing the worship of their subjects. In seizing the right to authorize religion, these rulers "robbed the true God of his honor." Williams traced this political idolatry to the example of Nebuchadnezzar, who "pretends honor to his golden image," while in reality he makes himself "the deity which all nations worshipped through the golden image which he had set up."[53]

Whether in ancient Babylon or in seventeenth-century New England, the result of political idolatry was the same: religious persecution. Williams argued that this story from Daniel 3 displayed the terror of such idolatrous persecution while also offering hope to God's faithful. In Williams's view, the three Jews served as examples for "God's true servants" in all ages of

---

[51] Williams, *Bloody Tenent Yet More Bloody*, in vol. 4 of *Complete Writings*, 199.

[52] Williams, *Examiner Defended*, in vol. 7 of *Complete Writings*, 210.

[53] Ibid., 214.

persecution, including his own.[54] As did faithful Christians who suffered under the sword of Christendom in the seventeenth century, these three Jews lived in bondage to hostile political forces. But they did not allow their civil rulers to rule their consciences. They "would neither be constrained to the worship of" the false religion endorsed by the state, nor would they be "restrained from" the worship of the true God as their consciences led them. Under such circumstances, Williams argued that all of God's people should follow these Jews in "not daring either to be restrained from the true, or constrained to false worship, and yet without breach of the civil or city-peace."[55] For God's witnesses under siege in Babylon or in New England, this story in Daniel 3 encouraged faithfulness and courage in the midst of persecution. The deliverance of these three witnesses demonstrated that God "is able to deliver" all of his persecuted followers "from such fiery threatenings and executions." This biblical story offered hope to any of God's servants who refused to "bow down to invented gods or worships" even when faced with "fiery trials."[56]

In response to the common accusation that religious dissenters threatened the civil peace, Williams again appealed to this story of the three witnesses in the fiery furnace. He emphasized that these Jews were not political radicals. They did not oppose the government itself, but only its unjust enforcement of its official religion. Indeed, the true sources of civil unrest in almost every situation were not religious dissenters but agents of persecution such as Nebuchadnezzar. Williams argued that civil magistrates who forced their subjects "to godliness or the worshipping of God" have caused "the greatest breach of peace, and the greatest distractions in the world." While the shape of such politically-sanctioned religions changed with time, they were all merely

---

[54] Williams, *Bloudy Tenent Yet More Bloody*, in vol. 4 of *Complete Writings*, 262.

[55] Williams, *Bloudy Tenent*, in vol. 3 of *Complete Writings*, 72.

[56] Williams, *Bloudy Tenent Yet More Bloody*, in vol. 4 of *Complete Writings*, 262.

variations on a theme similar to "Nebuchadnezzar's golden image" of "state worship."[57]

B. Naboth's Vineyard: Christendom as Political Hypocrisy

Alongside Nebuchadnezzar, Williams found additional Old Testament examples of persecuting rulers in King Ahab and Queen Jezebel. Like Nebuchadnezzar, Ahab and Jezebel misused their civil authority to punish the innocent. Moreover, as did Nebuchadnezzar, Ahab and Jezebel revealed the evil character that empires of persecution exhibit in all ages.

The biblical text under consideration (1 Kgs 21) described the situation of Israel during the reign of King Ahab. Although Ahab ruled God's covenanted people, the Hebrew scriptures condemned him for his dalliance with paganism and for his general unfaithfulness to the Lord. As the author of 1 Kings determined, "there was no one like Ahab" because he "sold himself to do what was evil in the sight of the LORD, urged on by his wife Jezebel" (1 Kgs 21:25, NRSV). The story of Naboth's vineyard demonstrated the corruption of Ahab's rule, describing him as an ungodly ruler who mistreated one of his poor subjects. The corrupt leadership of Ahab reminded Williams of the blatant misuse of power that so-called "Christian" nations exhibited in the seventeenth century.

The biblical account describes Naboth as a citizen who owned a vineyard that King Ahab wanted for himself. When Naboth refused to sell his vineyard, the dejected king told his wife Jezebel what had happened. Queen Jezebel then planned to entrap Naboth and to steal his vineyard. She used Ahab's seal of authority to issue proclamations for a time of religious fasting and assembly in the land. When Naboth joined the assembly during the fast, two evil men falsely accused him of blasphemy against God and the king. In response, the people took Naboth outside the city where they stoned him for his alleged crimes. The plan of Jezebel and Ahab had worked. With Naboth out of the way, Ahab was free to take possession of the coveted vineyard. But Ahab and Jezebel did not

---

[57] Williams, *Bloudy Tenent*, in vol. 3 of *Complete Writings*, 237.

escape punishment for their crimes. The prophet Elijah visited Ahab and proclaimed the Lord's judgment upon Ahab and Jezebel for their evil conspiracy against Naboth. Speaking through Elijah, the Lord told Ahab: "I will bring destruction on you; I will consume you, and will cut off from Ahab every male, bound or free, in Israel." As for Ahab's queen and accomplice, the Lord vowed that "the dogs shall eat Jezebel within the bounds of Jezreel" (1 Kgs 21:21–23).

In this story Williams found a classic illustration of how evil and ambitious magistrates used religion to persecute innocent citizens. Since Williams believed that the story had particular relevance to his controversies with New England's leaders, he used it to confront both John Cotton and the Puritan "Modell of Church and Civil Power." Most importantly, Williams believed that the Naboth story revealed the falsehood in Massachusetts Bay's claim that it did not engage in unjust religious violence. Puritan leaders were sensitive to the charge, alleged by Williams and other radicals, that they persecuted innocent people for cause of conscience. In defending themselves against this accusation, the authors of the "Modell" argued that they did not punish heretics outright. Instead, the "Modell" stipulated that magistrates first send such religious offenders to the church so that ministers could instruct them on their errors.[58] The goal of this practice was to teach the Puritan understanding of orthodoxy, which any righteous conscience presumably would accept. Puritans believed that the conscience needed such training in righteousness, because the conscience was free only if it was "rightly informed."[59] Thus, if

---

[58] Williams, *Bloudy Tenent*, in vol. 3 of *Complete Writings*, 271.

[59] Stout, *New England Soul*, 21. In this context, Stout observes that "the Puritans' suppression of heterodoxy was in keeping with their instrumental sense of liberty as the freedom to establish and maintain a Bible commonwealth. The state existed to wield power in the interests of gospel purity, and that meant prosecution of religious offenses as well as civil.... In New England, where all institutions were purified according to biblical precept and ordered by visible saints, there was no inherent contradiction between civic loyalty and godly sanctification. Thus, when a person knowingly transgressed the law of the land

heretics remained mired in their erroneous opinions after receiving proper instruction on divine truth, then they had no excuse for their sinful opinions, and the "Modell" advised magistrates to punish them accordingly. The "Modell" contended that, since righteous instruction preceded civil punishments, radicals such as Williams could not claim "that the magistrate persecutes men for their consciences, but that he justly" punishes heretics "for sinning against [their] conscience[s]."[60]

Williams believed that *any* use of civil power to punish persons for their religious beliefs was persecution. For him, the Puritan claim that they did not "persecute" the innocent but only "punished" the guilty demonstrated the hypocrisy of Christendom. After all, in the states of Christendom, ministers and civil officers conspired to set the boundaries of orthodoxy. They used their own guidelines to distinguish the innocent from the guilty and the religious saint who deserved praise from the heretic who deserved punishment. Williams took offense to the way the Puritans used their established churches to label those that the state could justly punish as heretics. He asserted that Puritan leaders were following the model of Ahab and Jezebel, who also used a religious assembly to entrap and murder a political enemy.[61]

---

or blasphemed its public institutions, that person sinned against his or her conscience, and it would be a perversion of charity *not* to punish him or her." See also Puritan minister Nathaniel Ward's comment that "the conscience is free insofar as it [remains] free from error" (*The Simple Cobbler of Aggawam in America*, ed. P. M. Zall [Lincoln: University of Nebraska Press, 1969] 11).

[60] "Modell of Church," in vol. 3 of *Complete Writings*, 271. See also the identical claim that Cotton made in response to the Murton epistle, John Cotton, "The Answer of Mr. John Cotton of Boston," in vol. 3 of *Complete Writings*, 42.

[61] Williams, *Bloudy Tenent*, in vol. 3 of *Complete Writings*, 278. In contrast to Williams's interpretation, the annotations to this passage in the Geneva Bible omit any reference to Ahab's and Jezebel's uses of religious ceremonies to commit civil crimes. However, the Geneva Bible annotations do condemn Ahab and Jezebel as tyrants for their murder of Naboth. (See *The Geneva Bible: A Facsimile of the 1560 Edition* [Madison: University of Wisconsin Press, 1969] 163.)

In Williams's view, Ahab and Jezebel demonstrated the evil that ensued when pagan rulers meddled in religion. Despite their orthodox claims and their displays of piety, the goal of such political officers was not to glorify God, but to honor themselves and to advance their own worldly kingdoms. Speaking of the empires of Christendom in his day, Williams remarked that "the kings and rulers of the earth commonly mind their own crowns, honors, and dominions, more than God's." Such leaders in Christendom's governments only "use God's name, and ordinances" just as "Jezebel used fasting and prayer, for the advancement of their own crowns," and to persecute "the innocent and righteous."[62] For Williams, the Naboth story revealed these evils of Christendom for what they were: abuses of both civil government and religious authority.

Williams's reading of the Naboth story exposed the hypocrisy of Christendom. Such revelation was necessary because persecutors never admitted their crimes. Instead, religious persecution nearly always happened under the guise of a righteous or holy purpose. Williams made this point, commenting on the tragic irony that persecutors often used God and his worship to persecute God's own people. Williams advised his readers to "search all scriptures, histories, records, monuments" and they would find that those who tormented God's people never admitted that they were religious persecutors. Instead, they attempted to hide their persecution behind "a mask or covering." Williams claimed that this was true of Old Testament persecutors like "Pharaoh, Saul, Ahab," and "Jezebel," in addition to New Testament figures such as the "Scribes and Pharisees," and later persecutors like "the bloody Neros," the Pope, and Satan himself.[63] In each case, persecutors blamed their actions on the persecuted. The story of Naboth provided an excellent example because Ahab and Jezebel justified Naboth's assassination on the false charge of blasphemy. In the

---

[62] Williams, *Bloody Tenent Yet More Bloody*, in vol. 4 of *Complete Writings*, 307–308.

[63] Williams, *Bloudy Tenent*, in vol. 3 of *Complete Writings*, 82.

process of their deception, Ahab and Jezebel used a religious ceremony to orchestrate Naboth's demise, and they used a religious condemnation to justify his stoning.[64] The case was similar with Christ because his enemies falsely accused him of being a religious radical, claiming that he was "a seducer of the people, a blasphemer against God, and traitor against Caesar."[65] The plight of Naboth was therefore precisely that of countless other true witnesses of God who received persecution at the hands of evil magistrates who claimed divine sanction to commit violent acts.

Williams lamented that his Puritan contemporaries in Massachusetts followed the model of Ahab and Jezebel in using religion to sanctify violent persecution. Even John Cotton, despite his "sincere intentions" to "aim at Christ," remained among those "who think they do God good service in killing the Lord Jesus in his servants."[66] For instance, in one of his early letters to Williams after the banishment, Cotton disavowed all blame on the part of the Colony for Williams's condition. Cotton informed the outcast that Massachusetts Bay had not expelled him so much as he had expelled himself because he had preached "corrupt doctrines, which tend to the disturbance both of civil and holy peace."[67] Williams believed that this way of reasoning placed Cotton and his colleagues alongside the model of Ahab and Jezebel. In this scenario, Williams counted himself among "all God's Naboths" who endured suffering for their resistance to persecuting states while their persecutors used a mask of piety and civil justice to commit heinous acts of violence.[68]

---

[64] Ibid., 278.

[65] Ibid., 83.

[66] Ibid., 83.

[67] John Cotton, *A Letter of Mr. John Cottons,* in vol. 1 of *The Complete Writings of Roger Williams* (Providence: Narragansett Club Publications, 1866; reprint, New York: Russell & Russell, 1963) 297–98.

[68] Williams, *Bloudy Tenent,* in vol. 3 of *Complete Writings,* 263. Williams was not alone in relating his persecuted experience to that of Naboth. John Goodwin also made a brief reference to Naboth's situation in relation to his own predicament as he came under attack from his polemical opponents (*Qeomacia,*

story also reveals God's condemn. of persecution

Even amid the tragedy of the Naboth passage, Williams asserted that the purpose of the story was to provide hope to the persecuted. Not only did the story detail the injustices that Naboth suffered, but it also revealed God's condemnation of such persecution, which the prophet Elijah revealed to Ahab and Jezebel. Williams colorfully paraphrased Elijah's proclamation, saying that God would "find both Jezebel and Ahab guilty, and make the dogs a feast with the flesh of Jezebel, and [would] leave not to Ahab a man to piss against the wall."[69] Consequently, the Naboth story revealed the hypocrisy whereby civil rulers use religious authority to justify their violent policies and to support their kingdoms.

> In that great battle between the Lord Jesus and the Devil, it is observable that Satan takes up the weapons of scripture, and such scripture which in show and color was excellent for his purpose.
>
> Roger Williams, 1644[70]

sum
fear-Satan gives bad readings

One of the fears of a biblically saturated culture is the realization that Satan is a deceitful interpreter of scripture. This anxiety plagued seventeenth-century New England—a society in which biblical interpretation provided the basis for social as well as individual life. Because the stakes were set so high, Roger Williams scrutinized the Bible, searching for its true meaning while remaining alert to Satan's deceptive exegetical snares. Williams found an instance of such biblical misinterpretation at the heart of civil governments in the seventeenth century, especially those in old and New England. Motivated by this conviction, Williams attacked the biblical foundations of Puritan society in his polemical writings. He filled his polemics with scriptural references and analysis because

---

Or, The Grand Imprudence of Men Running the Hazard of Fighting Against God, in Haller, vol. 3 of *Tracts on Liberty,* 5).

[69] Williams, *Bloudy Tenent,* in vol. 3 of *Complete Writings,* 278.
[70] Ibid., 84.

he believed that his opponents' primary errors stemmed from biblical interpretation. To be sure, Williams addressed issues of church, state, and religious persecution as biblical problems that needed biblical solutions, and we cannot understand Williams's statements on these critical issues without examining his unique interpretation of the Bible. Williams's radical opinions in the seventeenth century required biblical warfare against interpreters who defended the alliance of church and state.

One of the most crucial battles in this biblical warfare involved the political interpretation of the Old Testament. Williams's reading of the Old Testament challenged civil states that claimed to be "Christian nations" and protectors of God's rule on earth. Williams's struggle for religious liberty required a renewed appreciation of the relevance of the Old Testament to contemporary politics. The Old Testament was relevant, Williams believed, but not in the way that New England Puritans had hoped. Puritans were obsessed with the image of victorious Israel—God's chosen people that conquered political and religious enemies and built a holy nation. Confronting the Puritans' concentration on ancient Israel, Williams offered a vision of the Old Testament that opposed conventional politics in the New World. Williams could not abide the deep political divide that separated the Puritan emphasis on God's victorious nation of Israel in the Old Testament and the New Testament view of God's people as political outcasts—lowly and persecuted followers of a Lord who was executed by the state. But Williams did not conclude that the Old and New Testaments presented contradictory views of God's people and their relation to the civil state. Williams demonstrated that, like the New Testament, much of the Old Testament described God's people at odds with kings and magistrates. The stories of Artaxerxes, Nebuchadnezzar and the three witnesses, and Naboth's persecution by Ahab and Jezebel demonstrated that God's righteous people were often losers in the political world who served pagan masters. Williams believed that these stories provided relevant models to contemporary politics. Artaxerxes demonstrated that religious liberty was a wise and just policy in the state. The story of Nebuchadnezzar's golden image and fiery furnace revealed the idolatrous nature of any nation's attempt to force religious obedience on its citizens. The story of Ahab, Jezebel, and Naboth demonstrated that persecution was often the hypocritical attempt of civil rulers who used religion as a ruse to persecute God's people for political gain. Williams hoped that, once the echoes of Israel's glorious past had silenced, New and Old England would recover these models from the Old Testament that condemned religious persecution and proclaimed the necessity of religious liberty in the state.

Even greater challenges confronted Williams in his interpretation of the New Testament. Chief among the obstacles that Williams faced were the predominant views of Jesus' parable of the wheat and the weeds. This parable held a central place in controversies over religious liberty from Augustine's struggles with the Donatists to the Reformers' battles with Anabaptists. The next chapter examines Williams's encounter with this monumental parable and its many esteemed interpreters.

— Williams saw OT as supporting religious liberty and denouncing state persecutions on ppl not agreeing w/ state religion

Puritans
· Israel kings are model for Puritan magistrates
→ Israel is "type" that finds fulfillment in X; thus can't model alf Israel.

Williams
· Israel is only gov w/ link to God anyone claiming otherwise is illegit.

— Artaxerxes → Ps thought model ruler ble endorsed Giod. Ws model blc pagan who still ruled justly. Made him a better model to follow for 17th. Ps saw Ax saying to all practice Judaism while Ws thought he endorsed tolerance.

— Neb→ example of this is what happens when ppl forced to worship constant switching of religions, resorting to violence (shdd, Mech, Abind) to get that. Look @ native American treatment
    * exposed idolatrous claim of Xn Govs
· Ppl elect gov → no spiritual authority w/ ppl, thus none w/ gov; gov claiming that authority = idolatry → leads to persecution
— Ahab/Jez/Naboth — religion often used to persecute ppl for political gain → God against this

CHAPTER 3

A PARABLE OF RELIGIOUS LIBERTY:
CONTROVERSY OVER
THE WEEDS AND WHEAT

> That great and heavenly parable of the Tares [is] a knot
> about which so many holy fingers, dead and living, have
> been so laboriously exercised, all professing to untie, yet
> some by seeming to untie, have tied the knot the faster.
> Roger Williams, 1652[1]

Roger Williams knew that the Bible could inspire violence. The
religious wars and oppression that plagued the seventeenth-century
world distressed him greatly, and he considered these evils to be the
tragic effects of biblical misinterpretation. As he stated in the title
of his most famous book, religious persecution was rooted in a
"bloody tenet"—an evil teaching. He believed that this "doctrine of
persecution for cause of conscience" was "lamentably contrary to
the doctrine of Christ Jesus the Prince of Peace."[2] Thus, while
religious violence marred the political scene, Williams recognized
that it was first of all a biblical problem—a perversion of Christ's

---

[1] Williams, *The Bloody Tenent Yet More Bloody,* in vol. 4 of *The Complete
Writings of Roger Williams* (Providence: Narragansett Club Publications, 1870;
reprint, New York: Russell & Russell, 1963) 114–15.

[2] Williams, *The Bloudy Tenent, of Persecution, for Cause of Conscience,
discussed, in A Conference Betweene Truth and Peace,* in vol. 3 of *The Complete
Writings of Roger Williams* (Providence: Narragansett Club Publications, 1867;
reprint, New York: Russell & Russell, 1963) 425.

X
teaches
peace,
freedom

teaching in scripture. In Williams's view, Christ taught not violence and persecution, but peace and freedom in matters of conscience. Thus Williams used the Gospels to defend his interpretation of Christ against those who used scripture as an implement of persecution.

One of the most pivotal scriptural battlegrounds in Williams's defense of religious liberty concerned the proper interpretation of Jesus' parable about an infestation of weeds ("tares") in a field of wheat (Matt 13:24–30; 36–43). Long before Puritans cast ashore in New England, this parable had played a recurring role in controversies regarding religious liberty from Augustine's struggles with the Donatists to the magisterial Reformers' conflicts with Anabaptists.[3] The long history of interpretations of this parable was crucial to Williams's understanding of the wheat and weeds. Indeed, Williams knew that his dispute with Puritan minister John Cotton over this biblical text was but the latest chapter in a continuing interpretive conflict—one that held tragic consequences for Christ's faithful. For Williams, no passage was more vital to Christ's advocacy of religious liberty. Yet, much to Williams's horror, no passage had received worse treatment from interpreters than this parable of the weeds.[4]

---

[3] For an overview of the impact of this parable on the relationship between church and state, see Roland H. Bainton, "The Parable of the Tares as the Proof Text for Religious Liberty to the End of the Sixteenth Century," *Church History* 1/2 (1932): 67–89.

[4] The parable of the weeds was Williams's fourth most quoted biblical passage. Williams's interpretation of the parable is briefly treated in Gaustad, *Liberty of Conscience: Roger Williams in America,* ed. Mark A. Noll and Nathan O. Hatch, Library of Religious Biography (Grand Rapids: William B. Eerdmans Publishing, 1991) 72–74; Allen, "'The Restauration of Zion': Roger Williams and the Quest for the Primitive Church" (Ph.D. diss., University of Iowa, 1984) 212–14; and Paul Orrin Wright, "Roger Williams: God's Swordsman in Searching Times" (Ph.D. diss., Dallas Theological Seminary, 1968) 183–97. These brief treatments, however, do not fully assess Williams's exegesis of the parable, nor do they examine his exegesis in relation to other important interpretations since the Reformation.

Above all, Williams was appalled that this parable had been twisted in support of religious persecution by such otherwise "worthy witnesses" as John Calvin, Theodore Beza, and most recently John Cotton. In their readings of the parable, Williams believed that even these great Christian leaders proved that Satan was a subtle and deceitful interpreter who wreaked exegetical havoc, confusing the true meaning of the Bible.[5] Williams believed that misinterpretations of this parable had caused many states and churches to take the wide road of violence and religious persecution when they might have taken "paths" that were more peaceful.[6] The perversions of this parable through the ages caused many tragic deaths in violent attempts to "suppress all false religions."[7] Because of the immense consequences of this exegetical catastrophe, Williams attempted to vindicate this parable from "the violence" done to it. He invoked "the Lord's assistance" in examining this scripture at length because it was "of such great importance as concerning the truth of God, the blood of thousands, yea the blood of saints, and of the Lord Jesus in them."[8]

Williams interpreted the parable of the weeds in relation to other interpretations in the sixteenth and seventeenth centuries— most of which he opposed. This chapter analyzes Williams's interpretation of this parable in relation that of Protestant Reformers, Anabaptists, English Separatists, and Puritans. Among those who interpreted this parable, Williams cited John Calvin as perhaps the most respected reformer who misread it.[9] In opposing Calvin's interpretation, Williams joined Anabaptists who had rejected Calvin's view of the parable in the sixteenth century. The conflict between Calvin and the Anabaptists set the stage for Williams's later examination of the parable. In order to portray the Anabaptist

---

[5] Williams, *Bloudy Tenent,* in vol. 3 of *Complete Writings,* 97–98.

[6] Ibid., 113.

[7] Ibid., 98.

[8] Ibid., 99.

[9] Despite his disagreement with Calvin on this parable, Williams included Calvin among "those worthy witnesses whose memories are sweet with all that fear God" (*Bloudy Tenent,* in vol. 3 of *Complete Writings,* 97–98).

interpretation of the parable, I will focus on Menno Simons—one of the most influential Anabaptist theologians who challenged Calvin's view of the wheat and weeds. By including Simons's interpretation, I compare a radical view of the parable during the Reformation era with the radical interpretation offered by Williams a century later. The conflicting interpretations of Calvin and Simons also represent the variety of exegetical perspectives that Williams encountered when he engaged the parable in his argument for religious liberty.

Williams also interpreted the parable in light of the English Separatist movement of the late sixteenth and early seventeenth centuries.[10] In the view of English Separatists, this parable was an important defense of their separation from the Church of England, which they considered corrupt. Williams adopted the Separatist rejection of the Church of England and appreciated many Separatist writings, though he disagreed with their interpretation of the parable of the weeds. Moreover, Williams's disagreements with the Separatists' interpretation reflected the ways in which he was more radical than they in his view of the relationship between church and state.

Williams honed his interpretation of this parable in his conflict with Puritan leaders, most particularly John Cotton. Williams's debate with Cotton, which they waged via letters, began soon after Williams's banishment from the Bay Colony in 1635 and extended until Cotton's death in 1652. While some of their letters were private, Williams and Cotton also published several letters as tracts, thereby waging their debate in a public forum. Among these tracts are works with graphic titles such as Williams's *Bloudy Tenent, of Persecution, for Cause of Conscience* (1644); Cotton's reply in *The Bloudy Tenent, Washed And made white in the Bloud of the Lambe*

---

[10] For an interpretation of Williams's thought within the English Separatist tradition, see Spurgin, *Roger Williams and Puritan Radicalism in the English Separatist Tradition,* vol. 34 of Studies in American Religion (Lewiston NY: Edwin Mellen Press, 1989). See also Gaustad, "Roger Williams and the Principle of Separation," *Foundations* 1 (1958).

(1647); and Williams's rejoinder, *The Bloody Tenet Yet More Bloody* (1652). In their use of violent images, these titles revealed the crucial nature of the controversy in seventeenth-century old and New England. This imagery was typical of Williams, who often punctuated his arguments with "graphic sentences about murder, rape, the gouging of eyes, and the dashing of brains."[11] Such imagery underscored Williams's conviction that biblical interpretation was literally a matter of life and death.

It may be profitable to introduce this chapter by summarizing the parable that prompted such controversy. The text has two main divisions in Matthew 13: a parable (13:24–30) and Jesus' interpretation of some elements of this story to his confused disciples (13:36–43). In the narrative itself Jesus compares the kingdom of heaven to a master who planted good seed in his field. But while the master and his servants slept, an enemy invaded the field and sowed weeds among the seeds of wheat. Eventually, the servants noticed weeds as they grew alongside the good grain. Perplexed by this mixed complexion of the field, the servants asked the master where the weeds had come from. When the master responded that an enemy had sown the weeds, the servants offered to pluck the weeds from the field. The master denied this request, informing the servants that gathering the weeds would endanger the wheat, for the servants could accidentally uproot the good grain in their attempts to pull up the weeds. The master commanded an alternate strategy: allow the wheat and weeds to grow together until harvest. At that time, the master would instruct the reapers to remove the weeds from the field and burn them before gathering the wheat into the barn.

In response to inquiring disciples, Jesus identified several key terms and characters in the parable:

The one who sows the good seed is the Son of Man; the field is the world, and the good seed are the children of the kingdom; the

---

[11] Gilpin, "Roger Williams," in *Makers of Christian Theology in America*, ed. Mark G. Toulouse and James O. Duke (Nashville: Abingdon Press, 1997) 41.

weeds are the children of the evil one, and the enemy who sowed them is the devil; the harvest is the end of the age, and the reapers are angels. Just as the weeds are collected and burned up with fire, so will it be at the end of the age. The Son of Man will send his angels, and they will collect out of his kingdom all causes of sin and all evildoers, and they will throw them into the furnace of fire, where there will be weeping and gnashing of teeth. (Matt 13:37–43, NRSV)

I. THE PARABLE OF THE WEEDS IN THE REFORMATION

A. John Calvin (1509–1564)

Throughout his career as an interpreter of scripture, John Calvin remained committed to "lucid brevity." That is, he attempted to interpret the Bible as succinctly as possible, without undue speculation and exegetical wanderings. Apparently he believed that this approach was especially needed in an interpretation of the parable of the weeds because he noted that some interpreters had "investigated more subtly every minute detail" of the text. Calvin feared that such "indefinite discussions may lead us into foolishness" and he resolved "to be sparing in philosophising and to be satisfied with the simple and genuine sense."[12] Nevertheless, Calvin was obligated to wrestle at some length with this thorny parable of the weeds.

Calvin's most concise treatment of the parable was in the *Institutes*. There, he addressed the parable in criticism of those who separated from the church because of scandal within it. Specifically, Calvin had in mind Anabaptists, whom he considered

used parable to critique Anab, who separated

---

[12] John Calvin, *A Harmony of the Gospels Matthew, Mark and Luke,* vol. 2 of *Calvin's Commentaries,* ed. David W. Torrance and Thomas F. Torrance, trans. T. H. L. Parker (Edinburgh: Saint Andrews Press, 1972) 77. On Calvin's commitment to "lucid brevity," see David C. Steinmetz, *Calvin in Context* (New York: Oxford University Press, 1995) 14, 73.

contemporary representatives of the Donatist movement.[13] Calvin believed that Anabaptists, like the Donatists of the early church, were deluded with a false sense of their own purity, with some even believing themselves to be fully spiritual and free of sin. Whether out of "insane pride" or from an "ill-advised zeal for right-eousness," these radicals believed that no church existed without "perfect purity and integrity of life." Consequently, this delusion caused them to depart "out of hatred and wickedness from the lawful church," which Calvin believed existed anywhere the Word was preached and the sacraments were rightly administered.[14] Calvin believed that Anabaptists did not realize that the visible church was always "mingled of good men and bad," and he used the parable of the weeds to prove his point. For Calvin, the field signified the church, which was plagued with immoral "weeds" that grew alongside the moral "wheat." This parable, therefore, taught that Christians should accept the fact that the church would always "be weighted down with the mixture of the wicked" until the final judgment.[15]

Calvin examined the parable more thoroughly in his *Harmony of the Gospels*, which he first published in 1555. Here he expanded his exegesis, correcting some specific misinterpretations of others and engaging some of the problems posed by the parable. Calvin stressed that the weeds symbolized immorality within the church and not heresy. Unlike immoral persons, heretical beliefs were particularly dangerous because they threatened the gospel of Christ. Indeed, Calvin reasoned that Christ would never have forbidden his disciples to cast out doctrinal "weeds." Thus, Calvin asserted that the parable instructs the church to endure the moral faults of people, but not heretical beliefs. While the church may

---

[13] Edmund S. Morgan, *Visible Saints: The History of a Puritan Idea* (Ithaca: Cornell University Press, 1963) 21.

[14] John Calvin, *Institutes of the Christian Religion*, ed. John T. McNeill, trans. Ford Lewis Battles, 2 vols. (Philadelphia: Westminster Press, 1960) IV.i.13. On the marks of the church, see IV.i.9.

[15] Calvin, *Institutes*, IV.i.13.

excuse moral imperfections, it should exterminate heretical doctrines so that they do not corrupt "the purity of the faith."[16]

Above all, Calvin believed that the parable of the weeds contained valuable instruction on church discipline. The parable encouraged Christians to keep the faith when faced with evil persons within the body of Christ. Amid the mixture of good and bad members that inhabited all churches, the parable would calm "the zeal of those who think it is wrong to associate with any who are not pure angels."[17]

Calvin's argument that the parable had to do with church discipline rested on his belief that the field signified the church. This presented an embarrassing dilemma because, as Jesus himself explained, "the field is the world" (Matt 13:38). Calvin's exegesis of the parable therefore seemed to contradict the explanation that Christ gave to his disciples. In treating this delicate problem, Calvin argued that although Christ called the field the world, he intended "to apply" the field "to the Church, about which, after all, he was speaking."[18] Calvin pointed out that Jesus had introduced the parable by saying, "the kingdom of heaven may be compared to someone who sowed good seed in his field" (Matt 13:24, NRSV). In Calvin's view, this introductory comment indicated that the parable's scope was Christ's kingdom, the church, and not the world, which was the realm of Satan. Calvin solved the apparent

[margin note: valueable instruction on church discipline]

[margin note: claimed parable scope was X's king= church]

---

[16] Calvin, *Harmony of the Gospels*, in vol. 2 of Calvin's Commentaries, 75. Calvin was careful to guard against a possible heretical perversion of the parable. He cautioned that the parable did not teach that "God had sown good men at the creation and the devil evil men"—an interpretation that would support a Manichean dualism of two creative principles. Rather, Calvin argued that sin existed only as a corruption of good nature. Thus, Calvin stated that "the devil did not create evil men but depraves what God created and sows in the Lord's field what will harm the pure seed." And this work of the evil sower absolved God of responsibility for tares in the field. As Calvin put it, because the devil was the sower of evil in the church, "we learn to impute the blame for this evil to the devil," and not to God.

[17] Calvin, *Harmony of the Gospels*, in vol. 2 of Calvin's Commentaries, 76.
[18] Ibid., 75.

conflict by not taking literally Jesus' interpretation of the field as the world. Calvin claimed that Jesus "transfers by synecdoche to the world what is more apt of a part of it."[19] Jesus did not mean that the field was the world itself, but rather the church that existed within the world. This is an unusal interpretive move for Calvin. Despite his self-proclaimed preference to avoid figurative deliberations into the parable's details in favor of a commitment to "the simple and genuine sense," Calvin rejected a simple reading of Christ's interpretation of the field as the world, preferring instead a figural interpretation at this crucial juncture in the parable.[20]

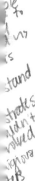

By interpreting the field as a symbol of the church, Calvin claimed that the parable had no relevance for the "world," which was the realm of civil magistrates. He clarified this position even further in his argument against Anabaptists who used this parable to forbid the civil magistrate's interference in religious matters. Calvin responded that this parable had nothing to do with the office of either ministers or magistrates. Rather, the parable was intended to console "the weak" who became offended when they saw that the church was not only the spiritual haven of the elect, but also the refuge of "impure dregs."[21]

B. Menno Simons (1496–1561)

While Calvin believed that the parable pertained only to the church, Anabaptists such as Menno Simons applied it to the civil

---

[19] Ibid. E. Brooks Holifield describes the "synecdoche" as an element of "proportional exegesis." Specifically, "the synecdoche—a figure in which a part represents a whole—enlarged the scope of a biblical rule or example" (see Holifield, *Era of Persuasion: American Thought and Culture, 1521–1680,* ed. Lewis Perry, Twayne's American Thought and Culture [Boston: Twayne Publishers, 1989] 48–49). For a discussion of the use of "synecdoche" by an English Separatist, see Robert Browne, *A Treatise upon the 23 of Matthewe,* in *The Writings of Robert Harrison and Robert Browne,* ed. Albert Peel and Leland H. Carlson (London: Allen and Unwin, 1953) 182–83, 195.

[20] Calvin, *Harmony of the Gospels,* in vol. 2 of Calvin's Commentaries, 77.

[21] Ibid., 76.

state.[22] The contrast in the two views appears most vividly in their interpretations of the field. Unlike Calvin, Simons took Jesus' explanation of the field literally (v. 38): the field did not signify the church, but the world, just as Christ said.[23] In so doing, Simons placed the relevance of the parable not in the church, but in the secular realm. Furthermore, Simons argued that the good seed sown by the householder signified the redemptive "word" that Christ sowed in the world, and the children of the kingdom were those who received this seed. Just as the good seed signified Christ's word and its growth in his righteous children, the weeds signified the devil's false doctrine, which grew to fruition in his evil children.[24] Consequently, the weeds represented not immorality within the church, but heresy in the world. The point for Simons was that both truth and heresy should coexist freely in the state, since "both wheat and tares grow together in the same field, namely, in the world."[25]

Given these presuppositions, the distinction between Calvin's and Simons's uses of the parable becomes clear. For Calvin, the command to let the weeds grow with the wheat pertained to the church, where overly zealous Christians were to accept the moral imperfections of fellow church members. This completely separated the parable from the authority of the magistrate. In contrast, Simons placed the parable in the world, the magistrate's realm of authority. In Simons's view, the parable commanded that magistrates leave heresy alone in the world, allowing it to grow

---

[22] Other Anabaptists shared Simons's interpretation of the parable. For example, see Dirk Philips, *Enchiridion or Handbook of Christian Doctrine and Religion*, in *The Writings of Dirk Philips*, ed. Cornelius J. Dyck, William E. Keeney, and Alvin J. Beachy (Scottdale: Herald Press, 1992) 214, 374–75; Balthasar Hubmaier, *On Heretics and Those Who Burn Them*, in *Balthasar Hubmaier: Theologian of Anabaptism*, ed. H. Wayne Pipkin and John H. Yoder (Scottdale: Herald Press, 1989) 61.

[23] Menno Simons, *Reply to Gellius Faber*, in *The Complete Writings of Menno Simons*, ed. John C. Wenger (Scottdale: Herald Press, 1956) 750.

[24] Simons, *Reply to Faber*, 750.

[25] Ibid.

unhindered until the judgment.[26] Above all, Simons directed his interpretation at supposedly "Christian" authorities who used this parable as a license to persecute heretics. He believed that such persecutors disobeyed the command of Christ by taking it upon themselves to "invade the province of the angels" whom Christ authorized to punish the unrighteous at the judgment. Thus the job of separating the wheat from the weeds belonged to angels—not so-called "Christian" magistrates.[27]

In sum, while Calvin argued that the parable applied only to the church, Simons explored its implications for life in the secular realm. Calvin argued that Jesus told the parable to limit overzealous claims for church purity. Simons asserted that Jesus told the parable to limit overzealous punishment of heretics in the world. Simons believed that a proper understanding of and obedience to this parable would have saved much innocent Anabaptist blood from the swords of persecutors. He recognized that both church and civil authorities constantly denounced the Anabaptists as "weeds," and used this parable to justify exterminating these radicals. In so doing, Simons believed that persecutors defeated the very purpose of the parable by destroying much "noble wheat" in their premature harvesting of the weeds.[28]

II. THE PARABLE OF THE WEEDS IN ENGLISH SEPARATISM

The parable of the weeds was a favorite text of religious radicals in England in the late sixteenth and seventeenth centuries. Like Simons and other Anabaptists, English Separatists used this parable to combat the conclusions of Calvin and others. Separatists disputed Calvin's view of the parable because they wanted to protect the purity of the church. But these English radicals did not

---

[26] Ibid.

[27] Menno Simons, *The Cross of the Saints*, in *The Complete Writings of Menno Simons*, 605; idem, *The Blasphemy of John of Leiden*, in *The Complete Writings of Menno Simons*, 48.

[28] Simons, *Reply to Faber*, 750.

simply adopt Simons's exegesis; their interpretations of the parable steered middle course between the views of Simons and Calvin. English Separatists shared Simons's desire to protect the purity of the church, but they also appreciated Calvin's need to retain the state's services in purifying and protecting the church from polluting elements. Unlike the Anabaptists, Separatists did not interpret the parable as an argument for complete religious freedom.

English Separatism arose around 1580 when Robert Browne and his followers separated from the Church of England to form a church of their own at Norwich. Browne argued the Separatist position in his appropriately-titled tract, *Reformation without Tarying for Anie.*[29] Frustrated with Elizabeth's ecclesiastical policies, Browne and his followers refused to wait for government to reform the Church of England. Instead, Separatists established their own churches on their conviction that a proper church should have a pure membership and that worship should be free of unscriptural elements.[30] The Separatist or "Brownist" movement spread throughout England in the late sixteenth and early seventeenth centuries, greatly influencing Roger Williams. By the time he arrived in Massachusetts in 1631, Williams had joined the Separatists in separating from the Church of England because of its corruption. This alignment with the Separatists put Williams at odds with his Puritan colleagues who hoped to reform the Church of England from within.[31] While Williams agreed with the Separatist rejection of the Church of England, he did not blindly adopt all of their convictions. As was often the case, Williams found much in Separatist theology and politics with which to disagree, particularly on the issues that were most important to

---

[29] Robert Browne, *A Treatise of Reformation without Tarying for Anie*, in *The Writings of Robert Harrison and Robert Browne*, ed. Albert Peel and Leland H. Carlson (London: Allen and Unwin, 1953) 150–70.

[30] Morgan, *Visible Saints*, 17.

[31] See Glenn LaFantasie's editorial essay in Williams, *The Correspondence of Roger Williams*, ed. Glenn W. LaFantasie, 2 vols. (Hanover: Brown University Press, 1988) 12–23.

him—religious liberty and the separation of church and state. These disagreements between Williams and the Separatists—as well as their agreements—are revealed in their interpretations of the parable of the weeds.

Henry Barrow (c. 1550–1593)

Williams arrived at the Separatist position primarily through reading books and tracts that Separatists had published in England and Amsterdam.[32] Foremost among these were the works of Henry Barrow, whom Edmund Morgan called "the fiercest spokesman for the Separatist position" in the late sixteenth century.[33] Not only was Barrow zealous, he was also articulate. Indeed, he and his associate, John Greenwood, provided the most complete expression of Separatist convictions in their controversial works from 1587 to 1593.[34] As was often the case in the sixteenth century, the zealous advocacy of controversial ideas came with a heavy price; Barrow and Greenwood were branded as subversives and executed in 1593.[35] Always mindful of the victims of violent persecution, Roger Williams praised Barrow and Greenwood as martyrs who "followed the Lord Jesus with their Gibbets on their shoulders, and were hanged with him and for him."[36] Williams admired their works during his years at Cambridge, 1626–1627.[37]

In his controversial writings, Barrow interpreted the parable of the wheat and weeds in direct opposition to Calvin's exegesis. Barrow vehemently opposed Calvin's interpretation of the field as

---

[32] See Spurgin, *Williams and Puritan Radicalism,* 123–38.

[33] Morgan, *Visible Saints,* 23.

[34] Timothy George, *John Robinson and the English Separatist Tradition* (Macon GA: Mercer University Press, 1982) 48.

[35] Spurgin, *Williams and Puritan Radicalism,* 66.

[36] Williams, *Mr. Cottons Letter Lately Printed, Examined and Answered,* in vol. 1 of *The Complete Writings of Roger Williams,* (Providence: Narragansett Club Publications, 1874; reprint, New York: Russell & Russell, 1963) 380–81; see also Williams, *Bloody Tenent Yet More Bloody,* in vol. 4 of *Complete Writings,* 331.

[37] Spurgin, *Williams and Puritan Radicalism,* 66.

the church, which allowed Calvin to claim "that seen and known tares shall grow and remain in the planted church, until God root them out."[38] To be sure, Barrow agreed with Calvin that the church would never be completely pure. But Barrow also believed that the church must do all that it could to condemn known sinners, purging them from the church if they refused to repent. To Barrow's disgust, however, Calvin used the parable to claim that the church was a mixed body, and that separation from the church because of visible sin was itself the sin of schism. Barrow argued that Calvin's interpretation of the field as the church reflected a faulty view of church discipline. As did other Separatists, Barrow rejected Calvin's claim that the church had only two identifying marks: preaching of the word and proper administration of the sacraments.[39] Separatists argued that Calvin neglected a third essential characteristic of any true church: the responsibility to discipline sinners and cleanse the church of error. In this important parable, Barrow found a biblical condemnation of Calvin's defective understanding of church discipline.[40]

Like Simons, Barrow used Jesus' explanation of the parable to combat Calvin's claim that the field signified the church. Both Simons and Barrow took Jesus' identification of the field as the world literally, not figuratively as Calvin read it. Furthermore, Barrow noted that this interpretation of the field as the world fit with the rest of scripture, and especially with the Genesis account of creation.[41] Barrow believed that the parable of the weeds was a

---

[38] Henry Barrow, *A Brief Discoverie of the False Church*, in *The Writings of Henry Barrow, 1587–1590*, ed. Leland H. Carlson (London: Allen and Unwin, 1962) 295.

[39] Ibid., 295.

[40] Ibid., 294–95.

[41] Ibid., 295. This literal appeal to Christ's explanation of the field as the world became a standard exegetical move for English Separatists and General Baptists. For example, see the anonymous tract, *Objections: Answered by Way of Dialogue* (n.p.: 1615). In this work, the author (probably John Murton) referred to Jesus' interpretation of the field as the world. The author's point was that if Christ had intended the field to be the church, Christ would have contradicted

symbolic retelling of the world's creation and the beginning of sin. According to this interpretation, before the weeds' appearance, the field represented the newly created world before the advent of evil. Moreover, as the enemy in the parable corrupted the field by sowing weeds, the serpent in the Garden of Eden corrupted the world through "fraud and malice." And, as the field must endure the weeds until harvest, the world must endure the remnants of sin until God's final judgment.[42] These parallels convinced Barrow that the field represented the world, not the church, just as Jesus stated in his explanation of the parable.

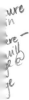

Through his understanding of the field as a reference to the world, Barrow read the parable as a command to endure sin in the civil sphere. He emphasized that the point of the parable was that God would purge sin from the world at the last judgment and that no human, "by a rash and inordinate zeal," is to judge prematurely. Barrow argued that Christ used this parable to teach "patience and

---

his directions for excommunication in Matt 18, as well as Paul's directives in 1 Cor 5 (18-19). On the authorship of this tract, see Leon McBeth, *English Baptist Literature on Religious Liberty to 1689* (New York: Arno Press, 1980) 49–50. While Barrow represented the majority opinion of Separatists in interpreting the field as the world, John Robinson was one leading Separatist who took more than one approach to the parable. Robinson was willing to concede Calvin's point that the field was the church. Robinson argued, however, that if the field represented the church, then the tares signified not scandalous sinners, but hypocrites who were hidden in the church. Thus Jesus' command to leave the tares in the field until harvest did not mean that the church had to endure notorious sinners in its midst. Instead, the parable simply warned that even the purest church contained some hypocrites hidden among its members. Accordingly, since these hypocrites were hidden, they could not be safely rooted out of the church. Just as rooting out the tares endangered the wheat, so rooting out supposed hypocrites threatened true Christians, for it was sometimes difficult to distinguish between the two. (See John Robinson, *A Justification of Separation from the Church of England,* in vol. 2 of *The Works of John Robinson,* ed. Robert Ashton [Boston: Doctrinal Tract and Book Society, 1851] 124.) For a General Baptist who interpreted the field as the church, see John Smyth, *Paralleles, Censures, Observations,* in vol. 2 of *The Works of John Smyth,* ed. W. T. Whitley (Cambridge: Cambridge University Press, 1915) 384–85.

[42] Barrow, *Brief Discovery,* in *Writings, 1587–1590,* 295.

sobriety towards all men," prompting disciples to pray that God may bring sinners to repentance. He believed that to purge sinners from the world prematurely would extinguish any hope of their repentance and "shut the door of God's grace." To further support his point, Barrow referred to Paul and Mary Magdalene, who were heinous sinners before being converted to serve God. Barrow asserted that it would have been tragic if these two had "been plucked up by the roots" as they grew among "the weeds and tares in the field of the world," prior to their eventual conversions.[43]

Barrow insisted that while the parable of the weeds forbade judging sinners in the world, it did not forbid disciplining sinners in the church. Barrow made this point with reference to Paul, observing that he directed the Corinthians not to judge those outside the church because that was God's responsibility (1 Cor 5:12–13). Thus, similar to the parable's command to leave sinners alone in the world until judgment, Paul encouraged restraint and patience, because God would judge the world at the appointed time. Yet Paul advised Christians to discipline sinners within the church and to excommunicate unrepentant violators (1 Cor 5:12–13). This appeal to the Pauline text strengthened Barrow's argument that the field was not the church because Paul commanded that the church be cleansed from all wicked persons. Barrow denied that the church was a field where "stinking weeds and noisome tares" grew. Instead, God provided "the weeding hook of his word, and the power" of Christ for the disciplining of his church. Contrary to Calvin's interpretation of this parable, the church was not a weed-infested field; it was a "garden" that needed careful weeding to maintain its beauty.[44]

In his zeal to weed the garden of the church, Barrow supported ministerial discipline with political power. He asserted that it was the duty of both ministers and magistrates to purify the church by

---

[43] Ibid., 296–97.
[44] Ibid., 297.

rejecting "the open ungodly."[45] Thus Barrow's interpretation of the parable of the weeds did not exclude the state's involvement with the church. As Michael Watts pointed out, "Henry Barrow" saw "nothing wrong in the state enforcing outward conformity in religion, provided that it was the religion approved by Henry Barrow."[46] And Barrow was not alone. He represented the typical Separatist belief that, as Edmund Morgan said, "the state *ought* to control religion, that the government *ought* to require everybody who worshipped to worship the way the Separatists did."[47]

In sum, Barrow's interpretation represented the standard Separatist view that, in contrast to Calvin's interpretation, the parable of the weeds did not teach that the church should be a mixed body of the elect with the openly sinful. This view of the church offended Separatists' convictions regarding discipline, which they considered an essential mark of any true church. Thus Separatists used the parable to defend church purity.

This view of the parable contrasts with that of Simons, who used it not only to deny interpretations such as that of Calvin, but also to support religious liberty. While Separatists agreed with Simons in preferring the literal interpretation of Christ's statement that the field is the world, Separatist writers never advocated complete religious liberty for all. Indeed, as the examination of

---

[45] Henry Barrow, "Barrow's Final Answer To Gifford—Marginalia," in *The Writings of John Greenwood and Henry Barrow, 1591–1593,* ed. Leland H. Carlson, Elizabethan Nonconformist Texts (London: Allen and Unwin, 1970) 194–95. See also Barrow's admonition that private citizens should not "stretch forth their hand by force to the reformation of any public enormities, which are by the magistrate's authority set up" (*The First Part of the Platforme, Writings, 1587–1590,* 229). See also Spurgin, *Williams and Puritan Radicalism,* 70–71. On this issue of church and state relations, Barrow echoed Robert Browne; see Spurgin, 111–12; Champlin Burrage, *The Early English Dissenters in the Light of Recent Research (1550–1641),* 2 vols. (Cambridge: Cambridge University Press, 1912) I:103–104.

[46] Michael R. Watts, *The Dissenters: From the Reformation to the French Revolution* (Oxford: Clarendon Press, 1978) 47.

[47] Morgan, *Roger Williams: The Church and the State* (New York: Harcourt Brace, 1967) 90.

needed
state to
aid
church
discipline

Barrow demonstrated, Separatists depended upon the state's powers to assist in church discipline. Consequently, Barrow and other Separatists steered a middle course between Simons and Calvin. As did Simons, Separatists denied Calvin's "mixed body" definition of the church. As did Calvin, however, the Separatists denied that the parable interfered with magistrates' responsibilities to punish religious violators. For Separatists, the parable did not inhibit church discipline, nor did it require religious freedom or the separation of church and state.[48]

III. JOHN COTTON: THE PARABLE OF THE WEEDS IN NEW ENGLAND PURITANISM

A. The Identity of the Weeds

In the parable of the weeds, John Cotton found a biblical defense of the Puritan commonwealth against Roger Williams's attacks. Cotton believed that the proper interpretation of the parable depended upon the definition of two key terms, the weeds and the field. The identity of the weeds revealed the nature of the evil that Jesus commanded his followers to tolerate "until the end of the age." As the previous discussion demonstrates, interpreters up to the seventeenth century were divided in their interpretations of the weeds in the parable. While Jesus identified the weeds as "the children of the evil one," this description confused as much as it

---

[48] Hugh Spurgin notes that Separatists "were concerned with certain, specific, religious grievances and with their own right to worship, not with the freedom of other unusual agitators" (*Williams and Radical Puritanism*, 123). The first English statements of religious liberty and separation of church and state came not from Separatists but from Baptists. These statements began with John Smyth in 1612. See John Smyth, *Propositions and Conclusions Concerning the True Christian Religion, 1612–1614*, in *Baptist Confessions of Faith*, ed. William L. Lumpkin (Valley Forge: Judson Press, 1969) 140; William Estep, "Sixteenth-Century Anabaptism and the Puritan Connections: Reflections upon Baptist Origins," in *Mennonites and Baptists*, ed. Paul Toews (Winnipeg: Kindred Press, 1993) 22–23.

clarified. As most Puritans recognized, evil "children" came in many forms, and surely Jesus did not intend that Christian churches and commonwealths should tolerate all varieties of satanic progeny! Here, then, was the significant question: what specific category of evil children did these weeds represent? Did Jesus consider these particular "children of the evil one" to be immoral hypocrites, flagrant heretics, or both? Cotton believed that the answers to these questions were critical to the parable's relevance in the seventeenth century.

In his attempt to identify the weeds, Cotton found a clue in the master's caution that pulling them up before the harvest would endanger the wheat (Matt 13:29). Why would the removal of the weeds threaten the wheat? Was the master concerned that the close proximity of the weeds and wheat made it impossible to remove one without uprooting the other? Or was it a problem of recognition, with the master doubting that his servants could tell the difference between the two types of plants? Cotton preferred the latter view, arguing that the master instructed his servants to leave the weeds alone because of the visible similarity between the weeds and the good grain. Cotton surmised that, unlike "briars and thorns," which were obviously undesirable weeds that the servants would have easily recognized, "tares" were a distinctive type of weed that resembled good grain. Thus, the master warned his servants not to pull up the tares because he feared they would pluck out some of the wheat due to mistaken identity.[49]

Cotton believed that this visible similarity between tares and wheat held important implications for the proper interpretation of the parable. While Jesus identified the tares as "the children of the

---

[49] In his *Bloudy Tenent*, Williams included an anonymous Baptist letter that was probably written by John Murton, as well as Cotton's response to that letter. Williams then devoted half of the *Bloudy Tenent* in response to Cotton's letter. This citation is taken from Cotton's letter as quoted in Williams's *Bloudy Tenent* (John Cotton, "The Answer of Mr. John Cotton of Boston," in vol. 3 of *Complete Writings*, 43). See also John Cotton, *The Bloudy Tenent, Washed, and Made White in the Bloud of the Lamb*, ed. Richard C. Robey, Research Library of Colonial Americana (London: 1647; reprint, New York: Arno, 1972) 40.

evil one" (13:38), Cotton believed that the visible similarity between the weeds and the wheat meant that these wicked children were similar in appearance to true Christians. Accordingly, while Jesus proclaimed that Christians should tolerate these "children of the evil one" until the end of the age, these wicked children were not gross violators of religious orthodoxy. For Cotton, the visible similarity between the weeds and the wheat was comforting because it implied that Jesus did not intend the unimaginable—that Christian churches and commonwealths should tolerate even the most destructive of heretics and pagans. After dismissing this radical interpretation, Cotton argued that the weeds represented hypocrites—children of Satan who appeared outwardly to be righteous Christians, although they were actually wicked in their hearts.[50] Just as weeds closely resembled the wheat, so did hypocrites appear to be faithful Christians.

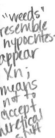

Furthermore, Cotton determined that the weeds represented not only hypocritical persons, but also certain erroneous doctrines and practices. Again, Cotton did not understand the weeds to signify obviously heretical doctrines and corrupt practices of worship. He insisted that obvious errors were easy to recognize, since the Bible was very clear about "fundamental and principal points of doctrine or worship." Cotton believed that any person who rejected these basic elements of orthodoxy did so purposefully, well aware of "the dangerous error of his way." Yet Cotton conceded that those who rejected the clear dictates of scripture and adopted heretical opinions should receive punishment only after the church warned them and gave them opportunities to repent, as Paul directed (Titus 3:10–11). If the commands of scripture and the warnings of the orthodox went unheeded by a stubborn individual, Cotton believed that both church and state rightly punished this sinner. But church and civil officers did not punish

---

[50] Thomas Hooker agreed with Cotton that the parable contained instruction about hypocrisy. See Thomas Hooker, *The Preface to William Ames's A Fresh Suit Against Human Ceremonies in God's Worship*, in *Thomas Hooker: Writings in England and Holland, 1626–1633*, 322.

this sinner "for cause of conscience, but for sinning against his own conscience." This was the case, since the true conscience received direction from scripture, which clearly detailed the major points of orthodox belief and practice. Cotton insisted that heresy usually did not result from ignorance, but from pride and stubbornness.[51] Heretics usually understood orthodoxy; they just chose to reject it. Indeed, heretics often recognized the wheat of the field, but they preferred the briars and thorns.

Cotton acknowledged that while the Bible clarified the most fundamental Christian beliefs and practices, less fundamental ones were sometimes harder to discern. He believed that this was an important lesson of the parable of the weeds. For him, the weeds represented errant opinions on less fundamental points that, while false, differed only slightly from the truth, just as the weeds differed only slightly from the wheat. Cotton knew that even good Christians often mistook such issues for the truth. Thus he believed that this parable did not condemn the good Christians in whom such weeds grew, because the good would then be burned for the sake of the bad, the wheat sacrificed on account of the weeds. Even so, Cotton cautioned that those who held their lesser errors enjoyed toleration only when they exhibited "a spirit of Christian meekness and love" and not "a boisterous and arrogant spirit" that disturbed the civil peace. This description of an "arrogant spirit" was undoubtedly a thinly-veiled reference to Williams. Nevertheless, Cotton argued that these kinds of Christians—slightly mistaken, but meek and peaceful—were "not to be persecuted, but tolerated," until God revealed his truth to them.[52] Cotton said that it was only in this limited sense that Christ called for religious toleration in the parable of the weeds.[53]

Essentially, then, Cotton believed that the weeds signified covert evil that had the appearance of righteousness. The weeds did

weeds = covert evil that looks righteous

---

[51] Cotton, "Answer of Mr. John Cotton," in vol. 3 of Williams's *Complete Writings*, 42–43.

[52] Ibid., 43. Cotton correlates this passage with Phil 3:17 and Rom 14:1–4.

[53] Ibid.

not signify obvious sinners, heretics, or openly false beliefs, but hypocritical wolves in sheep's clothing and false doctrines that closely resembled orthodoxy. Cotton surmised that Jesus would not have used "tares" to symbolize persons who lived openly heretical and scandalous lives and doctrines that were clearly false. Instead, Jesus would have referred to such gross offenders and false doctrines as "briars and thorns" because these were obvious weeds, clearly distinguishable from the wheat, and ready to be cast into the fire upon discovery. Consequently, the parable of the wheat and weeds did not concern the toleration of openly sinful and heretical persons or false beliefs in church and state.[54]

B. The Identity of the Field

The second critical issue concerned the identity of the field in the parable. While Jesus identified the field as the "world," this identification left room for conjecture. Was Jesus speaking literally or figuratively? Did Jesus use the term "world" to denote a secular realm that was distinct from the church? Alternatively, did Jesus consider "world" to be a figurative reference to the church as the "Christian world"—the universal community of his followers? Interpretations divided on this issue, with Calvin among those who regarded the field as the church, and Simons and the Separatists regarding the field as the world. The identity of the field was crucial because it determined the application of the parable: was the parable only relevant to discipline in the church, or did it contain instruction for life in the civil state?

In his interpretation of the field, Cotton opted for Calvin's interpretation: the field signified the church. He argued that since the householder signified Christ, his field was the church, the realm of his spiritual rule. Accordingly, Christ's decree to leave the tares alone until harvest was a command for the church to endure the presence of hypocritical Christians until the final judgment. The glaring difficulty with this interpretation was that it appeared to contradict Jesus' own interpretation of the parable, which

[54] Ibid., 42–43.

identified the field with "the world" (13:38). As did Calvin, Cotton negotiated this exegetical impasse by interpreting Jesus' explanation figuratively, claiming that Jesus did not mean that the field designated the world in its entirety, but (by [a] usual trope) the church—the professed followers of Christ who lived in the world.[55] In order to support this position, Cotton referred to some common biblical usages of "world," emphasizing scriptural pronouncements of Christ's love for the world (e.g., John 3:16), and his willingness to sacrifice himself for it (1 John 2:2).[56]

Cotton found support for his argument in the surprise of the servants. He noted that the servants of the householder were genuinely surprised that tares were in the field and this unexpected discovery led them to ask their master if he had sown only wheat in the field (Matt 13:27). Cotton reasoned that the surprise of the servants was inexplicable if the field symbolized the secular world. A worldly "field" littered with sinful "tares" would have surprised no one, for the world had been filled with all types of sinners ever since it was repopulated after the great flood of Noah's time.[57] Cotton argued that the servants' discovery of error and hypocrisy was surprising only if one allowed that the field signified the church.

This brought Cotton to the application of the parable: this story was a correction to those who were shocked at the sight of imperfection in the church. Even in a commonwealth populated by Puritans, this parable delivered a moderating word to overly zealous seekers of purity, for Christ commanded them to accept the minor imperfections of the church and to leave them alone until the final judgment. Cotton therefore removed the parable's application from the realm of civil authority, placing it exclusively

---

[55] John Cotton, *Bloudy Tenent, Washed*, 41. For another Puritan interpretation of the field as the church, see Thomas Shepard, *The Parable of the Ten Virgins*, vol. 2 of *The Works of Thomas Shepard* (Boston: Doctrinal Tract and Book Society, 1853; reprint, New York: A.M.S., 1967) 185–86, 188.

[56] Cotton, *Bloudy Tenent, Washed*, 41.

[57] Ibid., 42.

within the scope of church discipline. Christ's command to leave the tares alone until harvest was not a directive for magistrates to restrain from disciplining sinners, heretics, and pagans in the civil state. Instead, the parable was a correction to overly harsh discipline in the church—a reminder that, despite earnest attempts to cleanse the church of sin, ultimate perfection awaited the "harvest" of the final judgment.

IV. ROGER WILLIAMS: THE PARABLE OF THE WEEDS AND RELIGIOUS LIBERTY

In his encounter with the parable of the weeds—along with its controversial history of exegesis—Williams had three main concerns. Like most interpreters before him, Williams knew the importance of rightly identifying both the weeds and the field in the parable. Unlike most interpreters, however, Williams also was concerned to identify the parable's servants. In Williams's view, interpreters had wrongly supported religious persecution and Christendom by misinterpreting one or more of these three crucial elements of the text. Even so, he believed that a correct exegesis of these elements revealed the parable's advocacy of religious liberty.

A. The Identity of the Weeds

From the outset, Williams opposed Cotton's explanation that the weeds closely resembled the wheat. According to Williams's exegesis, the Greek word for tares (*zizanion*), also referred to cockle and darnel—weeds that knowledgeable farmers easily distinguished from good wheat.[58] Yet Williams observed that Cotton was an influential minister, and not a humble farmer. While Williams endured banishment to the wilderness, he often contrasted his situation with that of Cotton, who lived luxuriously, sitting "in as soft and rich a saddle as any throughout the whole country,

---

[58] Williams, *Bloudy Tenent*, in vol. 3 of *Complete Writings*, 101.

through the greatness and richness" of Boston.[59] Perhaps Williams suspected that Cotton's comfortable life in Boston had dulled his agricultural sensibilities and necessitated a refresher course in distinguishing wheat from weeds. Whether in contemporary fields of grain or in the pages of the Greek New Testament, Williams argued that the distinction between wheat and weeds was clear and that Cotton was mistaken to conclude otherwise.[60]

Besides evidence from agricultural terms, Williams pointed out that Cotton's exegesis did not explain the servants' ability to distinguish the weeds from wheat in the parable (Matt 13:26–27). If Cotton were correct in his claim that the weeds were indistinguishable from the wheat, how were the servants able to inform the householder of the weeds' presence in the field? Williams's answer was that the servants recognized the obvious weeds as they grew among the blades of wheat, and this alarming discovery led them to inform their master. Moreover, the servants' recognition of the weeds was not due to some miraculous revelation, but from common agricultural experience. As Williams observed, "as soon as tares and wheat are sprung up to blade and fruit, every husbandman can tell which is wheat, and which are tares and cockle."[61] Thus he concluded that the delay in pulling up

---

[59] Williams, *Bloody Tenent Yet More Bloody*, in vol. 4 of *Complete Writings*, 304.

[60] After being admonished by Cotton on this point, Williams admitted that *zizanion* could denote a particular type of weed that resembled the wheat while both were in a state of immaturity. See Cotton, *Bloudy Tenent, Washed*, 39–40; Williams, *Bloody Tenent Yet More Bloody*, in vol. 4 of *Complete Writings*, 119–20. Yet Williams replied that this did not compromise his main point: that it was not difficult for an experienced husbandman to distinguish the wheat from the tares when they had "grown up to blade and fruit" (*Bloody Tenent Yet More Bloody*, in vol. 4 of *Complete Writings*, 119).

[61] Williams, *Bloudy Tenent*, in vol. 3 of *Complete Writings*, 102–103. This was not the only interpretation of the tares offered by those who used the parable to argue for religious liberty. For instance, English pamphleteer Henry Robinson agreed with Cotton's interpretation that the tares might signify hypocrites. Thus, Robinson says that "the outward man may so conform himself if he will, as that it is impossible for the world to find him out, because they cannot arrive to the

the tares was not due to a problem with recognition. The servants identified the tares, but allowed these weeds to grow with the wheat because the master commanded them to leave the tares untouched.

Williams's rejection of the similarity of the wheat and the weeds threatened the basis of Cotton's interpretation of the parable. Cotton sought to reject the radical implications of the parable by minimizing the distinction between the weeds and the wheat. In arguing that the weeds were indistinguishable from the wheat, Cotton was able to claim that the weeds signified hypocritical sinners who resembled true Christians, and not radical pagans and heretics who directly challenged the Christian faith. In Cotton's view, Jesus advocated a policy of discretion in purging hypocrites from the church, and not an outright prohibition against the punishment of radicals who publicly opposed orthodox belief.

Williams, however, embraced this radical view of the parable and determined to prove that the evil children the weeds represented were "open and visible professors" of heretical religious convictions. Since tares were not subtle weeds, but "as bad as briars and thorns," obviously distinguishable from good wheat, they did not signify merely "unsuspected foxes"—deceitful hypocrites who hid their degradation. Instead, the tares represented religious offenders who were "as bad as those greedy wolves" that Paul warned about, for they intentionally used dangerous teachings to deceive Christians (Acts 20:28–31).[62] In opposition to Cotton's

---

heart," for "they work only upon the body, and cannot reach the soul." Even so, Robinson sides with Williams on the overall meaning of the parable, arguing that it "seems to me a full argument that the State should not be forwards in putting any to death...but this place makes especially against persecution for matters of Religion." (Henry Robinson, *Liberty of Conscience*, in vol. 3 of *Tracts on Liberty in the Puritan Revolution, 1638–1647*, ed. William Haller [New York: Columbia University Press, 1934] 167.)

[62] Williams, *Bloudy Tenent*, in vol. 3 of *Complete Writings*, 99–100, 103–104. Williams also denied Cotton's idea that the tares signified not only persons, but doctrines and practices as well. Again, Williams appealed to Jesus' explanation of the parable to make his point. Williams observed that Jesus specifically identified

position, therefore, Williams argued that the tares signified obvious enemies of Christianity. After all, Jesus identified the tares as "children of the wicked one," contrasting them with the "good seed," which signified "the children of the kingdom" (Matt 13:38, KJV). Williams reasoned that the wheat signified the righteous and the weeds denoted the opposite—the recognized followers of Satan. Far from hidden hypocrites, the tares signified heretics and Satanic "anti-Christians" who opposed Christianity directly and openly.

Williams argued that the parable of the weeds proposed the unsettling notion that faithful Christians must live among the enemies of Christ, including heretics, false Christians, "anti-Christians," and idolaters.[63] Contrary to the ambitious designs of Puritan Massachusetts, God endorsed no holy commonwealths, only holy churches. While Puritan leaders used biblical authority to construct a godly society, Williams attacked this Puritan civilization at its scriptural foundation. In the parable of the weeds, Williams discovered a biblical representation of life in a mixed society in which Christians held no authority over adherents to other religions in the civil state. In the terms of the parable, therefore, even the best of the wheat must share the field with the worst of the weeds until the reapers separate them at harvest.

---

the "good seed" as "the children of the kingdom," and he called the tares the "children" of the "wicked one" (v. 38; KJV and GB). Thus, the tares were not doctrines and practices. Instead, Jesus explained that both the good seed and the tares signified persons: the good seed denoted the children of Christ's kingdom and the tares identified the children of the evil one. Unlike Cotton, Williams was careful to limit his interpretation of the tares to the parameters set by Jesus' own explanation. Williams, *Bloudy Tenent*, in vol. 3 of *Complete Writings*, 100. Williams reiterated this point in *Queries of Highest Consideration*, in vol. 2 of *The Complete Writings of Roger Williams* (Providence: Narragansett Club Publications, 1867; reprint, New York: Russell & Russell, 1963) 274.

[63] Williams, *Bloudy Tenent*, in vol. 3 of *Complete Writings*, 107. See also Williams's *Queries*, in vol. 7 of *The Complete Writings of Roger Williams* (New York: Russell & Russell, 1963) 274.

B. The Identity of the Field

In taking issue with interpretations of the field offered by Calvin and Cotton, Williams sided with Anabaptist and Separatist interpreters, arguing that Jesus settled the issue with his statement: "the field is the world" (Matt 13:38, KJV, GB). In Williams's view, identifying the world as a figurative reference to the church was an immense exegetical mistake with profound political consequences. This confusion of the secular and sacred spheres in biblical texts was common among religious persecutors who "labored to turn this field of the world into the garden of the Church."[64] Williams compared the church to a beautiful garden that was both situated within the world and identifiable as holy and distinguishable from the world's sin. The world was, as this parable taught, comparable to a field strewn with righteous wheat mixed with sinful tares. While the garden of the church should remain pure, the field of the world was a habitat of both virtue and wickedness. The problem was that Christendom's magistrates and ministers confused the garden of the church with the field of the world. They vainly attempted to purify the world of religious violators. This tainted the church by enlisting the body of Christ as an accomplice in persecution and murder, and igniting religious wars that betrayed the command of Jesus in this parable.

For Williams, the confusion of church and world began with Emperor Constantine's political establishment of Christianity in the fourth century. Williams compared Constantine, who favored the church, with Emperor Nero, who persecuted Christians. Williams observed that, in their zeal to promote the church, Constantine and the other emperors who advocated Christianity "did more to hurt Christ Jesus" and his followers "than the raging fury of the most bloody Neroes." Williams's reasoning was that while Christians endured political persecution under Nero, at least they remained pure and faithful to Christ to the death, thereby retaining their integrity as disciples. Such was not the case in the

---

[64] Williams, *Bloudy Tenent*, in vol. 3 of *Complete Writings*, 105.

fourth century, when Christianity arose from its status as a minority religion to receive the sanction of the emperor. Williams believed that this apparent rise in church fortunes was actually a decline in faithfulness to Christ. Because they supported "their religion by the material sword," rulers like Constantine snuffed out the church and replaced Christianity with Christendom. Williams made this point vividly, noting that when Constantine drew "the sword of civil power in the suppressing of other consciences for the establishing of the Christian, then began the great mystery of the church's sleep, the gardens of Christ's churches turned into the wilderness of national religion, and the world (under Constantine's dominion) to the most unchristian Christendom."[65] The slumber of the church continued in the reigns of subsequent so-called Christian rulers, for "Christianity fell asleep in Constantine's bosom, and [in] the laps and bosoms of those Emperors professing the name of Christ."[66] Williams granted that Constantine and the bishops who assisted him had good intentions when they used civil power to punish pagans and enforce the Christian gospel. But in disobeying "the command of Christ Jesus to permit the tares to grow in the field of the world, they made the garden of the Church, and the field of the world to be all one."[67]

Williams believed that misinterpretations of the parable of the weeds proved that biblical exegesis had suffered a lethal blow with the political establishment of Christianity. He argued that the attempt to create a Christian empire led interpreters to confuse the distinction between ecclesiastical and civil realms of authority. As a result, interpreters commonly misunderstood biblical passages that Christ intended for the church as directions for the world and vice-versa. John Cotton's interpretation of the parable of the weeds was

---

[65] Ibid., 184; Williams, *Bloody Tenent Yet More Bloody*, in vol. 4 of *Complete Writings*, 442.

[66] Williams, *Bloudy Tenent*, in vol. 3 of *Complete Writings*, 184. For an analysis of Williams's view of the fall of the church see Allen, "The Restauration of Zion," 271–88.

[67] Williams, *Bloudy Tenent*, in vol. 3 of *Complete Writings*, 184.

a prime example of this kind of misuse. His defense of Christendom was based on interpreting the field as the church when Jesus had stated clearly that the field symbolized the world. Part of Christendom's corruption lay in its tendency to confuse church and world in the biblical text, thereby transforming sacred scripture into a dictate of persecution. The tragedy of this exegesis was that godly ministers such as Cotton believed that it was their duty to cleanse the world's field by plucking up its weeds prematurely. Williams claimed that church leaders, buoyed by their authority, believed "that they [were] ready to run to heaven and fetch fiery judgments" in order "to consume" heretics and "pluck them by the roots out of the world." Yet Williams argued that such actions contradicted the example and teachings of Christ, who was "the meek Lamb of God" who permitted "false Christians," and even "Antichristians," to remain in the world unhampered until the end of the world.[68]

C. The Identity of the Servants

Williams distinguished himself from Cotton and most other interpreters in his diligent attempt to identify the servants in the parable. The servants were the first to discover the weeds in the field. Upon making this discovery, they reported the weeds to their master, asking him whether they should pluck them up. The master ordered his servants to leave the weeds for fear of endangering the wheat. Williams wrestled with the question: did the servants signify magistrates or ministers? This problem was even more difficult because, unlike in the cases of the tares and the field, Jesus did not identify the servants in his explanation of the parable to his disciples. This was a puzzling omission given the importance of the servants to the parable. The servants were the primary actors in the parable—they alerted the master to the weeds' presence and they received the master's command to "leave the tares alone." Accordingly, Williams reasoned that the seventeenth-century equivalents to the servants were the ones to whom

---

[68] Ibid., 104.

Christ directed his command to resist persecuting heretics and pagans in the world.

Identifying the parable's servants produced a dilemma. On the one hand, if Williams determined that the servants signified ministers, this could imply that the field signified the church rather than the world. The church was, after all, the realm of ministerial authority. Williams had to be careful here, for this determination could undermine his contention that the parable's relevance extended beyond the church to encompass Christian behavior in the wider world.

On the other hand, an identification of the servants as magistrates was also problematic for Williams. If the servants signified magistrates, the implication was that Jesus' followers who actively did his bidding in the world were worldly rulers in the state rather than ministers in the church. This idea of a Christ-directed political state veered dangerously close to the Christendom that Williams abhorred. Here was Williams's dilemma. If he identified the servants as ministers, he risked supporting Cotton's argument that the field was the church and that the parable's authority extended only to the ecclesial realm. Yet, if Williams identified Christ's servants as magistrates, he would find himself supporting a Christian civil state.

Williams approached this delicate issue by identifying the servants in the parable as a figural reference to ministers—with the proviso that the parable concerned not their roles in the church but their responsibilities in the world.[69] The parable concerned how ministers were to deal with heretical "weeds" in the world's "field." This was the crux of Williams's radical reading of the parable. He argued that the parable commanded Christ's ministers to take a prophetic stance in relation to the civil governments of Christendom, advocating religious liberty in opposition to the coercive policies of the state. This was a decisive issue for Williams because his experience as a banished radical taught him that Christendom

---

[69] Ibid., 114. Williams cited Eph 5–6 and Col 3 as examples of directives for social roles in the New Testament.

demanded a cooperative church that aligned itself with the state and pliant ministers who willingly supported the civil government. In Massachusetts, Williams saw the violent consequences of ministers and magistrates who enshrined theological convictions into public policy. In place of this unholy alliance of Christendom, Williams asserted an alternative view of the minister's role in the civil realm that Christ outlined in the parable of the weeds. As the "servants" of Christ in the "field" of the world, ministers were to advocate religious liberty for all—including heretics and pagans.

Williams believed that the parable's command that ministers should leave heretical tares alone in the world's field had important implications. First, a minister was not to pluck up heretics by praying for their "temporal destruction." In making this point, Williams referred to a passage from the Gospels in which the disciples asked Jesus if he would command them to call down fire from heaven to consume the "heretical" Samaritans. Jesus replied with a stern rebuke (Luke 9:51–55). In Williams's view, Jesus' rejection of the disciples' request to burn the Samaritans was similar to the master's denial of his servants' offer to pluck the weeds from the field. In both texts, Christ advised his ministerial "servants" against condemning heretical "tares" in the world. Instead of such violent measures, Williams believed that Christ directed his followers to pray for all people, especially heretics and magistrates, and for civil peace.[70]

Second, Williams believed that this parable's message for ministers went beyond prayer to activism in society. He argued that this parable commanded ministers not to serve as accomplices in the state's prosecution of pagans and heretics.[71] Williams declared that God's ministers were not to provoke "civil magistrates, kings, emperors, governors, parliaments, or general courts or assemblies to punish and persecute all such persons out of the dominions and territories as worship not the true God according to the revealed

---

[70] Williams, *Bloudy Tenent*, in vol. 3 of *Complete Writings*, 115. Williams also cites comparative texts in Jer 29:7 and 2 Tim 2.

[71] Ibid.

will of God in Christ Jesus."[72]Thus the parable guided ministers not in disciplining sinners in the church, but in accepting heretics in the state. In the secular realm, ministers were to be "wisdom's maidens" who convicted sinners "with meek and loving, yet vehement *persuasions*," and not with violent and corrupt acts of *coercion*.[73] Williams probably had in mind ministers such as Cotton, who conspired with magistrates to banish those like Williams from the civil sphere because of their religious differences. In place of this persecuting model of ministry, Williams proposed an ethic of discipleship in which ministers followed Jesus' command in the parable of the weeds.

Williams's interpretation of the parable forbade Christians from persecuting heretics because such violence contradicted the example of "the King of Peace" who was "no author of civil force." Jesus did not come "to destroy men's bodies," not even "for the highest opposition made against him," including "that of calling him Beelzebub and charging him with sorcery, and casting out of devils by the devil himself." Williams believed that the parable of the weeds commanded Christ's followers to live according to his example. The support of religious persecution was not an option for Christians because Jesus "locked up the hands of all that call him Lord and Master" with his command to his servants: "let the tares alone until harvest."[74]

Thus, in Williams's view, this parable represented Christ's rejection of magistrates and ministers who would "permit not in the civil state, any religion, worship or conscience but their own"— a persecuting policy that became a hallmark of Christendom's desire to put "the whole world's neck under their imperial yoke." Christendom threatened citizens who did not obey the state's

---

[72] Ibid., 116.

[73] Williams, *Bloody Tenent Yet More Bloody*, in vol. 4 of *Complete Writings*, 152; emphasis added. Williams drew the imagery of "wisdom's maidens" from Prov 9:3.

[74] Williams, *Bloody Tenent Yet More Bloody*, in vol. 4 of *Complete Writings*, 152; *The Examiner Defended in a Fair and Sober Answer*, in vol. 7 of *Complete Writings*, 257.

religion, warning that they would "be cut off from all natural and civil being in the world, by fire and sword."[75] In his interpretation of the wheat and weeds, Williams opposed the "bloody and Antichristian doctrine" whereby ministers and magistrates have joined forces to persecute Christ and his followers. This was the fulfillment of Jesus' caution that plucking up the weeds prematurely would endanger the good wheat, for persecutors have always crucified Jesus and his followers "under pretense of punishing heretics, schismatics, and seditious persons."[76]

As Williams knew well, this parable represented a political strategy that challenged the accepted view that an orderly society required an official, state-sponsored religion. Indeed, authorities in the seventeenth century suppressed religious freedom because they considered it a subversive idea that threatened to engulf society in chaos. Williams argued that religious freedom was not a threat to peace. To the contrary, religious freedom was the only way to peace in the civil state. Regardless of popular and Puritan opinion, it was not religious liberty but Christendom's use of civil power to coerce the conscience that caused religious war and violence. This tragedy, in Williams's view, was a fulfillment of the parable's warning that rooting out the tares before harvest would endanger the wheat. His position was that violent attempts to punish heretics brought little peace, but instead endangered even true Christians, since they could be "plucked up and torn out of this world by such bloody storms and tempests."[77] Accordingly, world peace resulted not from the persecuting efforts of states, but from adherence to the peaceful parable of the weeds. As he asserted, "Obedience to the command of Christ to let the tares alone will prove *the only means*

---

[75] Williams, *Bloody Tenent Yet More Bloody*, in vol. 4 of *Complete Writings*, 125.

[76] Ibid., 147.

[77] Williams, *Bloudy Tenent*, in vol. 3 of *Complete Writings*, 111.

to preserve [the] civil peace, and without obedience to this command of Christ, it is impossible...to preserve the civil peace."[78]

Thus Williams argued that the parable of the weeds was immensely important because it concerned the responsibilities of ministers in society. The parable required ministers to venture outside ecclesiastical boundaries to promote religious liberty in the secular world. While they were not officials of the state, ministers had a civil role, a responsibility to advocate religious liberty in opposition to persecution, and a duty to oppose coercion with a peaceful strategy of persuasion. Ministers, in Williams's view, should urge civil magistrates to adopt religious liberty, which was the only means of attaining civil peace, and a combination of sensible politics with pure religion. This message of the parable was of critical importance because Christian ministers often played a crucial role in religious persecution. Williams realized that the religious persecution promoted by states of Christendom was only possible because of the support of ministers. Without ministerial accomplices, magistrates would lack the justification and the motivation to purge religious offenders from the state. Williams, therefore, used the parable of the weeds to undermine the alliance of church and state by forbidding ministerial participation in religious persecution.

§⒪

Biblical interpretation had a profound influence on political realities in the seventeenth century. Just as modern political debates focus on issues such as rights, justice, and equality, political controversies in Puritan New England engaged the Bible. The great authority that scripture held in society meant that exegesis was a perilous enterprise. Roger Williams believed that the Bible, if

---

[78] Ibid., 112, emphasis added. Williams cited evidence for this point in the example of "the States of Holland," which lived in peace even though they approved no official religion and allowed all citizens freedom in spiritual matters (*Queries,* in vol. 2 of *Complete Writings,* 274).

properly understood, provided divine guidance for society. But he was also painfully aware that, in the hands of unscrupulous or mistaken interpreters, the cultural authority granted to the Bible could contribute to the detriment of church and state. Into this turbulent exegetical context, Williams introduced a subversive political interpretation of scripture. He proclaimed that religious liberty was a biblical correction to religious persecution, which was rooted in a false doctrine—a perversion of Christ's revelation in scripture. The tragedy for Williams was that the Bible contained holy teachings that many interpreters used to serve unholy purposes. He protested that such faulty interpretation supported zealous persecutors who trampled "God's meekest servants" in the name of orthodoxy and religious uniformity, enacting Christendom's desire to unify church and state.[79] In the process of corrupting the church, Williams believed that Christendom had corrupted biblical exegesis by devising an interpretative method that supported the state's claim to authority over religious matters. In so doing, advocates of Christendom commonly confused church and world in biblical passages. When viewed through the lens of Christendom, therefore, the Bible transformed from a redemptive, liberating word to a divisive, violent force. Williams believed that Christendom had corrupted the Bible as part of a grand, devilish scheme to render the church impotent and to cast the world into disarray.

According to Williams, such was the case in Christendom's interpretations of the parable of the weeds and the wheat. Throughout much of Christian history, this parable was at the center of an exegetical firestorm, provoking controversy from Augustine's struggles with the Donatists to Roger Williams's battles with Puritan New England. Much to Williams's frustration, allies of Christendom often had the upper hand in the struggle for the meaning of the parable; respected divines such as John Calvin and John Cotton argued that the parable had nothing to do with

---

[79] Williams, *Bloody Tenent Yet More Bloody,* in vol. 4 of *Complete Writings,* 339.

religious liberty in the civil realm. Their contention was that Jesus' command to allow weeds to grow in the field was a warning to overzealous purists who threatened to separate from the church at the first sign of imperfection. Accordingly, Calvin, Cotton, and other advocates of the magistrate's authority in religious concerns argued that Jesus' command to leave the weeds alone pertained only to the church, not to civil officers' responsibilities to protect the state from heresy or paganism. Such interpretations were, in Williams's view, perversions of the parable, and had devastating consequences in so-called "Christian" nations that committed heinous acts of violence in the name of Jesus. In opposition to Christendom's interpretation, Williams argued that Jesus clearly defined the field in the parable as the world, not the church. Accordingly, Jesus' command to leave the weeds alone was his clearest advocacy of religious liberty in the civil realm. Heretics and pagans, while possibly mistaken and evil in their religious beliefs, were therefore entitled to the freedom to live and worship without fear of persecution at the hands of "Christian" magistrates.

Williams recognized that he did not battle alone in his struggle with interpreters over the parable of the weeds. We have considered Menno Simons as an example of an earlier interpreter who argued his case for religious liberty from the parable; we could have cited many more. And, while Williams did not quote Simons's interpretation of the parable, he did cite an anonymous English Baptist's reference to the parable in the *Bloudy Tenent*[80] This mention of the parable set the stage for Williams's much longer, more developed argument. We should not be surprised that Williams found a kinship in thought with Baptist colleagues. Years after he had founded the first Baptist congregation in America only to reject the Baptist church along with all others, he continued to honor Baptists, speaking highly of their characters in the face of persecution and quoting from their writings.

---

[80] While anonymous, the Baptist writer was probably John Murton. (Williams, *Bloudy Tenent*, in vol. 3 of *Complete Writings*, iv–v, 29–39.)

Williams's quotation of the Baptist letter reveals his engagement with previous interpreters of the Bible. Williams was not alone in his reading of the Bible—contrary to the view of some prominent historians in the last century. To the contrary, he was an astute participant in the exegetical controversies of his day. Williams often commented on the long history of interpreters who wrestled with the parable of the weeds, attempting to uncover its implications for church and state. His quotation from the Baptist letter proves that he recognized that he was part of a succession of interpreters who found Jesus' advocacy of religious liberty in this parable.

Did Menno Simons and other sixteenth-century Anabaptists directly influence Williams and other seventeenth-century Baptists? This question may never be answered to everyone's satisfaction.[81]

---

[81] The question of Anabaptist influence on English Baptists is contested. For the predominant view that there was no historical relation between Anabaptists and Baptists, see Winthrop S. Hudson, "Baptists Were Not Anabaptists," *Chronicle* 16 (1953): 171–78. For contrary interpretations, see Estep, "Sixteenth-Century Anabaptism and the Puritan Connections," 1–38; idem, *The Anabaptist Story: An Introduction to Sixteenth-Century Anabaptism*, 3rd ed. (Grand Rapids: William B. Eerdmans Publishing, 1996) 271–73; James Robert Coggins, *John Smyth's Congregation: English Separatism, Mennonite Influence, and the Elect Nation*, ed. Cornelius J. Dyck, Studies in Anabaptist and Mennonite History (Scottdale: Herald Press, 1991); Glen H. Stassen, "Anabaptist Influence in the Origin of the Particular Baptists," *Mennonite Quarterly Review* 36/4 (1962): 322–48; and Timothy George, "Between Pacifism and Coercion: The English Baptist Doctrine of Religious Toleration," *Mennonite Quarterly Review* 58/1 (1984): 30–49. Nevertheless, Williams was certainly influenced in his reading of the tares by at least one English Baptist tract, likely written by John Murton, though published anonymously. Indeed, Williams quoted a selection of this tract at the beginning of *The Bloudy Tenent*. While Murton did not make the detailed argument from this parable that Williams did, he did cite the parable as a proof text for religious liberty. (See *A Most Humble Supplication of Many of the King's Majesty's Loyal Subjects*, in *Tracts on Liberty of Conscience and Persecution, 1614–1661*, ed. Edward Bean Underhill [New York: Burt Franklin, 1966] 214.) See also an anonymous work that Murton probably helped to author, *Objections: Answered by way of Dialogue*, 14, 19. Another English Baptist who cited the parable as a proof text for religious liberty was Leonard Busher. Like Murton,

But it is clear that, in the interpretation of the parable of the weeds, Baptists spoke in unity with earlier Anabaptists in arguing that this parable proclaimed religious liberty. Williams never associated his interpretation of the parable with that of Menno Simons, but he certainly knew of the radical tradition of interpreters who shared his vision of this parable.

Williams did not merely repeat previous interpretations; he adapted them creatively to speak to his unique context in the seventeenth century. Written years after his banishment by ministers and magistrates in Massachusetts, his interpretation of the parable reflected his disdain for ministers who enabled the violent persecution of the state. His reading of the parable focused on the servants who received the master's command to "leave the weeds alone." He viewed these servants as ministers who had responsibilities beyond the church to ensure that the state did not use Christ's name to persecute anyone—regardless of their heretical religious convictions. No doubt Williams's special attention to the servants was due in part to his experience as one who was banished by Boston's ministerial "servants" who had failed to heed Christ's direction in the parable. In his colonial Providence, Williams endeavored to demonstrate to Boston that even a field littered with weeds could bear the fruit of civil peace without enforcing religious uniformity via the state's coercive means.

Williams's engagement with this parable and its interpreters reveals his proficient understanding of how interpretations of the Bible affected the religious and political realities of his time. The stakes were especially high in controversies over the parable of the weeds because this text concerned Jesus' view of religious liberty and the relationship between church and state. To be sure, Williams's biblical case for religious liberty pivoted on his inter-

---

Busher made only brief references to the parable; see Leonard Busher, *Religious Peace; or a Plea for Liberty of Conscience,* in *Tracts on Liberty of Conscience and Persecution, 1614–1661,* ed. Edward Bean Underhill (New York: Burt Franklin, 1966) 24, 77. See also Richard Overton, *The Araignement of Mr. Persecution,* in Haller, vol. 3 of *Tracts on Liberty,* 232.

pretation of Jesus; he could not allow his opponents to characterize Jesus as a religious persecutor. In the first lines of his *Bloudy Tenent*, Williams defended his view of Christ, arguing that "the blood of so many hundred thousand souls of Protestants and Papists, spilt in the wars of present and former ages, for their respective consciences, is not required nor accepted by Jesus Christ the Prince of Peace."[82] Williams strove to characterize Jesus not as a worldly persecutor, but as a humble Lord of peace, the son "of mean and inferior parents," and "a Carpenter" who:

> Disdained not to enter this world in a stable, amongst beasts, as unworthy [of] the society of men: who passed through this world with the esteem of a mad man, a deceiver, a conjurer, a traitor against Caesar, and destitute of an house wherein to rest his head: who made choice of his first and greatest ambassadors out of fishermen, tentmakers, &c. and at last chose to depart on the stage of a painful shameful gibbet.[83]

To be sure, Williams's interpretation of the parable of the weeds posed a significant challenge to predominant understandings of the New Testament, especially the depiction of Christ in the Gospels. Williams faced other imposing obstacles, however, because advocates of Christendom had at their disposal numerous other texts from the New Testament that seemed to justify the state's duty to protect orthodoxy and to prohibit heresy. One of the chief weapons in Christendom's biblical arsenal was St. Paul. As the chief architect of the New Testament church, Paul had a profound influence in Puritan commonwealths that strove to imitate the earliest church in all of its details. Accordingly, if Williams were to make a biblical case for religious liberty that would stem the tide of religious persecution, he would have to overcome the challenge of Paul with a decisive reinterpretation of the great apostle. The next

---

[82] Williams, *Bloudy Tenent*, in vol. 3 of *Complete Writings*, 3.
[83] Williams, *Mr. Cottons Letter*, in vol. 1 of *Complete Writings*, 317.

chapter explores Williams's Pauline argument for religious liberty and its implications for Puritan New England.

Calvin: Field = church which will always be full of non/sinners
valueable info on church discipline — tolerate sinners,
exterminate heretical beliefs

Simmons: Civil authorities leave heretics alone — parable limits
overzealous persecution of AnaB by world

Sep/Barrow: church won't be pure but must condemn
sinners; parable is a recap of Gen.
-endure sin in the civil sphere b/c God will purge @ judge.
• can't discipline sinners in world, but can in church
* Gov should control religion and make everyone worship
as Seps did

Cotton: weeds = evil ppl who appear righteous; ≠ openly
heretical / obviously evil
- Field = church; parable directive for church not to
be overly harsh on church discipline; okay for magistrates
to discipline + punish

Williams:
• weeds = overt heretics
servants — can recognize diff, but don't pull up
* charge for Xns/heretics to live together w/o punishment
• field = world; problem is that magistrates (constantine)
enforced religion, making church and field as one → now
too difficut to determine the difference
• servants = those to whom X commanded to resist the
persecuting of heretics
* figural reference to ministers
→ ministers should stop supporting state persecutions of
heretics viz would strip state justification

w/Cotton - parable applied to church → leave heretics alone
- state can persecute

CHAPTER 4

ST. PAUL AND CIVIL GOVERNMENT IN THE PURITAN COLONIES

In October 1636, just over a year after the Massachusetts Bay Colony expelled him for his radical opinions, Roger Williams wrote a letter to his accusers that expressed his interpretation of his banishment. Williams wrote in response to a letter of admonition that Governor John Winthrop had written on behalf of officials in the Bay Colony.[1] In his letter to Williams, Winthrop had inquired about Williams's questionable spiritual condition. Williams acknowledged that Winthrop had intended well—that his letter was not that of a "Pharisee," but rather that of "a physician to the sick."[2] Nevertheless, Williams insisted that it was not he, but Massachusetts Bay that needed a physician. Williams said that Winthrop and his colleagues remained mired in "the Dungheap of this Earth" because they refused to separate from the corrupt Church of England. Most importantly, Williams criticized the Bay Colony for their willingness to persecute those, like Williams himself, who disagreed with them on religious matters. Williams said that, among all of God's people, Massachusetts Bay was "the

---

[1] See Glenn LaFantasie's editorial notes in Roger Williams, *The Correspondence of Roger Williams*, 2 vols. (Hanover NH: Brown University Press, 1988) 61. Winthrop's letter to Williams was similar to one that Massachusetts Bay later wrote to Anne Hutchinson following her banishment for antinomianism (see David D. Hall, ed., *The Antinomian Controversy, 1636–1638: A Documentary History* [Middletown: Wesleyan University Press, 1968] 390–95).

[2] Williams, *Correspondence*, 65.

worst by far" because they "smite and beat" their "fellow servants," and "expel them" from their "coasts."[3] Williams obviously considered himself a victim of religious persecution at the hands of Winthrop and his colleagues in the Bay Colony.

Williams's letter also demonstrated that he had found a biblical means of interpreting his banishment in the New Testament record of the life and words of Paul. Indeed, in his letter to Winthrop and the Bay Colony, Williams presented himself as a seventeenth-century Paul.[4] Williams continually paralleled his persecuted state with that of Paul, whose ministry was replete with struggles that he endured on behalf of Christ. Despite losing friends, respect, and the other benefits of life in the Bay Colony, Williams, like Paul, willingly sacrificed these worldly gains for the cause of Christ (see Phil 3:7–8).[5] Furthermore, while Paul was ready not only to face imprisonment, but to die in Jerusalem for Christ, Williams was "ready not only to be banished, but to die in New England for the name of the Lord Jesus" (cf. Acts 21:13).[6]

Williams's experience also resonated with that of Paul in his willingness to serve those who had rejected him. Paul wrote to the Corinthians that he would "very gladly spend and be spent for you; though the more abundantly I love you, the less I be loved" (2 Cor 12:15, KJV). Williams adapted Paul's words in his epistle to the Bay Colony, vowing that he would "rejoice to spend and be spent in any service (according to my conscience) for your welfares."[7] Williams did continue to serve Massachusetts Bay. As he reminded Winthrop in this letter, Williams had recently returned from a diplomatic mission on behalf of the Bay Colony, wherein he

---

[3] Ibid., 68.

[4] Ibid., *Correspondence*, 62. Williams's emphasis on Paul is evident from the letter's abundant references to Pauline epistles, as well as references to Paul's experiences as recorded in Acts. Thus, in a short letter of just over four pages, Williams made twelve references to Pauline epistles and one reference to Paul in Acts. See LaFantasie's notes in Williams, *Correspondence*, 70–72.

[5] Williams, *Correspondence*, 66.

[6] Ibid., 67.

[7] Ibid.

W letter
like
Pauline
epistle

prevented the Pequot and Narragansett tribes from aligning themselves against the English in the fall of 1636.[8] Thus, as Williams conceived it, his letter to Winthrop was similar to a seventeenth-century Pauline epistle, since Williams paralleled his treatment by the Bay Colony to Paul's treatment by his persecutors in the New Testament. Williams's identification with Paul was not limited to this letter.[9] His argument for the separation of church from state depended on his interpretation of Paul's instruction on the civil magistrate.[10] Williams dealt most extensively with Paul's teaching in Romans 13, and with the story of Paul's appeal to Caesar in Acts 25. But Williams also selected other Pauline texts to make a case for religious liberty against the persecuting states of Christendom. Williams's interpretation of Paul played a crucial role in his defense of the separation of church and state and religious liberty in seventeenth-century New England.

I. PAUL AND THE CIVIL MAGISTRATE: ROGER WILLIAMS'S INTERPRETIVE TRADITION

Roger Williams based his argument for the separation of church and state on a radical understanding of the civil magistrate. Unlike magisterial Reformers, New England Puritans, and English

---

[8] Ibid., 65, 70.

[9] John J. Teunissen and Evelyn J. Hinz, "Roger Williams, St. Paul, and American Primitivism," *The Canadian Review of American Studies* 4/2 (1973): 121–36. This study argues that "Williams saw more than a general affinity between himself and St. Paul." Furthermore, this study of Williams's other writings, especially his *Key Into the Language*, reaches conclusions that are similar to the ones I have drawn from this discussion of Williams's letter to Winthrop. For instance, Teunissen and Hinz observe that "like Paul, Williams found himself accused of sedition, mutiny, and civil disobedience; indeed, he found himself banished by his own in much the same way that Paul found his chief persecutors in the Pharisees" (123).

[10] In his published works, Williams cited the Pauline epistles 680 times. Note that this figure does not include his 180 citations from Acts, many of which dealt with Paul. By way of comparison, his second most cited biblical genre was the Gospels, which he cited 414 times.

Separatists, Williams argued that the civil magistrate's jurisdiction did not extend to religious matters. In making this argument, Williams contended with Paul's commands concerning obedience to authorities in Romans 13. The fact that Williams's understanding of the role of the civil magistrate centered on his exegesis of Romans 13 is not surprising because this text was often a pivotal passage for Christian interpretations of civil authority.[11] Moreover, Williams not only had to contend with Paul, but also with the interpretations of Paul that John Cotton and other divines had placed in his path. Partly because of this history of interpretation and partly because of the passage itself, Romans 13 was a problematic text for Williams. He wrestled extensively both with the passage and with its interpreters in his effort to depict Paul as a champion of the separation of church and state.

The passage under discussion is Paul's admonition to the Roman Christians concerning obedience to authorities:

> Let every person be subject to the governing authorities; for there is no authority except from God, and those authorities that exist have been instituted by God. Therefore whoever resists authority resists what God has appointed, and those who resist will incur judgment. For rulers are not a terror to good conduct, but to bad. Do you wish to have no fear of the authority? Then do what is good, and you will receive its approval; for it is God's servant for your good. But if you do what is wrong, you should be afraid, for the authority does not bear the sword in vain! It is the servant of God to execute wrath on the wrongdoer. Therefore one must be subject, not only because of wrath but also because of conscience. For the same reason you also pay taxes, for the authorities are God's servants, busy with this very thing.

---

[11] Indeed, David C. Steinmetz's recent discussion of Calvin's view of the civil magistrate was essentially an examination of Calvin's interpretation of this chapter from Romans (*Calvin in Context* [New York/Oxford: Oxford University Press, 1995] 199–208).

Pay to all what is due them—taxes to whom taxes are due, revenue to whom revenue is due, respect to whom respect is due, honor to whom honor is due. (Rom 13:1–7, NRSV)

Paul left no doubt that Christians should obey worldly authorities. But there was some ambiguity in the text that needed clarification. The first issue for interpreters concerned the identity of the "governing authorities." Was Paul writing of civil officers, ecclesiastical officers, or a combination of both? Sixteenth-century interpreters had disagreed over how to settle this issue.[12] Both Cotton and Williams, however, judged that Paul was speaking solely of civil rulers and magistrates. Read in this way, Paul's words to the Romans placed civil authority on a lofty plane. Rulers were divinely ordained, obedience to them was a religious duty, and disobedience to them was no less than disobedience to God. When necessary, magistrates dealt with disobedience violently, for God had ordained the magistrate's use of the sword to punish evildoers. Thus Paul instructed Christians to recognize that rulers and magistrates were God's servants, and to obey them accordingly. Christians owed princes and magistrates their due taxes, respect, and honor.

Paul's strong claims for civil authority in Romans 13 disturbed many interpreters in the Reformation period. Even Calvin and Melanchthon, who defended the magistrates' power in religious affairs, were uncomfortable with Paul's seemingly unqualified claims for civil authority in this passage.[13] If even Calvin and Melanchthon thought Paul's advocacy of state power in this passage was too strongly stated, we might wonder what Roger Williams's reaction was. Such an exalted description of the state's

---

[12] David Steinmetz illustrated this exegetical division. He noted that Thomas de Vio Cardinal Cajetan, Girolamo Cardinal Seripando, John Calvin, and Philip Melanchthon believed that Paul referred solely to civil magistrates in Romans 13. In contrast, Martin Luther believed that Paul had both secular and ecclesiastical authorities in mind. (Steinmetz, *Calvin in Context*, 202.)

[13] Steinmetz, *Calvin in Context*, 207.

power posed a serious problem for Williams's desire to forbid civil officers from meddling in religious affairs. In Romans 13, Paul seemed to leave little room for such limitations on magisterial authority. In light of this passage, how could Williams hold Paul in high esteem as a champion of religious liberty and the separation of church and state? *problem: Paul leaves little room for disobed*

A. English Separatists on Paul and the Civil Magistrate

Williams's exegetical dilemma is made even more acute when we consider that English Separatists, even some who were major influences on Williams, used this passage to justify the magistrate's responsibilities in religious affairs. Among these was Henry Ainsworth, the pastor of an English Separatist congregation that immigrated to Amsterdam to escape persecution in 1595. Ainsworth was a rarity in that both John Cotton and Roger Williams admired him. Though he detested Ainsworth's Separatism, Cotton praised both his humility and his useful commentary on the Pentateuch.[14] Williams also admired Ainsworth's exegetical scholarship. Furthermore, ever the advocate of the lowly and the persecuted, Williams also appreciated Ainsworth because he was a "despised" Separatist who was knowledgeable about the scriptures despite his lack of impressive scholarly credentials.[15]

As did most Separatists, Ainsworth negotiated a middle course between the Church of England and the Anabaptists. As Leland H. Carlson claimed, Separatists attempted "to steer between the rocks

---

[14] John Cotton, *The Way of the Congregational Churches Cleared*, in *John Cotton on the Churches of New England*, ed. Larzer Ziff (Cambridge: Belknap/Harvard University Press, 1968) 180–81.

[15] Williams, *The Bloudy Tenent, of Persecution, for Cause of Conscience*, discussed, in *A Conference Betweene Truth and Peace*, in vol. 3 of *The Complete Writings of Roger Williams* (Providence: Narragansett Club Publications, 1867; reprint, New York: Russell & Russell, 1963) 307–308. See also Williams, *Mr. Cottons Letter Lately Printed, Examined and Answered*, in vol. 1 of *The Complete Writings of Roger Williams* (Providence: Narragansett Club Publications, 1874; reprint, New York: Russell & Russell, 1963) 382.

of popery and the quicksands of Anabaptistry."[16] In order to refute accusations that he and his followers were political rebels, Ainsworth cited Romans 13 to demonstrate that Separatists honored biblical teachings on obedience to civil rulers.[17] In his interpretation of the passage, Ainsworth argued that Paul's command to obey governing authorities meant that magistrates were responsible for expelling "all false ministries, voluntary religions, and counterfeit worship of God" from the civil state.[18] Ainsworth also stressed that Paul held the civil magistrate responsible for supporting both "pure religion and true ministry." He believed that, in this passage, Paul regarded the magistrates as God's "lieutenants" on earth who judged in both civil and ecclesiastical affairs.[19] Ainsworth argued that just as the magistrate ensured peace in the civil sphere, so should he promote "mutual peace and concord in the communion of saints."[20] As the example of Ainsworth demonstrates, this passage from Romans was critical in Separatist claims for magisterial authority in religious matters.[21]

---

[16] Leland H. Carlson, "Introduction," in *The Writings of Henry Barrow, 1587–1590*, ed. Leland H. Carlson (London: Allen and Unwin, 1962) 33. While Carlson was speaking specifically of Henry Barrow, his statement is true of most other Separatists as well.

[17] Williston Walker emphasized the importance of this kind of argument for Ainsworth. Indeed, Ainsworth's primary purpose in his *Confession of 1596* was to defend his congregation against charges that they were schismatics and political rebels. (See Williston Walker, "The Second Confession of the London-Amsterdam Church, 1596," in *The Creeds and Platforms of Congregationalism*, ed. Williston Walker [Philadelphia: Pilgrim Press, 1960] 43).

[18] *A True Confession of the Faith*, in *The Creeds and Platforms of Congregationalism*, 71. This confession was reprinted in [Henry Ainsworth and Francis Johnson], *An Apologie or Defence of Such True Christians as Are Commonly (but Unjustly) Called Brownists* (Amsterdam: 1604) 4–29.

[19] Ainsworth, *True Confession*, 72.

[20] Henry Ainsworth, *Communion of Saints* (London: John Bellamie and Ralph Smith, 1641) 315; see also 276, 312–14. Ainsworth also cites Romans 13 in *Counterpoyson* (London: n.p., 1642) 86, 136.

[21] I call this *the* Separatist interpretation of Romans 13 because Ainsworth's interpretation was representative of Separatists as a whole. For example, see Henry Barrow, *A Brief Discoverie of the False Church*, in *The Writings of Henry*

B. John Cotton on Paul and the Civil Magistrate

John Cotton's interpretation of the passage was similar to that of
Ainsworth. Prompted by his disagreement with Williams, however,
Cotton examined the passage more thoroughly than Ainsworth
had. The first issue that Cotton engaged concerned the relationship
between Romans 13 and the Ten Commandments. Cotton referred
to the traditional division of the Commandments into two tables of
the law. According to this scheme, the first table concerned those
duties that people owed to God. These included not worshipping
other gods or idols, not misusing God's name, and remembering
the Sabbath (Exod 20:3–11). The second table consisted of duties
that people owed to one another, which included honoring parents
and laws against murder, adultery, stealing, bearing false witness,
and coveting (Exod 20:12–17).

Cotton characterized Paul's comments on obedience to civil
authority in Romans 13 as duties of the second table of the law,
since that was the civil ruler's domain—the relationships among
people in society. Yet, Cotton insisted that the duties of both tables
were interrelated. For example, he noted that an essential part of
the Christian duty of honoring civil rulers included praying for
them (see 1 Tim 2:1–2). This meant that prayer, which was a
religious activity belonging to the first table, might also be a duty of

Barrow, 1587–1590, ed. Leland H. Carlson (London: Allen and Unwin, 1962)
563–64, 289, 405–406, 412; idem, *Reply to Dr. Some's <u>A Godly Treatise</u>*, in
Writings, 1587–1590, 158, 168. For other citations of Romans 13 in Barrow's
works, see *The First Part of the Platforme*, in *Writings, 1587–1590*, 238, 245; idem,
A Plaine Refutation, in *The Writings of Henry Barrow, 1590–1591*, ed. Leland H.
Carlson (London: Allen and Unwin, 1966) 132; idem, *A Refutation of Mr.
Giffard's Reasons*, in *Writings, 1590–1591*, 350. For Francis Johnson's agreement
with Barrow on this point, see Francis Johnson, *Francis Johnson to Lord Burghley,
June 2, 1593*, in *The Writings of John Greenwood and Henry Barrow, 1591–1593*,
ed. Leland H. Carlson (London: Allen and Unwin, 1970) 439; idem, *Fraunces
Johnson for his Writing, John Greenwood and Henry Barrow*, 462.

the second table when Christians prayed for their civil rulers.[22] Likewise, while heresy was a religious sin committed against the first table, the task of punishing heretics was "a duty of the second table" that the civil magistrate was responsible to carry out.

Cotton reasoned that Paul's commands in Romans 13 resonated with the second table of the law because both passages concerned righteousness in the civil state. Paul admonished the Roman Christians to obey civil authorities as God's ministers who were responsible for societal good (Rom 13:4). For Cotton, this meant that civil rulers had religious tasks. Rulers were charged to promote the "truth of doctrine, holiness of worship," and "purity of church government" in the civil state because these were essential elements of a Christian society. Cotton believed that nothing was more perilous to civil welfare than heretical doctrine, idolatrous worship, and tyrannical church polity. The magistrate's responsibility to safeguard the righteousness of the community required the use of the sword to banish such dangerous religious elements from the state.[23] This command for obedience to magisterial authority included obedience in religious as well as in civil matters.

This interpretation of Romans 13 required Cotton to deal with the problem of Christians' obedience to pagan rulers in religious affairs. Cotton acknowledged that Christians throughout history had served rulers who did not share the faith. Under such unfriendly political circumstances, how could Paul's command for absolute obedience to the civil ruler stand? How could Christians expect pagan rulers to judge wisely in religious affairs?

Cotton responded that Christ never commanded a duty without providing the necessary means of its accomplishment. In order to fortify magistrates to judge in religious cases, Christ had provided the Bible for the magistrates' instruction. Cotton also

---

[22] Cotton, *The Bloudy Tenent, Washed, and Made White in the Bloud of the Lamb*, ed. Richard C. Robey, Research Library of Colonial Americana (London: 1647; reprint, New York: Arno, 1972) 99.

[23] Ibid., 99, 104.

argued that magistrates were to judge only the most basic religious cases. Any civil officer with even the slightest degree of spiritual discernment would be able to recognize and to punish gross heresy. Cotton believed that church history verified this fact because even pagan rulers had often been able to distinguish between true Christians and seditious heretics.[24] Thus Paul's command for the magistrate's authority in religious affairs was dependent upon the ordination of God and not upon the spiritual competence of the magistrate.[25]

Cotton supported his interpretation of Paul's view of the magistrate with Acts 25. In this passage, Paul appealed to Caesar's judgment in response to accusations leveled against Paul by Jewish leaders. Cotton cited this passage as an example of Paul acting on his conviction that rulers had authority to judge religious cases. In Cotton's opinion, Paul's appeal to the emperor proved three points that remained important guidelines for Christians in their relations with political officials. First, it demonstrated that civil magistrates could be helpful allies for Christians during times of need. Paul accepted the legitimate authority of the civil ruler and acknowledged the benefits of civil authority. Second, it proved that ecclesiastical officers must submit to the jurisdiction of civil rulers. Third, Cotton argued that Paul sought Caesar's judgment in religious cases as well as civil ones.[26] Paul reported that the Jews had accused him not only of political sedition, but also of religious crimes against both Jewish law and the Temple (Acts 25:8). For Cotton, the fact that Paul requested a trial before Caesar in these religious cases proved that Paul accepted the ruling of civil officers on religious issues.[27]

---

[24] Ibid., 101.

[25] Ibid., 107.

[26] Ibid., 102–103.

[27] Ibid., 103. Cotton was careful to emphasize that Paul did not appeal to Caesar so that the emperor could judge whether Paul's theological position and ministerial actions were divinely ordained. Instead, Paul only requested Caesar's judgment on whether or not Paul had broken any Jewish or imperial laws. Thus, Cotton argued, while Paul asked for Caesar's judgment in religious cases, Paul

II. ROGER WILLIAMS ON PAUL AND THE CIVIL MAGISTRATE

Roger Williams described Romans 13 as "a fort" that had been a point of contention in many religious controversies, with numerous interpreters seeking "to gain and win it."[28] Among these interpreters was John Cotton, whose exegesis of this passage threatened Williams's portrayal of Paul as an advocate of religious liberty and the separation of church and state. Williams lamented that Cotton, along with "so many excellent servants of God," had misinterpreted Romans 13 in order to justify religious persecution. As a result, Williams believed that these faulty interpreters had led "to their own and others' temporal destruction by civil wars and combustions in the world." He endeavored to clarify the confusion that "the great juggler Satan" had caused among interpreters of this text.[29] Williams took this task seriously, for Romans 13 ranks as his second most cited passage from scripture in his published works.[30]

One of Williams's most important interpretive challenges was to deal with Paul's strong advocacy of civil authority. Paul claimed that civil rulers were divinely ordained, and that any disobedience to them was no less than a sin against God. Williams accounted for Paul's extravagant claims for civil power by referring to the original setting of the text. Williams surmised that Paul's first readers had a negative opinion of civil authority due to their experience as a persecuted group in the Roman Empire. As Williams said, Christians in the first century suffered under emperors who were

---

did not appeal to Caesar's theological or spiritual competence. Paul sought Caesar's competence as a political officer, and not as a theologian. Thus, Cotton's view of Paul's appeal to the emperor supported Cotton's interpretation of Paul's commands in Rom 13. Civil rulers did not need to be theologians or even Christians to judge fundamental religious issues such as the distinction between orthodoxy and heresy, and whether or not persons had violated specific religious laws.

[28] Williams, *The Bloody Tenent Yet More Bloody*, in vol. 4 of *The Complete Writings of Roger Williams* (Providence: Narragansett Club Publications, 1870; reprint, New York: Russell & Russell, 1963) 262–63.

[29] Williams, *Bloudy Tenent*, in vol. 3 of *Complete Writings*, 150.

[30] Williams cited this passage 40 times in his published works.

"cruel and bloody persecutors of the name and followers of Jesus."
These rulers were not content "with the majesty of an earthly
throne, crown, sword [and] scepter," so they seized the "throne" of
religious authority as well. Williams reasoned that, under these
hostile circumstances, Paul's first readers were "tempted to despise
civil governors, especially such as were ignorant of the Son of God,
and persecuted him in his servants."[31] In this situation, Williams
recognized that Paul's strong advocacy of civil authorities was
appropriate advice for persecuted Christians. While Paul did not
excuse the emperors' meddling in religious affairs, he emphasized
that God had ordained rulers to keep the peace in the civil sphere
by punishing those who violated the laws of the state.[32] Paul
reminded Roman Christians that the religious persecution they
endured was no cause to neglect the proper use of civil authority.
Christians were not to be political subversives, despite the fact that
pagan rulers had wrongly persecuted them.[33]

Williams argued that while Romans 13 asserted the
magistrate's authority in the state, it did not justify the magistrate's
interference in religious affairs. Unlike John Cotton, he argued that
Romans 13 applied strictly to the second table of the Ten
Commandments. Williams observed that from Romans 12:9
through chapter 13, Paul treated "the duties of the saints"
regarding the second table, including their words and activities in
the state. Williams denied any reference to Romans 13 regarding

*31 c. - note to persecuted Xns to remind them that
just b/c being persecuted didn't mean ignoring civil mag
- CMags still kept state laws / peace
* doesn't justify interference in religion*

---

[31] Williams, *Bloudy Tenent*, in vol. 3 of *Complete Writings*, 156.

[32] Ibid., 59, 108–109, 146–47.

[33] Calvin had made similar comments in his interpretation of Romans 13.
David Steinmetz notes that "since the Roman Empire was involved in the
persecution of early Christian communities, it seemed doubly absurd to many
Christians to render obedience to authorities who were 'contriving to snatch the
kingdom from Christ.' In Calvin's view it was, therefore, particularly important
for Paul to lay great stress on the authority of magistrates" (Steinmetz, *Calvin in
Context* [New York: Oxford University Press, 1995], 201).

state not to be in charge of first tablet of 10

the first table, which concerned religious duties that Christians owed to God.[34]

In order to support his argument that Romans 13 pertained only to civil authority, Williams made a surprising move: he enlisted the exegetical insights of John Calvin. Williams certainly understood the great polemical value of citing Calvin in a controversy with John Cotton. Even so, the reference to Calvin seems curious, given the fact that Cotton was closer than Williams to Calvin's position on the magistrate's involvement in religious affairs. Williams admitted that Calvin held magistrates responsible for enforcing both tables of the Ten Commandments, which included defending Christianity against heresy.[35] Despite Calvin's persecuting theology, however, Williams observed that "the light of truth so evidently shined upon" Calvin's interpretation that he

---

[34] Williams, *Bloudy Tenent*, in vol. 3 of *Complete Writings,* 151. On this point, Williams's interpretation of Romans 13 agreed substantially with that of Menno Simons. While Simons did not use the language of the Tables of the Law, he argued that Paul's command informed the magistrate that his or her authority came from God. Furthermore, this awareness should lead civil rulers not to "invade and transgress against Christ" and his authority by using the "iron sword" to interfere "in that which belongs exclusively to the eternal judgment of the Most High God, such as in faith and matters pertaining to faith" (*Reply To False Accusations,* in *The Complete Writings of Menno Simons,* ed. John Christian Wenger [Scottdale: Herald Press, 1956] 550). See also in *The Complete Writings of Menno Simons: Foundation of Christian Doctrine, 1539,* 200; *Christian Baptism,* 285; and *Why I Do Not Cease Teaching and Writing,* 304. An anonymous pamphlet published in England one year after Williams's *Bloudy Tenent* offered a similar interpretation of Romans 13 to that of Williams. The author cited this chapter to prove that the magistrate's work deals with "not faith, but facts, not doctrines, but deeds" (*The Ancient Bounds* [London: Henry Overton, 1645] 16). English pamphleteer Henry Robinson agreed with Williams's interpretation of this passage. While Robinson did not engage the text at length, he summarily judged that Paul's command to be subject to civil rulers "only is meant in civil matters, and not such as may concern the inward governing and regalement of the soul" (*Liberty of Conscience,* in vol. 3 of *Tracts on Liberty in the Puritan Revolution, 1638–1647,* ed. William Haller [New York: Columbia University Press, 1934] 159).

[35] Williams, *Bloudy Tenent,* in vol. 3 of *Complete Writings,* 153.

"absolutely denied" that Romans 13 pertained to the duties of the first table.[36]

This strategy demonstrated the importance of Paul to Williams's understanding of religious liberty and the separation of church and state. Williams quoted Calvin's exegesis in order to clear Paul from the accusation that Romans 13 advocated the magistrate's authority in religious affairs. This was important because Williams's biblical argument depended largely on Paul's vote as an apostolic champion of religious liberty and the separation of church and state. Consequently, while Williams admitted that Calvin would have agreed with Cotton on the issue of the magistrate's religious role, Calvin would have disagreed with Cotton's interpretation of Paul's commands in Romans 13. Williams quoted Calvin not to support his advocacy of religious liberty, because he knew that Calvin would have disagreed with him on that position. Instead, Williams quoted Calvin to support his interpretation of this specific Pauline passage.

Williams cited Calvin's assertion that interpreters should not use Romans 13 to tyrannize the conscience because this text pertained only to civil government.[37] Applauding this statement,

---

[36] Williams made this statement to refer to both Calvin and Beza. Williams, *Bloudy Tenent*, in vol. 3 of *Complete Writings*, 153–55. Calvin also agreed with Melanchthon on this point. According to David Steinmetz, "Paul has in mind only secular magistrates [in Romans 13]. Whatever needs to be said about offices and order in the institutional church (and Melanchthon and Calvin agree that a good deal needs to be said) is simply not the subject of this passage" (Steinmetz, *Calvin in Context*, 202).

[37] Williams, *Bloudy Tenent*, in vol. 3 of *Complete Writings*, 153. Williams's quotations can be found in John Calvin, *Iohannis Calvini Commentarius in Epistolam Pauli ad Romanos*, ed. T. H. L. Parker, vol. 22 of Studies in the History of Christian Thought (Leiden: E. J. Brill, 1981) 285. Williams quoted from the Latin text and provided a translation. For an alternate translation, see John Calvin, *The Epistles of Paul the Apostle to the Romans and to the Thessalonians*, ed. David W. Torrance and Thomas F. Torrance, trans. Ross Mackenzie, *Calvin's Commentaries* (Grand Rapids: Wm. B. Eerdmans Publishing, 1960) 283. Williams made essentially the same point in two other quotations from Calvin: see Williams, *Bloudy Tenent* in vol. 3 of *Complete Writings*, 154–55; Calvin,

Williams castigated interpreters such as John Cotton who had indeed used this passage to tyrannize the conscience when they used it to justify their allowance of "no other religion nor worship in their territories, but one." These advocates of Christendom, Williams believed, defended "their faith from reproach and blasphemy of heretics by civil weapons, and all that from this very 13 of the Romans." In Williams's view, such use of scripture was blasphemous, and interpreters who advocated it would be found guilty of misinterpreting Paul "before the Tribunal of the most High."[38] When Paul wrote of the sword in Romans 13, he meant the civil sword of worldly rulers, which was rightly used to keep the peace in the state by punishing civil offenders.[39] Williams denied that Romans 13 gave the civil magistrate any authority to discipline religious offenders, for civil rulers had no authority to judge religious cases.

What, then, was to be made of Paul's appeal to Caesar? Was Cotton not correct in observing that Paul had appealed to Caesar to judge the religious charges that the Jews had brought against him? Williams responded that while the Jews had charged Paul with both civil and spiritual crimes, Paul appealed to Caesar's judgment in the civil accusations only.

In defense of this position, Williams cited Acts 23, which recorded the letter that Roman tribune Claudius Lysias wrote to Governor Felix regarding Paul. Lysias wrote that the Jews had accused Paul of religious violations of Jewish law, but that Paul "was charged with nothing deserving death or imprisonment" (Acts 23:29, NRSV). Williams reasoned that, in stating that Paul's

Acts 25
-Paul appealed to Caesar on civil accusations

Commentarius, 286–87; Calvin, *Epistles of Paul*, 285–86. English Puritan William Perkins had a similar interpretation of the passage. For him, Paul's admonition in Romans 13 spoke to the specific issue of obedience to magistrates in "body and goods and outward conversation," adding that the passage did not proclaim "a subjection of conscience to men's laws" (Perkins, *A Discourse of Conscience*, in *William Perkins, 1558–1602*, ed. Thomas F. Merrill [Nieuwkoop: B. De Graaf, 1966] 26).

[38] Williams, *Bloudy Tenent*, in vol. 3 of *Complete Writings*, 154.
[39] Ibid., 59, 108–109.

crimes against the Jewish religion were not punishable by imprisonment or death, Lysias was admitting that Paul's religious violations were not punishable by civil means. Furthermore, Williams noted that Paul went before civil officials only to defend himself against civil accusations. Paul later testified before Governor Felix that he had not caused a riot in Jerusalem, which would have been a civil offense (Acts 24:12).[40] Paul further demonstrated that he was no subversive by appealing to the emperor's authority. He even declared his willingness to suffer the death penalty if the emperor declared that he deserved execution for his crimes (Acts 25:11). In light of these passages, Williams interpreted Paul's appeal to Caesar in the context of Paul's commands regarding submission to rulers in Romans 13. As a good citizen, Paul appealed to the emperor to judge any civil offense, and Paul was willing to accept the emperor's decision, even if it meant execution. Nevertheless, this was an appeal to Caesar's judgment in civil and not religious matters. [41]

Williams found it inconceivable that Paul would have appealed to Caesar in religious matters because Caesar was not qualified to judge religious cases. Williams emphasized Caesar's religious incompetence, arguing that he was "an idolatrous stranger from the true God, and a lion like bloody persecutor of the Lord Jesus, the Lamb of God." If Paul had appealed to Caesar's tribunal to judge in religious cases, Paul would have been "appealing to darkness to judge light, to unrighteousness to judge righteousness, the spiritually blind to judge" a dispute over "heavenly colors." Such an appeal was absurd because Paul would have been appealing to a spiritual inferior.[42] In discussing Paul's spiritual superiority to Caesar, Williams cited Paul's statement that "apostles and prophets" were the "foundation" of the church (Eph 2:20). In Williams's view, this meant that apostles and prophets were

---

[40] Williams, *Bloody Tenent Yet More Bloody*, in vol. 4 of *Complete Writings*, 274.

[41] Ibid., 273–74.

[42] Williams, *Bloudy Tenent*, in vol. 3 of *Complete Writings*, 157.

apostles +prophets higher authority than Caesar

spiritual authorities to which "Caesar himself ought to have appealed" in any religious issue. Williams determined that even if Caesar had been a Christian ruler, he still would have lacked the authority to judge in religious matters. Paul's comment to the Ephesians meant that even Christian rulers had to be subject to Christ's authority, which was placed "in the hands of the apostles and churches" so that they could judge all spiritual issues.[43]

Williams argued that Christ gave apostles and churches the authority to judge spiritual cases because they possessed a special ability to discern spiritual truths. Williams again made this point with reference to Paul, who wrote that Christians understood a mysterious wisdom that worldly "princes" did not know, "for had they known it, they would not have crucified the Lord" (1 Cor 2:8, KJV). In light of this statement, Williams determined that Paul could not have appealed to Caesar to judge in religious matters. Such an appeal would have been "a prostitution of spiritual things to carnal and natural judgments, which are not able to comprehend spiritual matters."[44]

Paul advocating two spheres of authority

Thus Williams believed that Paul advocated two separate spheres of authority, civil and religious. In Romans 13, Paul declared that civil rulers had authority over all citizens, including apostles and church leaders, in civil matters. Yet, in both Ephesians 2 and 1 Corinthians 2, Paul indicated that though apostles and other church leaders may be "poor and mean despised persons in civil respects," they had the authority over all worldly rulers in judging religious issues.[45]

Williams concluded that Paul rightly appealed to the emperor to judge accusations that Paul had committed crimes against the state. The emperor, in Williams's view, was responsible for defending "Paul from civil violence, and slanderous accusations about sedition, mutiny, civil disobedience," or any other civil crimes. Paul set the example for all Christians to appeal to civil

---

[43] Ibid., 158.
[44] Ibid., 159.
[45] Ibid., 158.

rulers for protection and civil justice, whether these rulers were "the Roman Caesar," an "Egyptian Pharaoh," or "an Indian Sachem."[46] Williams even advanced the radical claim that civil magistrates owed protection not only to Christians but also to heretics and pagans. Paul's support for the magistrate's protective role in Romans 13 meant that the civil sword was intended to protect representatives of any religious perspective.[47] Williams claimed, therefore, that the proper role of a magistrate was to be not a persecutor but a protector who guarded citizens from any violent opposition to their religious opinions.

III. ROGER WILLIAMS ON PAUL AND RELIGIOUS LIBERTY

Williams's interpretation of Paul was not limited to arguments for the separation of spiritual and civil spheres of authority. In Williams's view, Paul also advocated religious liberty in response to persecutors who used violence to punish religious violators. Williams portrayed Paul as a former persecutor who rejected the use of violence in serving the cause of Christ. Instead of wielding the physical sword, Paul advocated the power of spiritual weapons. Williams seized this Pauline insight in his case for religious liberty, arguing that spiritual weapons were far superior to the civil sword in combating religious errors.

A. The Superiority of Spiritual Weapons

Williams believed that Paul distinguished between the civil sword of Romans 13 and a spiritual sword, which was the only appropriate means of confronting heretics and pagans. Paul advocated the spiritual sword's use in both church and state. In the church, the spiritual sword included excommunication, through which those members who persisted in their errors after due warning were cast out of the community. This was the subject of Paul's command in 1 Corinthians 5, where he admonished the

---

[46] Ibid., 159.
[47] Ibid., 373.

Corinthians: "I am writing to you not to associate with anyone who bears the name of brother or sister who is sexually immoral or greedy, or is an idolater, reviler, drunkard, or robber. Do not even eat with such a one. For what have I to do with judging those outside? Is it not those who are inside that you are to judge? God will judge those outside. 'Drive out the wicked person from among you'" (1 Cor 5:11–13, NRSV). Williams argued that this was Paul's advocacy of the spiritual sword's proper use as an instrument for "the spiritual killing or cutting off by excommunication" any person in the church who persisted in immorality or unorthodox belief.[48] Excommunication was the chief spiritual weapon that the

 excomm = spiritual sword to keep church pure

---

[48] Williams, *Bloudy Tenent*, in vol. 3 of *Complete Writings*, 91. Here Williams echoed an interpretation of this passage that was common among English Separatists, and somewhat less common among orthodox Puritans. For Separatist interpretations of 1 Cor 5, see Robert Harrison, *A Treatise of the Church and the Kingdome of Christ*, in *The Writings of Robert Harrison and Robert Browne*, ed, Albert Peel and Leland H. Carlson (London: Allen and Unwin, 1953) 33, 35, 41, 43; idem, *A Little Treatise Uppon the Firste Verse of the 122 Psalm*, 86, 120; Robert Browne, *A Treatise of Reformation Without Tarying for Anie*, in *The Writings of Robert Harrison and Robert Browne*, 169; idem, *A Treatise upon the 23 of Matthewe*, 215; idem, *A True and Short Declaration*, 406; idem, *An Answere to Master Cartwright His Letter for Joyning with the English Churches*, 437–38, 441, 443, 445–46, 466–67, 505; idem, *An Aunswer to Mr. Flowers Letter*, 525–27; Henry Ainsworth, *Communion of Saints*, 100, 106–107, 300, 348, 350; idem, *Counterpoyson*, 16, 30, 51, 70–72, 85, 100–101, 104; idem, *Arrow Against Idolatry* (n.p.: 1640) 74; Henry Ainsworth and John Ainsworth, *The Trying Out of the Truth* (N.P., 1615) 79; Henry Ainsworth, *A Defence of the Holy Scriptures* (Amsterdam: Giles Thorp, 1613) 6, 51, 106; John Robinson, *A Justification of Separation from the Church of England*, in vol. 2 of *The Works of John Robinson*, ed. Robert Ashton (Boston: Doctrinal Tract and Book Society, 1851) 21, 70, 165–66, 170–79, 216–17, 219–20, 226–27, 234–35, 237–44, 322–23, 342–43, 345–46, 354, 367–68, 464; John Canne, *The Snare is Broken* (London: M. Simmons, 1649) 43; idem, *A Necessity of Separation from the Church of England*, ed. Charles Stovel (London: Hanserd Knollys Society, 1849) 219, 230, 307; idem, *A Stay Against Straying* (Amsterdam: n.p., 1639) 43; John Greenwood, *A Breife Refutation of Mr. George Giffard*, in *The Writings of John Greenwood and Henry Barrow, 1591–1593*, 19, 35; idem, *A Fewe Observations*, in *John Greenwood and Henry Barrow*, 70; Henry Barrow, *Final Answer to Gifford*, in *John Greenwood and Henry Barrow*, 194; idem, *A Plaine Refutation*, in *Writings, 1590–1591*,

church used to maintain its purity. Williams maintained that this
Pauline text provided the clearest biblical teaching of this use of the
spiritual sword.[49]

103–13, 135–39, 153, 177, 205; idem, *A Refutation of Mr. Giffard's Reasons*, in
Writings, 1590–1591, 353; idem, *A Brief Discoverie*, in *Writings, 1587–1590*,
292–97, 325, 385, 520–21, 613, 638–40; idem, *Profes of Aparant Churche*, in
Writings, 1587–1590, 73, 75, 80; idem, *Reply to Dr. Some's*, in *Writings,
1587–1590*, 157. Like his Separatist antecedents and contemporaries, Williams
used Paul's command in 1 Cor 5 to justify excommunication. See also Williams's
other citations of this passage: Appendix. For interpretations of the passage by
orthodox Puritans, see William Ames, *The Marrow of Theology*, ed. John D.
Eusden, trans. John D. Eusden (Boston: Pilgrim Press, 1968) 200; Thomas
Hooker, *The Carnal Hypocrite*, in *Thomas Hooker: Writings in England and
Holland, 1626–1633*, ed. George H. Williams et al. (Cambridge MA: Harvard
University Press, 1975) 110; Richard Mather, *Church-Government and Church-
Covenant Discussed*, in *Church Covenant: Two Tracts*, ed. Richard C. Robey (New
York: Arno Press, 1972) 10–11, 17, 38, 45–53.

[49] Another passage that was often cited to endorse excommunication was
Matt 18:15–17. But Williams preferred 1 Cor 5. He cited Matt 18 only 14 times,
compared to 32 citations of 1 Cor 5. In interpreting Matt 18 as a command for
excommunication, Williams followed an exegetical tradition of the Anabaptists
of the sixteenth century and English Separatists. For Anabaptist interpretations,
see Menno Simons, *A Clear Account of Excommunication*, in *The Complete
Writings of Menno Simons*, 457, 468–70, 472; idem, *Reply to Gellius Faber*, 724,
745, 751–52; idem, *Instruction on Excommunication*, 982. For Separatist interpretations, see Robert Harrison, *Treatise of the Church*, 45; idem, *A Little Treatise
Uppon the Firste Verse of the 122 Psalm*, 120; Robert Browne, *Reformation
without Tarying*, 155; idem, *Treatise upon the 23 of Matthewe*, 207; idem, *True
and Short Declaration*, 399, 420; idem, *Answere to Master Cartwright*, 437,
442–44, 446, 456, 463–65, 487, 491; idem, *Aunswere to Mr. Flowers*, 526–27;
Henry Barrow, *Plaine Refutation*, in *Writings, 1590–1591*, 59, 139–40, 142, 152,
205; idem, *A Refutation of Mr. Giffard's Reasons*, in *Writings, 1590–1591*, 351;
idem, *Profes of Aparant Churche*, in *Writings, 1587–1590*, 72; idem, *Reply to Dr.
Some's*, in *Writings, 1587–1590*, 157; idem, *A True Description out of the Worde of
God, of the Visible Church*, in *Writings, 1587–1590*, 220–22; idem, *First Part of the
Platforme*, in *Writings, 1587–1590*, 244; idem, *Brief Discoverie*, in *Writings,
1587–1590*, 317, 319, 506, 509, 511, 519, 625, 639; idem, *Barrow's Final Answer*,
in *Writings, 1591–1593*, 135, 153, 184, 194; John Greenwood, *A Breife Refutation*,
in *John Greenwood and Henry Barrow*, 35; Henry Ainsworth, *Communion of
Saints*, 61, 100, 253, 271, 276, 290, 347–48, 359–60, 362; *Apologie or Defence*

spiritual
sword
also
powerful
weapon
against
religious
error in
state

The spiritual sword, however, not only cleansed the church of false belief and improper behavior; it was also a powerful weapon against religious error in the state. Again, Williams turned to Paul, emphasizing two passages that were especially provocative descriptions of the spiritual sword. The first was 2 Corinthians 10, which was crucial to Williams's understanding of Paul, evidenced by the fact that it was one of his most cited Pauline texts.[50] Here Paul wrote that Christians "do not war after the flesh," because "the weapons of our warfare are not carnal, but mighty through God to the pulling down of strongholds." Paul continued, saying that this Christian warfare consisted of "casting down imaginations, and every high thing that exalteth itself against the knowledge of God, and bringing into conformity every thought to the obedience of Christ" (2 Cor 10:3–5, KJV).

(Amsterdam: n.p., 1604) 8, 21, 25–26, 43–45, 47, 60, 62–63, 98; Henry Ainsworth and John Ainsworth, *The Trying Out of the Truth* (N.P., 1615) 47, 79, 101; Henry Ainsworth, *Arrow Against Idolatry*, (n.p., 1640) 74; idem, *Counterpoyson*, 16, 55, 69, 70–71, 81, 85, 103–104; John Canne, *Necessitie of Separation*, ed. Charles Stovel (London: Hanserd Knollys Society, 1849) 97, 147, 219; idem, *A Stay Against Straying*, (Amsterdam: n.p., 1639) 31; John Robinson, *A Just and Necessary Apology of Certain Christians*, in vol. 3 of *The Works of John Robinson*, ed. Robert Ashton (Boston: Doctrinal Tract and Book Society, 1851) 32. For Baptist interpretations, see Thomas Helwys, *A Short Declaration of the Mistery of Iniquity* (n.p.: 1612) 59, 155; idem, *An Advertisement or Admonition unto the Congregations* (n.p.: 1611) 41, 9.

[50] In his published works, Williams made 21 references to 2 Corinthians 10. Ephesians 6 was also a favorite passage of Williams's, with 13 citations in his published works. In his interpretation of these passages, Williams likely appropriated the insights of some English Baptist writers, although they did not give the passages as much attention as Williams did. For examples of English Baptist interpretation of 2 Cor 10, see: Leonard Busher, *Religious Peace; or a Plea for Liberty of Conscience*, in *Tracts on Liberty of Conscience and Persecution, 1614–1661*, ed. Edward Bean Underhill (New York: Burt Franklin, 1966) 16, 28, 56, 76; [John Murton], *Persecution for Religion Judged and Condemned*, in *Tracts on Liberty of Conscience*, ed. Edward Bean Underhill (New York: Burt Franklin, 1966) 85–86, 108; *A Most Humble Supplication*, in *Tracts on Liberty of Conscience and Persecution*, 215. For an English Baptist interpretation of Eph 6, see Busher, *Religious Peace*, 16, 19.

The second Pauline text that Williams used to explain the power of spiritual weapons was Ephesians 6:10–20.[51] Here, Paul wrote that "our struggle is not against enemies of blood and flesh, but against the rulers, against the authorities, against the cosmic powers of this present darkness, against the spiritual forces of evil in the heavenly places. Therefore take up the whole armor of God, so that you may be able to withstand on that evil day, and having done everything, to stand firm" (Eph 6:12–13, NRSV).

Paul described this "armor of God" with images such as the "belt of truth," the "breastplate of righteousness," the "shield of faith," the "helmet of salvation," and "the sword of the Spirit, which is the word of God" (Eph 6:14–17).

Williams argued that 2 Corinthians 10 and Ephesians 6, when compared to Romans 13, demonstrated Paul's advocacy of "a two-fold state, a civil state and a spiritual state."[52] Paul intended to distinguish these two states and their respective officers, weapons, and punishments. In Williams's interpretation, these Pauline texts taught that the civil and spiritual states were "of different natures." Williams's comparison of these passages was also crucial to his argument "that civil weapons are most improper and unfitting in matters of the spiritual state and kingdom, though in the civil state most proper and suitable."[53]

In Williams's writings, the spiritual weapons that Paul described included biblical arguments that Christians used to combat heretical doctrines (2 Cor 10:5). Williams argued that Paul's spiritual weapons were not the "civil or corporeal" tools of

---

[51] For Williams's exegesis of Eph 6, see *Bloudy Tenent*, in vol. 3 of *Complete Writings*, 114, 149–50, 160, 255, 361–63; *Bloody Tenent Yet More Bloody*, in vol. 4 of *Complete Writings*, 88, 248, 278; *George Fox Digg'd out of His Burrowes*, in vol. 5 of *The Complete Writings of Roger Williams* (Providence: Narragansett Club Publications, 1872; reprint, New York: Russell & Russell, 1963) 456, 494; *Queries of Highest Consideration*, in vol. 2 of *The Complete Writings of Roger Williams* (Providence: Narragansett Club Publications, 1867; reprint, New York: Russell & Russell, 1963) 269.

[52] Williams, *Bloudy Tenent*, in vol. 3 of *Complete Writings*, 147.

[53] Ibid.

the state, but "they were the reprehensions, convictions, exhortations, and persuasions of the Word of the eternal God." The Christian's spiritual weapons were persuasive, not coercive. Christians used these weapons not to harm the body, but to afflict "the conscience" in the name of Christ.[54]

Much to Williams's consternation, persecutors rejected Christ's spiritual sword in correcting heretics, choosing instead to "run to borrow Caesar's" physical sword. Williams argued that despite Paul's glorious advocacy of spiritual weapons, "commanders in Christ's army" have cowardly depended upon the "sword of steel" instead of Christ's spiritual sword.[55] This was the error of Christendom in general and of John Cotton in particular. In combating heresy, Cotton believed that "the sword of the Spirit is too weak, and the sword of the magistrate must help."[56] In response to this lack of faith in spiritual artillery, Williams appealed to the example of Christ, using images from Paul's admonition in Ephesians 6. Here, Williams's questions were rhetorical: "will the Lord Jesus (did he ever in His own person practice, or did he appoint to) join to His breastplate of righteousness the breastplate of iron and steel?" Did Jesus support his "helmet of righteousness and salvation in Christ" with a "helmet and crest of iron, brass, or steel?" Did Jesus need to add "a target of wood to his shield of faith?" Finally, asked Williams, did Jesus support his sword of the Spirit with "the material sword, the work of smiths and cutlers?"[57]

Instead of this spiritual cowardice in appealing to civil weapons, Williams defended the propriety and power of the spiritual sword in combating heresy. Williams argued for "the sufficiency of [Christ's] spiritual power in his church, for the purging forth and conquering of the least evil," and for "bringing every thought in subjection unto Christ Jesus," as Paul had taught in 2

---

[54] Ibid., 90.
[55] Williams, *Bloody Tenent Yet More Bloody*, in vol. 4 of *Complete Writings*, 223.
[56] Ibid., 380.
[57] Williams, *Bloudy Tenent*, in vol. 3 of *Complete Writings*, 149–50.

Corinthians 10.[58] Against persecutors who feared that heresy would corrupt Christian society without the civil sword's enforcement, he cited Paul's admonition that Christ's sword was powerful "to break down the strongest holds," and "to defend itself against the very gates of earth or Hell."[59]

B. Williams and Paul on
Religious Freedom and the Possibility of Conversion

Williams contended that while the spiritual sword could help to convert heretics and pagans to Christianity, the physical sword was useless in converting unbelievers. Williams illustrated this with a passage from 2 Timothy 2 that he considered critical to Paul's treatment of heretics. Paul advised Timothy on the treatment of two heretics, Hymenaeus and Philetus, who erred in teaching that the general resurrection had already taken place (2 Tim 2:17–18). Williams pointed out that Paul did not advise Timothy "to stir up the secular power" to punish Hymenaeus and Philetus so that they would not infect society with their dangerous beliefs. To the contrary, Paul cautioned Timothy to correct these and all opponents with gentleness, waiting patiently for God to lead them to repentance.[60] Williams used this example as a guideline for Christian dealings with religious difference in the world. For him, Paul's command in this passage made it "incredible that any servant or messenger of the King of peace should stir up the civil magistrate to cut off [heretics] by the civil sword." Instead, this passage advised Christians "to wait" patiently for God to deliver heretics and pagans from their errors while "bearing in the interim their oppositions and gainsayings."[61] Thus, instead of persecution, Paul advocated patience and gentle correction for dealing with religious errors in the world.

---

[58] Ibid., 285.

[59] Ibid., 111.

[60] Williams, *Bloody Tenent Yet More Bloody*, in vol. 4 of *Complete Writings*, 185.

[61] Ibid., 152; see also, *Bloudy Tenent*, in vol. 3 of *Complete Writings*, 135.

use spiritual weapon for gentle persuasion

Williams believed that, in this passage, Paul advocated the use of the spiritual weapon of gentle persuasion based on biblical argumentation. This strategy contrasted with the persecuting tactic that punished heretics with the civil sword. A benefit of spiritual persuasion was that it kept in sight the ultimate goal of converting heretics' souls and not killing their bodies. Such was not the case with the persecuting strategy. Williams used this Pauline text to emphasize the ineffectiveness of civil weapons for converting heretics and pagans. As Williams pointed out, Paul said that only God could grant repentance to false teachers and save them from Satan's clutches (2 Tim 2:25–26). Consequently, the threat of the physical sword could not convert an errant conscience to orthodoxy. That was the work not of the sword of steel in the hands of the magistrates, but of "the sword of the Spirit in the hands of his spiritual officers."[62] Accordingly, persecutors who attempted to enforce orthodoxy with the sword only succeeded in creating either hypocrites or martyrs. When faced with the threat of the sword, some heretics became hypocrites, pretending to convert to Christ-

civil enforcement condemns heretics to die

ianity in order to avoid persecution.[63] Other heretics became martyrs, enduring persecution and death rather than feigning adherence to the state's religion. In the latter case, civil enforcement of religion condemned heretics and pagans to die in their errors. Williams argued that "civil wars and combustions" only succeeded in killing heretics and pagans, thereby ending any chance that they may have repented of their errors.[64] Thus, the use of the civil sword to enforce orthodoxy, which persecutors intended as means to correct and to convert heretics and pagans, became an impediment to conversion.

In contrast to this bleak picture of religious persecution, Williams interpreted 2 Timothy 2 as Paul's command that Christians should correct heretics and pagans with gentle persuasion and not violent coercion. Only through this peaceful strategy could Christ-

---

[62] Williams, *Bloudy Tenent*, in vol. 3 of *Complete Writings*, 136.

[63] Ibid., 136.

[64] Ibid., 208.

ians eventually lead errant souls to orthodoxy. For Williams, this passage demonstrated that religious liberty kept the hope of conversion alive. Perhaps he even had Paul's own conversion experience in mind in his reading this passage. Indeed, Williams remarked that the person who had experienced God's mercy in deliverance from a "former blindness, opposition and enmity against God, cannot but be patient and gentle toward" all variety of heretics and pagans. Williams, therefore, used this passage to advocate the religious freedom of all faiths. Civil rulers, Williams asserted, should grant religious freedom to Jews who both denied Christianity and justified their predecessors' crucifixion of Jesus, Moslems who subordinated Christ to Muhammad, all kinds of "Antichristians" who created "false Christs," and even the "wildest sorts of" pagans. In dealing with these groups, Williams supported a policy of gentleness and patience that he credited largely to the Apostle Paul.[65]

ℰℴ

If we consider St. Paul's traditional reputation as a Roman citizen who defended the divinely-granted authority of the civil magistrate, it is surprising that Roger Williams perceived a commonality between himself and the Apostle. In his letter to Governor John Winthrop and the Massachusetts Bay Colony in October 1636, Williams interpreted his recent banishment in Pauline terms. Like Paul, who often suffered on behalf of his faith, Williams saw himself as a victim of religious persecution banished by Massachusetts Bay because of his beliefs. As part of this perceived kinship with Paul, Williams drew heavily on Pauline texts in describing his banished condition to the colony that had evicted him. Williams did not adopt a Pauline stance for mere dramatic effect. Instead, his sense of connection with Paul was essential to Williams's self-understanding throughout his career, as evidenced by the fact that he cited the Pauline epistles more than any other

[65] Ibid., 92–93.

biblical genre in his writings. Indeed, Williams's references to Paul were so prominent that his polemical treatises reveal a distinctive Pauline vision for the separation of church and state and religious liberty.

Williams's interpretation of Paul challenged the dominant political interpretation of the New Testament in the seventeenth century. Just as Williams challenged Christendom's understanding of Jesus in the parable of the weeds, he also undermined a view of Paul that had supported alliances of churches and states through-out the sixteenth and seventeenth centuries. Yet, Williams's biblical argument for religious liberty would have been incomplete without a reassessment of the book of Revelation, which captivated people in all ranks of society in the seventeenth century. Williams shared this fascination with the book of Revelation, evidenced by the fact that his writings contain over three hundred citations from it—more than from any other biblical book. He expended much effort in deciphering the apocalyptic visions in the Revelation because he believed that they were pivotal to his opposition to religious persecution in the seventeenth century. The following chapter examines Williams's apocalyptic rationale for religious liberty.

- Paul clearly supports civil authority → who is that?
  ° Separatists – CA should support peace in civil state + religion
  ° Cotton - connected R 13 to 2nd Table of 10; obed in civil + religious
    matters; used Acts 25 as Paul demonstrating going to the
    CA for help
  ° Williams - context = persecuted Xns, remind that CA can help
    in civil issues (demo in Acts 25)
    - apostles, church leaders higher than CA, Caesar to defer

- Religious Liberty
  ° diff. weapons for church/state
    - church = spiritual sword   - state = physical
    - correct heretics via gentle persuasion

CHAPTER 5

THE APOCALYPTIC STRUGGLE AGAINST COLONIAL PERSECUTION: VIOLENCE, LIBERTY, AND THE BOOK OF REVELATION

The book of Revelation captivated Puritans in the seventeenth century and was essential to their fascination with an unfolding cosmic drama that would culminate in Christ's millennial rule.[1]

---

[1] While few studies have focused exclusively on Puritan exegesis of Revelation, abundant studies have centered on the related theme of Puritan millennialism. T. D. Bozeman correctly observes that "during the latter 1970s and the 1980s the American Puritans' Errand into the Wilderness was remodeled along eschatological lines" with studies that attributed the migration to millennial motivations. See Bozeman, *To Live Ancient Lives: The Primitivist Dimension in Puritanism* (Chapel Hill: University of North Carolina Press, 1988) 193. Bozeman, however, refutes the idea that millennialism dominated early Puritan thought (236). For studies of Puritan millennialism, see Bercovitch, "New England's Errand Reappraised," in *New Directions in American Intellectual History,* ed. John Higham and Paul K. Conkin (Baltimore MD: Johns Hopkins University Press, 1979) 93; *The American Jeremiad* (Madison WI: University of Wisconsin Press, 1978); and "Typology and Puritan New England: The Williams-Cotton Controversy Reassessed," *American Quarterly* 19 (1967), especially 189; James F. Maclear, "New England and the Fifth Monarchy: The Quest for the Millennium in Early American Puritanism," in *Puritan New England: Essays on Religion, Society, and Culture,* ed. Alden T. Vaughan and Francis J. Bremer (New York: St. Martin's Press, 1977) 66–91; Philip Gura, *A Glimpse of Sion's Glory: Puritan Radicalism in New England, 1620–1660* (Middletown: Wesleyan University Press, 1984) 13.

Roger Williams shared the Puritans' attraction to the book of Revelation and the tendency to view the seventeenth century as part of an apocalyptic drama. Clark Gilpin has pointed out that "Williams considered Revelation a symbolic presentation of historical development from the time of Christ to his own age."[2] The fact that he quoted from Revelation much more often than from any other biblical book demonstrates the importance of the book to Williams's thought.[3]

The two passages from Revelation that Williams cited most often were Revelation chapters 2–3 and chapter 17. The first of these passages comprised letters to seven churches in Asia, which contained Christ's introductory praises, admonitions, and warnings to the recipients of the apocalyptic visions that followed. The second passage that interested Williams contained the vision of the whore and the great beast.[4] This vision painted a picture of a powerful and detestable whore who enlisted the aid of a great beast to persecute Christ's faithful witnesses. Williams believed that both

---

[2] Gilpin, *The Millenarian Piety of Roger Williams*, (Chicago: University of Chicago Press, 1979) 82. Gilpin's excellent book centered on Williams's distinctive understanding of the millennium. Gilpin argued that Williams's interpretation was distinct from two dominant forms of Puritan millenarianism from the civil wars to Restoration in two essential characteristics. The first was Williams's "extreme primitivism." He believed that the millennial rule of Christ would be the restored church in its apostolic form. This was different from most English millennialists who followed Thomas Brightman in understanding the 1000-year reign of Christ as comprehensive over both state and church, a "holy commonwealth" in which Christians would exercise political and ecclesiastical power. Second, Williams believed the restored church members would express "spirituality" via primitive ecclesiastical ordinances. This was a departure from many radical Puritans who saw millennium as the "establishment of an entirely new form of Christianity" (61).

[3] Williams quoted from Revelation 306 times in his published works. By comparison, his second most quoted book was Matthew, which he quoted 214 times.

[4] While Gilpin focuses on Williams's millenarian thought, he does not concentrate on Williams's interpretation of the book of Revelation. For instance, Gilpin only mentions Revelation 2 once; see *Millenarian Piety*, 88. Furthermore, Gilpin never treats Williams's interpretation of Revelation 17.

of these passages had been misused to support the state's enforcement of orthodoxy through violence. In response, Williams presented his interpretation of these apocalyptic texts. Evidently, he believed that these texts were important because they were among his most cited of all biblical passages.[5]

Most of Williams's predecessors and contemporaries de-emphasized Revelation 2–3 and Revelation 17. This chapter attempts to explain why these passages were so crucial to Williams despite the fact that many others considered them minor pages in an otherwise captivating apocalyptic book. While many interpreters neglected these apocalyptic scenes, they were crucial to Williams's arguments against religious persecution and in favor of separation of church and state and religious liberty. He deemed these texts to be critical revelations that cast needed light on the seventeenth century.

I. THE LETTERS TO THE SEVEN CHURCHES IN ASIA (REVELATION 2–3)

Revelation 2–3 comprises Christ's letters to the churches in Ephesus, Smyrna, Pergamus, Thyatira, Sardis, Philadelphia, and Laodicea. The letters share a common organizational pattern. Each begins with a description of Christ's glory and authority. Christ then praises each community for its good works, except in Laodicea, where he finds nothing to commend. Next Christ scolds each church for deficiencies such as immorality, heretical doctrines, and lack of faith. The exceptions are in the letters to Smyrna and Philadelphia, where Christ finds nothing to condemn. Finally, Christ concludes each letter with praise and encourage-

---

[5] Revelation 2–3 was Williams's most cited biblical passage in all of his published writings, and Revelation 17 was his third most cited text.

ment to those in the communities that prove themselves conquerors in the face of approaching evil.[6]

In the seventeenth century, the letters to the seven churches were not very important for English Separatists and Baptists.[7] For them, these apocalyptic letters were minor proof texts for church purity, but not arguments against Christendom or in defense of religious liberty. The neglect of Revelation 2–3 by Williams's like-minded predecessors and contemporaries begs the question: why was this passage Williams's most cited biblical text in his published works? Williams knew the writings of major Separatists and Baptists, and that these writings influenced his biblical interpretation.

---

[6] For a summary of the fourfold scheme of each letter, see G. B. Caird, *A Commentary on The Revelation of St. John the Divine*, ed. Henry Chadwick, Harpers New Testament Commentaries (New York: Harper and Row, 1966) 27.

[7] For example, in Henry Barrow's most important book, *Brief Discoverie of the False Church*, which spans some 410 pages, he mentioned Revelation 2 on only 6 pages. In each case, Barrow attempted no extended exegesis, but only cited the passage as a proof text for the necessity of church discipline (in *The Writings of Henry Barrow, 1587–1590*, ed. Leland H. Carlson [London: Allen and Unwin, 1962], 154, 297–98, 483, 520, 613,). Other Separatists and Baptists shared Barrow's disinterest in Revelation 2. For example, Robert Harrison and Robert Browne only cited the passage three times in their writings. See Robert Harrison, *A Treatise of the Church and the Kingdome of Christ*, in *The Writings of Robert Harrison and Robert Browne*, ed. Albert Peel and Leland H. Carlson (London: Allen and Unwin, 1953) 37; idem, *A Little Treatise Uppon the Firste Verse of the 122 Psalm*, 100; Robert Browne, *A Treatise upon the 23 of Matthewe*, 200. John Canne provides a similar example. In his most important work, *A Necessitie of Separation From the Church of England* (ed. Charles Stoval [London: Hanserd Knollys Societies, 1849]), which spans over 300 pages, he cited Revelation 2 on only 2 pages: see 177, 187. The most citations of Revelation 2 that I found in any book by an English Separatist were in Henry Ainsworth's *Communion of Saints* (London: John Bellamie and Ralph Smith, 1641). In that 400-page book, Ainsworth cited the passage on 22 pages; vii, 39, 81, 110, 178, 201, 241, 301–302, 334, 340, 366–67, 369, 375–76, 383–86, 388–89. Importantly, English Baptists, with whom Williams was closest in thought, gave even less attention to Revelation 2. For example, Thomas Helwys cited the passage on only three pages of his most important work, *Mistery of Iniquity* (n.p.: 1612); 63, 133, 176.

Why, then, was this passage a most visible exception? What did Williams see in Revelation 2–3 that other Separatists and Baptists overlooked?

The difference is that, unlike other Separatists and Baptists, Williams encountered John Cotton, whose interpretation of Revelation 2–3 posed a formidable threat to Williams's position. Cotton's exegesis of Revelation 2–3 was particularly challenging to Williams because Cotton argued that Christ himself wrote these letters to condemn religious toleration and warn his followers that they should not allow heretics and pagans to infect their communities. Williams recognized that if this portrayal were convincing, it would undercut his defense of religious liberty and the separation of church and state. As a previous chapter on Williams's interpretation of the weeds parable demonstrated, Williams based his arguments for religious liberty and the division of church from state on his conviction that these were "doctrines of Christ." Thus, he had to defend his portrayal of Christ against Cotton's depiction of Christ as a religious persecutor.

A. John Cotton: Christ's Threats against Religious Toleration

Cotton cited Revelation 2–3 to oppose arguments for religious liberty that appeared in a tract by an anonymous English Baptist.[8] Cotton later claimed that Williams had sent him the tract and requested his response. Cotton then replied to Williams in "a private letter." Cotton, therefore, was unpleasantly surprised to discover this private response to Williams in print when Williams published it along with a selection from the Baptist tract in his *Bloudy Tenent of Persecution.*[9] Williams later denied both that he

---

[8] *A Most Humble Supplication of Many of the King's Majesty's Loyal Subjects,* in *Tracts on Liberty of Conscience and Persecution, 1614–1661,* ed. Edward Bean Underhill (New York: Burt Franklin, 1966) 181–231. Although the tract is anonymous, most scholars have followed Underhill in attributing it to John Murton. See editor's remarks on 187.

[9] John Cotton, *Bloudy Tenent, Washed, and Made White in the Bloud of the Lambe,* ed. Richard C. Robey (London: 1647; reprint, New York: Arno Press, 1972) 2. For Cotton's response, see John Cotton, "The Answer of Mr. John

had sent the tract to Cotton and that Cotton's response was private.[10] But Williams made no secret of the fact that he admired the contents of this Baptist's work as well as the fortitude of its writer. Williams observed that the Baptist author wrote the book while he was imprisoned in Newgate for his "witness of some truths of Jesus," and that, because he had no pen or ink, he wrote in milk. Writing in milk had its advantages, because words written in milk were undetectable unless someone heated the paper. This clever Baptist was therefore able to smuggle his book to his colleagues on the outside. Williams could not resist the symbolism, pointing out that, like the milky ink that wrote them, the Baptist's arguments contained spiritual "milk, tending to soul nourishment even for babes and sucklings in Christ." Williams contrasted these arguments in milk, which were "spiritually white, pure, and inno-cent" as well as "soft, meek, peaceable and gentle," with Cotton's response, which was written in "blood" with "bloody and slaught-erous conclusions."[11]

 In his work, the Baptist writer had cited the African Church Father Tertullian's claim that authorities should not compel people to adopt religious opinions. Tertullian had argued that such forced compliance was unnecessary, for what any individual believed about God neither hindered nor helped anyone else. Furthermore, Tertullian said that coercion was contrary to the nature of worship, which by definition had to be freely offered to God.[12]

Cotton of Boston," in vol. 3 of *The Complete Works of Roger Williams* (New York: Russell & Russell, 1963) 41–54.

[10] Williams, *The Bloody Tenent Yet More Bloody*, in vol. 4 of *The Complete Writings of Roger Williams* (Providence: Narragansett Club Publications, 1870; reprint, New York: Russell & Russell, 1963) 24.

[11] Williams, *The Bloudy Tenent, of Persecution, for Cause of Conscience, discussed, in A Conference Betweene Truth and Peace*, in vol. 3 of *The Complete Writings of Roger Williams* (Providence: Narragansett Club Publications, 1867; reprint, New York: Russell & Russell, 1963) 61–62.

[12] *A Most Humble Supplication*, in *Tracts on Liberty of Conscience*, ed. Edward Bean Underhill (New York: Burt Franklin, 1966) 220. The Tertullian quote is from Tertullian, *To Scapula*, in vol. 10 of *The Fathers of the Church: A*

In response, Cotton agreed that no one should force religious orthodoxy upon those who would not accept it. Cotton pointed out that he and his colleagues in the Bay Colony respected this rule by allowing "the Indians to continue in their unbelief."[13] Idolaters and heretics could worship privately as long as they neither practiced their beliefs publicly nor attempted to propagate their erroneous teachings in the commonwealth. As Cotton claimed, religious error was acceptable in private, but "it will not therefore be lawful openly to tolerate the worship of devils or idols, or the seduction of any from the truth."[14]

Above all, Cotton feared the seductive potential of idolatry and heresy. He believed that religious liberty for all would sound the death knell for true Christianity because erroneous teachings, if allowed to grow openly in the commonwealth, would cause "the ruin and desolation of the church."[15] In making this point, Cotton appealed to Revelation 2, which contained Christ's threats to punish the seven churches of Asia if they tolerated idolatry or heresy in their midst.[16] For instance, Christ commended his followers in Ephesus for not tolerating "evildoers," and for despising false apostles (Rev 2:2, 6). According to the same standard of nontoleration, Christ warned the people of Pergamum and Thyatira for allowing the heretical "teaching of Balaam" (2:15), "the teaching of the Nicolaitans" (2:15), and the false prophet Jezebel to contaminate their communities (2:20). Cotton applied these "threats of Christ" to the Christian communities of his day, arguing that these letters revealed Christ's judgment that any who "blaspheme the true God, and his true religion" should "be severely punished."[17]

Cotton insisted that such punishment of heretics and idolaters was a Christian duty and not religious persecution. He defined

---

New Translation, ed. Roy J. Deferrari (New York: Fathers of the Church, Inc., 1950) 152.

[13] Cotton, "Answer of Mr. John Cotton," in vol. 3 of Complete Writings, 49.

[14] Ibid.

[15] Ibid.

[16] Ibid., 49–50.

[17] Ibid., 49–50; see also 46.

perse.

religious persecution as wrongly punishing an *innocent* person for his or her religious beliefs. Of course, this definition excluded heretics and idolaters from charity, because to punish a heretic or an idolater was not to persecute "an innocent," but rather to punish "a culpable and damnable person." Such persons were not persecuted for cause of "conscience, but for persisting in error against the light of conscience," which was rightly guided by Christian truth.[18] Thus Cotton interpreted the letters to the churches in Asia as instances of Christ's zeal to punish heresy and idolatry for the sake of the truth. Such disciplinary means were necessary to protect the integrity of Christian witness in the world. As Cotton expressed it, persons who persist in "sinning against [the] light of faith and conscience, may justly be censured by the church with excommunication, and by the civil sword also, in case they shall corrupt others to the perdition of their souls."[19]

punish idolaters for truths sake

Cotton believed that Christ's condemnation of improper belief in Revelation 2–3 justified Massachusetts Bay's banishment of Roger Williams for his erroneous and subversive opinions. Soon after Williams's banishment, Cotton wrote a letter to Williams that defended the Colony's action in condemning him. Cotton took this opportunity to cite Christ's letter to Pergamum, in which Christ had commanded errant teachers to "repent" of their heresy. Christ warned that, if they persisted in their error, he would "make war against them with the sword of [his] mouth" (Rev 2:16, NRSV).[20] Based on this passage, Cotton justified the Bay Colony's banishment of Williams. Cotton chastised Williams for his "corrupt doctrines," which caused "the Lord Jesus to fight against you with the sword of his mouth (as he himself speaketh, Rev 2:16)."[21] Cotton duly informed Williams that Christ's sword had justly

---

[18] Ibid., 49.

[19] Ibid., 51.

[20] John Cotton, "Letter From John Cotton (1636)," in vol. 1 of *The Correspondence of Roger Williams,* ed. Glenn W. LaFantasie (Providence: Brown University Press, 1988) 34.

[21] Ibid.

condemned him through the "testimonies of the Churches and Brethren" in Massachusetts Bay. Thus, in citing Revelation 2, Cotton enlisted Christ's support of Williams's banishment. The colony had rightly banished Williams because his "corrupt doctrines" had threatened to disturb both the "civil and holy peace."[22]

B. Roger Williams: Revelation 2–3 and Christendom's Violent Biblical Interpretation

Cotton's use of Revelation 2–3 to depict Christ as supporting state punishment of religious error particularly disturbed Williams. In his view, Cotton had misinterpreted Christ's messages in Revelation 2–3. Williams found the root of Cotton's interpretive problem in his failure to realize that these apocalyptic letters applied only to the church and not to the state. Williams argued that Christ directed his warnings against toleration to the churches in these cities and not to the cities as a whole. "Christ's charge," Williams asserted, "is not against the civil magistrate of Pergamus, but the messenger or ministry of the church in Pergamus."[23] Consequently, Christ's letters to the churches had nothing to do with civil rule and punishment, but only with church government and purity. Christ intended his threats against tolerating improper beliefs as a means to motivate ministers to purify their churches, not to motivate magistrates to eliminate heresy and idolatry from their commonwealths.[24] In keeping with his vision of Christ's aversion to religious persecution, Williams emphasized that Jesus "never appointed the civil sword" as an "antidote" for religious poisons in the state.[25] Williams was astonished that "the Father of

---

[22] Ibid.

[23] Williams, *Bloudy Tenent,* in vol. 3 of *Complete Writings,* 173. Here, Williams followed the common interpretation of the "angels" in the churches as the churches' ministers and leaders; see also *The Geneva Bible: The Annotated New Testament, 1602 edition* (Cleveland: Pilgrim Press, 1989) 125. Geneva Bible marginal note on 2.1.

[24] Williams, *Bloudy Tenent,* in vol. 3 of *Complete Writings,* 173–74.

[25] Ibid., 127.

lights" would "darken and veil the eye of so precious a man" as John Cotton to the extent that Cotton could misinterpret this passage as applicable to the civil magistrate.[26]

Similar to his complaint about misinterpretations of the parable of the weeds, Williams lamented that Cotton's approach to Revelation 2–3 reflected Christendom's corruption of biblical interpretation, which had plagued churches and states for centuries. Under the influence of Christendom's blending of church and state, interpreters misapplied biblical messages to the state although Christ had intended them as directions for the church alone.[27] Williams, therefore, asserted that interpreters such as Cotton misrepresented the Bible as a scripture of persecution that supported the state's enforcement of orthodoxy. Williams lamented that Cotton's "perverse" misapplication of Revelation 2–3 to the state demonstrated how "the Christian World (so called)" had "swallowed up Christianity." Cotton had read Christ's message for the churches as directions for the state because Christendom had made "the church and the civil state" into "one flock of Jesus Christ."[28] This meant that "Christ's sheep" were not distinguished from the "unconverted wild or tame beasts and cattle of the world."[29] Williams understood this as a biblical tragedy. It

---

[26] Ibid., 173. Williams probably would have been no happier with Thomas Hooker's interpretation of this passage. Like Cotton, Hooker seemed to make no sharp distinction between church and state in the application of the letters to the seven churches. For instance, Hooker used Christ's warnings to the churches in the context of a sermon that warned seventeenth-century hearers not to assume that they are God's chosen. In 1629, Hooker warned against the presumption that God would not punish the English because "we have the gospel," and "no nation under heaven [has] so many in it that fear the Lord as our nation hath." Hooker drew a parallel between the English nation and the church of Ephesus in Revelation 2, which Christ first favored and then threatened (see Rev 2:2, 4–5). Thomas Hooker, *The Faithful Covenanter*, in *Thomas Hooker: Writings in England and Holland, 1626–1633*, ed. George H. Williams et al., (Cambridge MA: Harvard University Press, 1975) 195–96.

[27] Williams, *Bloudy Tenent*, in vol. 3 of *Complete Writings*, 127.

[28] Ibid., 174.

[29] Ibid.

perverted Christ's message and misused his name to wage wars and to persecute heretics and idolaters.

1. The Suffering of the Faithful in Apocalyptic Times. Williams believed that Cotton's assumption that Christians held the political power to persecute heretics in these seven Asian cities was wrong. Williams argued that these apocalyptic letters depicted the Christians not as persecutors but as the persecuted. These letters warned Christians that they should expect religious persecution. From Williams's perspective as an exile, this was good advice for Christians who endured Christendom's persecution not only in first-century Asia but also in seventeenth-century England and New England. He cautioned that Christians of his day should heed Christ's advice to the church at Smyrna: "Do not fear what you are about to suffer. Beware, the devil is about to throw some of you into prison so that you may be tested.... Be faithful until death, and I will give you the crown of life" (Rev 2:10, NRSV). Williams interpreted this passage as a warning that any who were "too near of kin to the Prince of Peace" would not "escape the hunters" for long.[30] Christendom's persecution would throw "all Christ's witnesses into prison" and "murder and sling out the carcasses of the saints to shame and injury."[31] In enduring such persecutions, the saints shared the suffering of Christ, for Christendom "would cast Christ himself into prison again, and to the gallows again, if he came again in person into any...persecuting state in the world."[32]

Williams applied this exegesis of Revelation 2 to "the saints" that Christendom's state of England had cast into prison. He asserted that, by "not tolerating the idolater and heretic," the English government was guilty of "not tolerating" Christ, who lived on "in his followers." Thus, in not allowing so-called heretics and idolaters their freedom, England had hunted and persecuted Christ

---

[30] Williams, *Bloody Tenent Yet More Bloody*, in vol. 4 of *Complete Writings*, 44.

[31] Ibid., 45.

[32] Ibid., 159.

by not allowing hunters/ppl freedom actually persecuting X

("out of the world."[33] Williams judged that, far from being a license to persecutors, the letters to the seven churches in Asia were Christ's advice and encouragement to the persecuted.

2. Spiritual "Conquerors." While these churches experienced persecution, their cause was not lost. Williams emphasized that *letters gave hope* these letters proclaimed the hope that would survive the harshest trials. The conclusions to the letters inspired strength and promised deliverance to all who conquered amid the trials of persecution.[34] For example, Christ inspired the church at Thyatira, saying, "For he that overcometh and keepeth my works unto the end, to him will I give power over nations" (Rev 2:26, GB). In light of Christendom's alignment of church and state, the question arose concerning what this "overcoming" entailed. Obviously, Williams did not interpret Christ's words as an encouragement to military or physical conquest. Rather, he believed that these charges to "overcome" referred to Revelation 12:11, where "God's servants overcame the Dragon or Devil in the Roman Emperors by three weapons: the blood of the Lamb, the word of their testimony, and the not loving of their lives unto the death."[35] For Williams, this clarified the sense in which Christ encouraged his faithful to "overcome." Far from relying on magisterial power, Christ's servants were to conquer their enemies by using the three spiritual *demand to use spiritual weapons* weapons mentioned in Revelation 12:11. This proved that "God's servants are all overcomers when they war with God's weapons in God's cause and worship."[36] In Revelation 2–3, therefore, Williams found an apocalyptic demand for the exclusive use of spiritual weapons in combating evil doctrine.[37]

---

[33] Williams, *The Examiner Defended in a Fair and Sober Answer*, in vol. 7 of *The Complete Writings of Roger Williams* (New York: Russell & Russell, 1963) 277.

[34] Williams, *Bloudy Tenent*, in vol. 3 of *Complete Writings*, 190.

[35] Ibid. See also Rev 12:11.

[36] Williams, *Bloudy Tenent*, in vol. 3 of *Complete Writings*, 190.

[37] To use another of Williams's images, spiritual maladies needed that "good physician Christ Jesus," who supplied his church with "spiritual antidotes

Williams emphasized this interpretation by placing Revelation 2–3 alongside Paul's appeal for spiritual weapons in Ephesians 6. The letters to the seven churches, in Williams's view, confirmed Paul's command that Christians contend with evil not through physical violence but with spiritual weapons. Williams asserted that Christian "men and women fight under the great Lord general, the Lord Jesus Christ," whose "weapons, armor, and artillery" were "spiritual," as Paul said in Ephesians 6. Similarly, "in all the 7 churches of Asia," Christ's followers were "spiritual conquerors" who overcame the challenges that heretics, idolaters, and persecutors had set before them.[38] This comparison of Williams's interpretation of Ephesians 6 and Revelation 2–3 reveals the consistency of Williams's biblical vision for religious liberty. The success of his argument depended upon his ability to persuade opponents that religious liberty was a political doctrine that encompassed all of scripture, uniting seemingly discordant voices such as Paul's advice to the Ephesians and the Apocalyptic letters to the seven churches.

3. Christ and Jezebel: A Pattern for Christian Patience amid Heresy and Idolatry. Cotton had argued that these letters proved a fundamental rule of Christ—that it is evil "to tolerate notorious evil doers, whether seducing teachers or scandalous livers." Cotton found an example of this rule in Christ's condemnation of Thyatira "for tolerating Jezebel to teach and seduce."[39] Here Williams seized an opening and attempted to capitalize on a weakness in Cotton's exegesis. Williams pointed out that before Christ ordered Jezebel's punishment, he had tolerated Jezebel for a time in hopes that she would repent (Rev 2:21). In Williams's view, Christ's patience with Jezebel was an example of "God's wonderful toleration" of sinners, which scripture recounted in numerous other passages. Williams

---

and preservations against the spiritual sicknesses, sores, weaknesses, [and] dangers" that threatened his people. Williams, *Bloudy Tenent,* in vol. 3 of *Complete Writings,* 127.

[38] Williams, *Bloudy Tenent,* in vol. 3 of *Complete Writings,* 362–63.

[39] Cotton, "Answer of Mr. John Cotton," in vol. 3 of *Complete Writings,* 46.

*God
endures
the
heretics* asserted that, while God was holy, he still endured graciously "all the idolaters and profanations, all the thefts and rapines, all the whoredomes and abominations" in hopes that even the worst of sinners would repent. Thus, Williams contended that these apocalyptic letters displayed not only Christ's opposition to error, but also his tolerance of it. Revelation 2–3 exemplified not only Christ's judgment, but also his patience.[40]

Williams believed that one of Cotton's problems with this passage resulted from his failure to distinguish between approval and toleration. Williams asserted that, in these letters, Christ did not approve of Jezebel's heresy, but he tolerated it for a time. While Christ never approved of evil, he advocated a "suffering or permission" of it in the world until judgment.[41] In Williams's understanding, it did not transgress "an absolute rule" of the Lord "to permit and tolerate…the souls and consciences of all men in the world."[42] Thus Williams argued that Christ's patience with Jezebel provided a model for Christians to follow in their relations with heretics and idolaters in the world.

4. Religious Freedom and the Civil Peace. Williams found no basis in this passage for Cotton's fear that heretics and idolaters would disrupt the civil peace if authorities allowed them to remain in the state. To the contrary, Williams insisted, these letters showed that civil peace was possible in cities that were religiously diverse. The city of Smyrna was a prime example. In that city, Christ's church endured "slander on the part of those who say that they are Jews and are not, but are a synagogue of Satan" (Rev 2:9, NRSV). Whether this "synagogue of Satan" depicted literal Jews or false Christians, this group obviously stood apart from Christ's church in Smyrna.[43] But Williams observed that the passage gave no evidence that these "spiritual oppositions" within Smyrna created

---

[40] Williams, *Bloudy Tenent*, in vol. 3 of *Complete Writings*, 166.
[41] Ibid., 165.
[42] Ibid., 167.
[43] Ibid., 74.

any civil opposition between citizens. Far from being a city that suffered for its religious diversity, Smyrna was a biblical example of a religiously diverse city that enjoyed civil peace and order.[44]

For Williams, this civil peace amid religious diversity taught Christendom a lesson that it sorely needed: civil peace never depended upon the presence of Christianity in the state. He observed that many great cities flourished without Christian rulers. To be sure, Native Americans and the "wildest pagans keep the peace of their towns or cities" even though one cannot find "a true church of God" among any of the native peoples.[45] Williams illustrated this by comparing the church to "a corporation, society, or company" that existed within a city. He noted that corporations operated independently, administered their own affairs, and kept their own records. Moreover, corporations sometimes endure conflicts that cause them to "divide, break into schisms and factions," and even to "dissolve into pieces and nothing." Yet corporations may undergo these divisions and disruptions without disturbing the city of which they are a part because "the essence or being of the city…is essentially distinct from those particular societies" that operate within it.[46] Comparing this illustration to Revelation 2–3, Williams concluded that the church in Ephesus was like a society within the city of Ephesus. Thus even if Christ condemned the church in Ephesus outright, discrediting it for its errors (as he threatened to do), "all this might be without the least impeachment or infringement of the peace of the city of Ephesus."[47] This reading of Revelation 2–3 supported Williams's view that Jesus commanded magistrates "not to persecute, and to see that none of their subjects be persecuted and oppressed for their conscience and worship," as long as these citizens were "otherwise subject and peaceable in civil obedience."[48]

---

[44] Ibid., 74.
[45] Ibid., 72–73.
[46] Ibid., 73.
[47] Ibid., 74.
[48] Ibid., 188.

*religious
confirm=
moral
uniform*

Williams acknowledged that one of Christendom's fears was that religious diversity would lead to moral anarchy. Interpreters such as John Cotton believed that religious uniformity was necessary in order to ensure moral uniformity in the common-wealth. If individuals were free to follow their own consciences in religious matters, what prevented them from following their own consciences in ethical matters? In response, Williams cautioned that religious freedom did not imply ethical freedom. He granted that if heretical or idolatrous beliefs issued in immoral or sub-versive actions, then magistrates were right to discipline the per-petrators. For instance, if "Balaam's or Jezebel's doctrine" taught "corporal fornication," then the officers of the cities of Per-gamum and Thyatira should have suppressed "not only such practices," but also the teachings that supported these immoral actions.[49] But Williams doubted that this qualification had any relevance to these apocalyptic letters. He surmised that when Christ warned the church of Thyatira not to tolerate Jezebel's "fornication," Christ did not mean "corporal whoredoms," but rather "spiritual whore-doms."[50] Furthermore, as long as "Balaam's teach-ers or Jezebel" only "seduce" church members to idolatrous and heretical beliefs and worship and not immoral actions, the civil magistrate has no jurisdiction to punish them.[51]

*conquer
tempt. w/
spiritual
weapons*

In sum, Williams believed that these apocalyptic messages con-tained valuable information about Christ's attitude toward re-ligious diversity in the state. While Christ encouraged his followers to conquer amid their afflictions, he advised them to do so with spiritual weapons, not the state's civil sword. Equipped with their spiritual weapons, these churches had the resources to endure their oppressions, and to purify their communities of polluting ele-ments. Moreover, these letters demonstrated that, contrary to Cotton's interpretation, Christ was capable of tolerating heresy—

---

[49] Ibid., 173.

[50] Williams, *Bloody Tenent Yet More Bloody*, in vol. 4 of *Complete Writings*, 146.

[51] Williams, *Bloudy Tenent*, in vol. 3 of *Complete Writings*, 173.

even the dire heresy of Jezebel—without exterminating it from the state. Williams also argued that these Asian cities disproved Christendom's theory that civil peace depended on religious uniformity. While these cities exemplified religious diversity, they did not degenerate into moral or political chaos.

II. THE WOMAN AND THE BEAST (REVELATION 17)

The apocalyptic vision of the "Great Whore of Babylon" in Revelation 17 captivated Williams's attention. He repeatedly referred to this passage, quoting from it in his writings and interpreting its significance for the seventeenth century. The passage features a graphic description of an adorned whore, her scarlet beast, and the blood of their innocent victims. Is there any wonder that Williams found this text so riveting and so useful in his depiction of the disastrous consequences of religious persecution? The crux of the text deserves quotation:

> I saw a woman sitting on a scarlet beast that was full of blasphemous names, and it had seven heads and ten horns. The woman was clothed in purple and scarlet, and adorned with gold and jewels and pearls, holding in her hand a golden cup full of abominations and the impurities of her fornication; and on her forehead was written a name, a mystery: "Babylon the great, mother of whores and of earth's abominations." And I saw that the woman was drunk with the blood of the saints and the blood of the witnesses to Jesus. (Rev 17:3b–6, NRSV)

In his reading of this vision, Williams followed many Protestant interpreters who identified the whore and her "scarlet beast" with the Roman Catholic Church.[52] Puritans needed look no

---

[52] As Christopher Hill has argued, "the identification of the Pope and Antichrist won very general support in the Church of England" during the years 1530–1640 (*Antichrist in Seventeenth-Century England* [London: Oxford

further than the annotations to the *Geneva Bible* to read that "the harlot" was the Church of Rome, which they also knew as "spiritual Babylon."[53] The *Geneva Bible* marginal notes even attributed the beast's scarlet hue to the fact that "the Romish clergy were so much delighted with this color."[54] Williams argued that the true identifying mark of the woman was that she drank from the "golden cup" of religious persecution. He repeatedly cited John's observation that "the woman was drunk with the blood of the saints and the blood of the witnesses to Jesus" (Rev 17:6, NRSV). In this grotesque image, Williams found a clear representation of Roman Catholicism's "persecuting Spirit." He asserted that there could be no "one religious state known in the world that" better represented "that woman drunk with the blood of the saints, and witnesses of Jesus comparably so near as doth the estate of the Romish Church and profession."[55] So Williams discovered the genesis of Christendom in this apocalyptic vision. Christendom formed when political rulers "committed fornication" with the Roman whore, drank from her "golden cup full of abominations," and became drunk on the blood of Christ's persecuted saints (Rev 17:2, 4, 6, NRSV).

Williams also recognized a symbol for religious violence in the mysterious name on the whore's forehead (Rev 17:5). This "blasphemous character" represented Christendom's claim that the

---

University Press, 1971] 40). Puritans and Separatists interpreted this passage in terms of papist elements of worship that were idolatrous. See John Greenwood, *Briefe Refutation*, 13, 15, 28; idem, *A Fewe Observations*, 61; Henry Barrow, *A Few Observations to the Reader of M. Giffard His Last Replie*, in *The Writings of John Greenwood and Henry Barrow, 1591–1593*, ed. Leland H. Carlson (London: Allen and Unwin, 1970) 98; idem, *Letter to an Honorable Lady and Countesse of His Kindred Yet Living*, in *The Writings of John Greenwood and Henry Barrow, 1591–1593*, 244; idem, *A Plaine Refutation*, 35, 46, 129, 265, 288, 319; idem, *A Refutation of Mr. Giffard's Reasons*, 337; idem, *First Part of the Platforme*, 245; idem, *Brief Discoverie*, 275, 338–39, 432, 446, 491, 498, 537, 564, 668.

[53] *Geneva Bible* (1602), 133.

[54] Ibid.

[55] Williams, *George Fox Digg'd*, in vol. 5 of *Complete Writings*, 207.

state had both civil and spiritual authority. Williams argued that Christendom's blasphemy consisted in the false assumption that kings, queens, and magistrates "are sacred (or holy) persons, their majesties sacred, their crowns sacred, their thrones sacred, and their very kingdoms and empires sacred."[56] He believed that the "great whore" of Rome instigated this blasphemy in her claim to be the "sacred or *holy* Roman Empire."[57] The whore's blasphemy had seduced the clergy to reject Jesus in favor of Christendom's alliance of church and state. The whore's clergy, "like some proud and dainty servants," refused "to serve a poor despised Christ, a carpenter, one that came at last to the gallows." Instead, the sacrilegious clergy of Christendom preferred "rich and lordly, pompous and princely, temporal and worldly Christs."[58] Williams believed, therefore, that the whore of Revelation 17 exemplified Christendom perfectly, both in its blasphemous claim for a divine state, and in its resulting persecution of Christ and his saints.

A. The Ten Horns of the Beast (vv. 3, 12–14)

Williams also paid close attention to the whore's beast, believing that this was another striking picture of religious persecution. As John described, the woman was sitting on a scarlet beast that had seven heads and ten horns. John explained that the beast's ten horns represented the "ten kings" that yielded "their power and authority to the beast." Further, he observed that the beast and its kingdoms would "make war on the Lamb" of God, Jesus Christ (Rev 17:12–14, NRSV). In interpreting this vision, Williams surmised that, since the whore represented Roman Catholicism, the beast and its kingdoms depicted the nations that the papists had "converted" by force.[59]

---

[56] Williams, *Examiner Defended*, in vol. 7 of *Complete Writings*, 234.

[57] Ibid.; emphasis added.

[58] Williams, *Bloody Tenent Yet More Bloody*, in vol. 4 of *Complete Writings*, 381.

[59] Williams, *George Fox Digg'd*, in vol. 5 of *Complete Writings*, 348.

Williams believed that kingdoms of the beast were not only Catholic nations, but also all nations of Christendom that supported the whore's doctrine of persecution. Read in this way, the point of the vision was not merely to condemn Catholicism, but to condemn religious persecution in any form. Williams believed that the Catholic states exemplified most clearly the religious violence and persecution that marred the seventeenth century. But he also stressed that Catholicism had spread its persecuting doctrine to Protestant states of Christendom. He believed that the ten horns signified any kingdoms—Catholic or Protestant—which, "under pretense of fighting for Christ Jesus, give their power to the beast against him."[60] Against Christendom's blasphemous claims that a state-enforced Christianity furthered Christ's witness, Williams asserted that "to force the consciences of the unwilling is a soul-rape."[61] Any land that justified such persecution in the name of Christ did so in opposition to Christ's true Spirit and word. Williams warned the seventeenth century that any nation that claimed "the title of Christ's land, or Christian land" was in fact one of the kingdoms of the beast and one of "those countries whereon the whore sitteth" (Rev 17:5).[62]

Greatly to the dismay of Massachusetts Bay authorities, Williams identified one such kingdom as that of King Charles I. In December 1633, John Winthrop noted that Williams had written a treatise in which he "did personally apply to our present King Charles" this passage about kings that had yielded their power to

---

[60] Williams, *Bloudy Tenent*, in vol. 3 of *Complete Writings*, 150. One year after Williams published *The Bloudy Tenent*, English revolutionary John Lilburne wrote a letter in which he interpreted this passage in a way similar to Williams. Lilburne argued that the prophecy in which the kings of the earth shall grant power to the beast had been fulfilled with rulers who had assisted "the Pope, to join the Ecclesiastical and Civil State together, making the golden Laws of Christ, to depend upon the leaden Laws of man" (*A Copie of a Letter to Mr. William Prinne ESQ*, in vol. 3 of *Tracts on Liberty in the Puritan Revolution, 1638–1647*, 184).

[61] Williams, *Examiner Defended*, in vol. 7 of *Complete Writings*, 268.

[62] Williams, *Bloudy Tenent*, in vol. 3 of *Complete Writings*, 320.

the beast.[63] For Williams, Charles demonstrated that he was one of the beast's kings when he used his status as a "Christian King" to justify his seizure of American lands without the permission of their Native American owners. In Williams's opinion, this was yet another crime of Christendom—yet another instance in which a ruler falsely claimed divine favor to achieve corrupt goals. Williams could hardly have offered an interpretation that proved more offensive to Massachusetts Bay. In calling King Charles an exploiting king of the beast, Williams had denied the legitimacy of the Massachusetts Bay charter.

Williams did not stop there. He extended his assault by reading his Puritan adversaries into this apocalyptic diatribe against Christendom. While Charles represented one of the "Ten Horns," the Bay Colony itself represented another in its violent advocacy of Christendom. Williams demonstrated this by exposing the persecuting arguments of John Cotton in his polemical writings. While Cotton abhorred Catholicism, Williams asserted that Cotton was a religious persecutor who had sipped "at the bloody cup of the great whore," and that he had not "recovered from the drunkenness of the great whore, who intoxicateth the nations."[64] Williams believed that the authorities of Massachusetts Bay had been under the influence of this violent intoxication when they banished him.

---

[63] In addition to Rev 17:12–13, Winthop said that Williams also applied two other passages to Charles: Rev 16:13–14, and Rev 18:9. John Winthrop, *The Journal of John Winthrop, 1630–1649*, ed. Richard S. Dunn, James Savage, and Laetitia Yeandle (Cambridge: Belknap Press of Harvard University Press, 1996) 107. See also James F. Maclear, "New England and the Fifth Monarchy," in *Puritan New England: Essays on Religion, Society, and Culture*, ed. Alden T. Vaughan and Francis J. Bremer (New York: St. Martin's Press, 1977) 71; Allen, "'The Restauration of Zion': Roger Williams and the Quest for the Primitive Church" (Ph.D. diss., University of Iowa, 1984) 134–35. Williams's treatise has been lost.

[64] Williams, *Bloody Tenent Yet More Bloody*, in vol. 4 of *Complete Writings*, 107; *Bloudy Tenent*, in vol. 3 of *Complete Writings*, 192.

What Williams most detested about Christendom was its feigned Christianity. Christendom was particularly dangerous because its political governments pretended to be Christian and pretended to persecute heretics and idolaters in Christ's name. Yet, in yielding their authority and power to the beast, "all these nations" were not Christian, but were only "guilded over with the name of Christ."[65] While they claimed to persecute erroneous believers for Christ's sake, Christendom's kingdoms only donned an executioner's mask to persecute Christ with a "subtle, secret and gentle violence."[66]

Williams believed that this "gentle violence," committed against Christians in Christ's name, was Christendom's hallmark. Such "gentle violence" was worse than outright persecution of the church. In this sense, Nero's blatant violence against the church was less damaging than Constantine's persecutions that he intended as an aid to Christ's cause.[67] Such was the persecution of Christendom in Revelation 17, in which the "great whore," pretending that she drank the blood of heretics, instead became "drunk with the blood of the saints and witnesses of Jesus" (Rev 17:6).[68]

Williams lamented that the whore and her beast established their own orthodoxy and then used it to judge Christ and his followers for their "heresy." This was the familiar pattern that nations used to justify religious persecution. In Christendom, "the cruel beast armed with the power of kings sits judge in his own quarrels against the Lamb."[69] Williams saw this exemplified in John Cotton, who supported Massachusetts Bay's right to decide which version of Christianity was true and which versions deserved the state's punishment. To Williams, this meant that Cotton merely

---

[65] Williams, *Bloudy Tenent*, in vol. 3 of *Complete Writings*, 335.

[66] Ibid.

[67] Ibid., 184.

[68] Williams, *Examiner Defended*, in vol. 7 of *Complete Writings*, 277.

[69] Williams, *Bloody Tenent Yet More Bloody*, in vol. 4 of *Complete Writings*, 522.

wanted to be sure that the magistrates would "draw their swords for *his* conscience, church," and doctrine, so that they could punish any other religious positions "as heretical."[70] In this way, Cotton and his colleagues defined proper belief according to their own standards. Cotton defended the process, arguing that they punished a heretic, not for cause of conscience, "but for sinning against his conscience."[71] Williams found it despicable and arrogant that Cotton allowed his version of truth to define the shape of all legitimate consciences.

B. The Whore's Destruction (vv. 16–18)

This apocalyptic vision takes a strange turn when the beast and his kings ("ten horns") betray the whore. They turn from supporting the whore to hating her, and finally they "devour her flesh and burn her up with fire" (Rev 17:16, NRSV). In killing the whore, the beast and his kings, who at first opposed Christ and his kingdom, turn and do Christ's bidding. For Williams, who interpreted the ten kings as evil models of Christendom, this shift posed an exegetical problem. How was he to account for the fact that the very Christendom that he abhorred became the instrument of the whore's demise? Even more seriously, how could he account for the fact that these kings of Christendom apparently defeated the whore with physical rather than spiritual weapons, devouring "her flesh" and burning "her up with fire"? Did this mean that kings rightly used physical weapons to fight Christ's battles?

Williams recognized the problems that this text posed to his argument. Many interpreters, he noted, used this apocalyptic passage to support the use of "carnal weapons in spiritual cases."[72] Unfortunately for Williams, these interpreters came not only from hostile opponents such as John Cotton, but also from the usually friendly ranks of English Separatism. One such Separatist was John Robinson. In 1614, Robinson used this passage as part of his

---

[70] Ibid., 44; emphasis added.
[71] Ibid., 522.
[72] Williams, *Bloudy Tenent*, in vol. 3 of *Complete Writings*, 421.

response to several English Baptists who argued that the civil magistrate had no jurisdiction in religious affairs. Robinson stated that civil officers had a divinely-appointed responsibility to enforce true Christianity in their commonwealths. In Robinson's view, this power was exemplified in Revelation 17:16, which stated that the kings would kill the whore not with spiritual power of the church but with the civil weapons of the state.[73]

While John Cotton disagreed with Robinson's Separatism, he agreed with his interpretation of Revelation 17:16. Cotton used this passage as ammunition against Williams's acceptance of all religious views in the state until Christ returns to judge them. Cotton responded that "it is not the will of Christ" that heretics and idolaters "should be tolerated in the world until the end of the world."[74] Like Robinson, Cotton cited this account of the kings' killing the whore as part of the biblical rationale for non-toleration, arguing that these kings would do the work of Christ in eliminating the whore's idolatry and heresy from the world. Because of this service, the kings signify "faithful princes" who will answer the call of God in the fulfillment of their religious duties.[75] By killing the whore, these kings will help to prepare the way for "a visible state of a New Jerusalem, which shall flourish many years upon the earth, before the end of the world."[76]

Williams dismissed Cotton's claim that these kings will be "faithful princes" that God will ordain to do his bidding. Williams reminded Cotton that, far from being "faithful" disciples, these kings would hate both the whore and Christ, the Lamb of God. As the vision detailed, these kings "will make war on the Lamb, and the Lamb will conquer them, for he is Lord of lords and King of

---

[73] John Robinson, *Of Religious Communion, Private and Public*, in vol. 3 of *The Works of John Robinson*, ed. Robert Ashton (Boston: Doctrinal Tract and Book Society, 1851) 277.

[74] Cotton, *The Bloudy Tenent, Washed, And made white in the bloud of the Lambe*, ed. Richard C. Robey, Research Library of Colonial Americana (London: 1647; reprint, New York: Arno, 1972) 42.

[75] Ibid., 42–43.

[76] Ibid., 43.

kings" (Rev 17:14, NRSV).[77] Thus, although these kings served Christ's purpose by killing the whore, they were not followers of Christ and, therefore, their "hatred of the whore" was not "a true, chaste, Christian hatred against Antichristian whorish practices."[78] In fact, these kings had accepted anti-Christian practices by drinking from the whore's cup (Rev 17:2). Williams therefore argued that these kings were not acting on Christ's behalf when they destroyed the whore. Instead, they killed the whore because of their own self-interest, following their evil natures and their tendency toward destruction and violence.[79] Thus Williams perceived that God would destroy the whore not by commissioning his faithful disciples to carry out the task, but by providentially using these kings' evil natures against her. Williams anticipated that this would happen when, as "with all whores and their lovers, the Church of Rome and her great lovers shall fall out, and by the righteous vengeance of God upon her...these mighty fornicators shall turn their love into hatred, which hatred shall make her a poor desolate naked whore, torn and consumed."[80]

Williams observed that this was not the first time that God had used evil persons to accomplish good purposes. The Old Testament King Jehu was "both hypocritical and idolatrous," but he served God's purpose both when he "dashed out the brains of that great whore Jezebel" by having her thrown out of a window, and when he "executed judgment on Baal's priests" (see 2 Kgs 9:30–37).[81] The same was true of Henry VIII, a more recent "Jehu," who rejected Roman Catholicism in England and thereby "threw the whore Jezebel the Church of Rome out of England's window." Even so, like Jehu, Henry VIII was no godly servant. While Henry fought the

---

[77] Williams, *Bloody Tenent Yet More Bloody*, in vol. 4 of *Complete Writings*, 127.

[78] Williams, *Bloody Tenent*, in vol. 3 of *Complete Writings*, 422.

[79] Ibid.

[80] Ibid.

[81] Williams, *Bloody Tenent Yet More Bloody*, in vol. 4 of *Complete Writings*, 128–29.

papacy, he also "continued to burn the saints of Jesus upon his six popish and bloody articles."[82]

Williams further argued that the kings of Revelation 17 could not be God's servants because they murdered the whore in a particularly heinous way and cannibalized her remains. Who could believe that Christ would command his servants "to make a woman naked (though a whore) and to eat her flesh" as these kings will do?[83] Such detestable violence was far from the methods of Jesus, the prince of peace. Besides, Williams pointed out that these same kings who hated and killed the whore in Revelation 17 would "weep and wail over her when they see the smoke of her burning" in Revelation 18.[84]

Based on this examination, Williams concluded that Cotton and others were wrong to interpret the kings' punishment of the whore as a proof text for magisterial authority in religious affairs. These kings were certainly not Christian rulers because, while they hated the whore in one scene, they joined her in persecuting Christ's servants in another. Furthermore, even after they had killed the whore, they repented of their action and mourned her demise. In light of these observations, Williams contended that these kings did not represent Christian rulers. These kings of the beast did not "prove it lawful for people to give power to their kings and magistrates thus to deal" with the consciences of their citizens. Neither did this vision license Christians "to kill and slaughter and burn" anyone in Christ's name, even if the offender was the worst of idolaters or heretics.[85]

---

[82] Williams, *Bloody Tenent Yet More Bloody*, in vol. 4 of *Complete Writings*, 129. Williams here referred to Henry VIII's "Six Articles" of 1539 whereby he imposed traditionally Catholic rites on England's Church.

[83] Williams, *Bloody Tenent Yet More Bloody*, in vol. 4 of *Complete Writings*, 128.

[84] Rev 18:9, NRSV; Williams, *Bloudy Tenent*, in vol. 3 of *Complete Writings*, 422–23.

[85] Williams, *Bloudy Tenent*, in vol. 3 of *Complete Writings*, 423.

§

In his interpretation of the book of Revelation, Roger Williams opposed interpreters who had used apocalyptic visions to support the persecuting states of Christendom. As was usually the case, Williams's primary exegetical opponent was John Cotton. In these texts, as in various other biblical passages, Williams believed that Cotton had mangled the biblical word into a justification of Christendom and its bloody doctrine of persecution. Cotton's interpretation of Revelation 2–3 was typical, for he interpreted Christ's command to oppose religious heresy as a policy for the civil state rather than the church. This interpretation depicted Christ as an advocate of the magistrate's role as religious disciplinarian. In Williams's view, this made Christ the author of religious persecution. Cotton's exegesis of Revelation 2–3, therefore, directly challenged Williams's understanding of Christ as the Lord of the persecuted, not an advocate of persecution. Williams opposed Cotton's interpretation, arguing that Christ intended these letters to motivate churches to purify themselves, not to empower magistrates to punish religious undesirables. Williams also read these apocalyptic letters as justifications of the compatibility between religious freedom and civil peace and the adequacy of spiritual weapons in spiritual battles.

Williams interpreted the graphic vision of the whore and the beast (Revelation 17) as a symbolic representation of the genesis of Christendom. Like many Protestants, Williams interpreted the whore as a symbol for the Roman Church. But Williams expanded the whore's application to include all nations that used civil force to maintain religious uniformity, including the persecuting governments of Charles I and Massachusetts Bay. Williams's criticism of King Charles was particularly severe, for he condemned the king for using his status as a "Christian" and "civilized" ruler to justify his seizure of American territories from so-called "pagan" and uncivilized Native Americans. In Williams's view, King Charles's theft of Native American lands was yet another example of Christendom's arrogance and injustice, yet another instance in which a ruler used so-called "Christian" status to justify violent persecution. Williams's association of King Charles with the beast shook the foundations of Massachusetts Bay, calling into question the Puritans' right to the land upon which their colony was built.

Williams believed that these apocalyptic texts were among those that advocates of Christendom had perverted for violent purposes. He saw his exegetical task as a redeeming effort whereby he opposed the bloody interpretations of these texts and clarified their true meanings. Williams asserted that apocalyptic visions and graphic symbols of the book of Revelation provided an enlightening perspective on the evils of violent persecution. Furthermore, these images of persecution were neither theoretical nor irrelevant, for Williams did not hesitate to apply the visions of persecution in the book of Revelation to specific governments and rulers in the seventeenth century. One could ask for no clearer example of the great political implications of biblical interpretation in Williams's lifetime.

- Thought letter to 7 churches written by X → don't let ppl
 (i.e. heretics) affect communities

- Cotton: heretics can worship in private, not public
   – punishment of heretics is Xn duty; religious persecution=
 punishing innocent for beliefs
   – thought X's condemnation justified w/ banishments

— W: letters only deal w/ church, not state or civil authority
   * letters to suffering community; persecution = persecuting X
   * suppose to be spiritual conquers
   · God tolerated Jez b/f condemned
   · letters show civil peace possible in places of religious tolerance
   – cities were religiously diverse + not in chaos

- Whore = RCC who instigates blasphemy in claim to be sacred
  or "holy Roman other"; = RCC b/c claim on state + b/c persecuting

- Beast = papists converted by force
   · 10 horns = any land that justifies persecution for Xnity
     * King Charles → this claim meant Mass. Bay illegit b/c taken from Indi
   · Kings kill whore ≠ no toleration; kings were evil ppl, not
 Xn rulers, used by God to do God's will.

CHAPTER 6

ROGER WILLIAMS'S BIBLICAL CHALLENGE TO AMERICA

How does the preceding picture of Roger Williams illuminate his importance for America? This book has delved into the seventeenth century, exploring a world in which the Bible was the paramount guide in all of life, the ultimate foundation of civil and religious authority, and the last word in every controversy. Understandably, then, Williams made his case for religious liberty in biblical terms. But does the biblical nature of his thought that made him so provocative in the seventeenth century render him irrelevant to today, when debates over religious liberty no longer center on the Old Testament, the parable of the weeds, the Apostle Paul, or the whore of Babylon?

On one level, Williams's relevance to contemporary discussions of church and state lies not in the nature of his thought but in his conclusions—Williams made the first sustained defense of religious liberty in American history. Over a century before Jefferson and Madison proclaimed that religious liberty was essential to the new nation, Roger Williams had waged his own polemical war for the cause. Perry Miller was correct: "later generations may not always have understood his thought," but "they could not forget him or deny him" because "he was always there to remind Americans that no other conclusion than absolute religious freedom was feasible in this society."[1] To be sure, America

---

[1] Perry Miller, *Roger Williams: His Contribution to the American Tradition* (New York: Russell & Russell, 1953) 254.

has not forgotten Williams. He is the subject of hundreds of books written since the eighteenth century, ranging from scholarly works in history, politics, and religion to books written for children.[2] Several times during the twentieth century, the Supreme Court cited him in cases involving church and state.[3] Whether they quote him properly or not, modern Americans rightly remember Williams because he addressed enduring issues that are as lively and problematic today as they were in the seventeenth century—including questions such as: "Does faith have anything to fear from government sponsorship?" and "must government rely upon religious belief to inculcate the virtues necessary to sustain a stable polity?"[4]

These questions rose to national prominence yet again in 2001 with President George W. Bush's "Faith-Based Initiative," which encouraged the government to support religious institutions that performed social services. This proposal received some bipartisan support in Congress but faced strong opposition from those who believed it was an inappropriate alliance of church and state. A self-professed born-again Christian, Bush had trumpeted religious themes throughout his campaign and promised these initiatives as a fresh approach to the use of religious organizations to treat an ailing nation. These initiatives—and the controversy they provoked—reveal that the issues dividing Williams from New England Puritans continue to divide Americans today. Anywhere politicians and ministers attempt to draw the lines between religion and politics, church and state, Roger Williams's words are relevant.

Still, Williams is relevant not only because of his conclusions regarding religious liberty, but also because of the biblical nature of his thought. His biblical case for religious liberty remains instructive for America's continued struggles to come to terms with

---

[2] An example is the recent biography for teenagers, Edwin S. Gaustad, *Roger Williams: Prophet of Liberty* (New York: Oxford University Press, 2001).

[3] Timothy Hall, *Separating Church and State: Roger Williams and Religious Liberty* (Urbana: University of Illinois Press, 1998) 1–3.

[4] Ibid., 146.

its First Amendment heritage. His biblical thought remains relevant because the Bible is an enduring presence in American society. To be sure, America has not always been the biblically saturated culture that Puritan New England was. But the Bible has not been as absent from American society as it may appear on the surface. Rather, the Bible is so intertwined with the fabric of American society that it is sometimes hardly noticeable. As one scholar notes, "Scripture has been nearly omnipresent in the nation's past," appealing to the masses as well as the elite, and studied for spiritual guidance as well as pilfered for political gain.[5] National leaders—especially presidents—routinely quote from the Bible or refer to its greatness. Even skeptical presidents like Thomas Jefferson and John Adams could not leave scripture alone. The Gospels fascinated Jefferson to the point that he edited his own version of Jesus' teachings, stripped of the miraculous features that he could not accept. Adams, likewise, praised the Bible's teachings, calling it the primary source of his personal philosophy.[6] In the following century Abraham Lincoln, one of America's most beloved presidents, praised the scriptures as humanity's greatest "gift" from God.[7] Contemporary leaders express similar praise for the scriptures, and biblical references are common sources for presidential addresses to the nation. The inauguration of each president highlights the Bible's status as a national symbol as the president-elect places a hand on the Good Book while swearing to uphold the duties and ideals of the nation's highest office. Perhaps, as Edwin Gaustad observes, frequent political appeals to biblical images and themes reflect an attempt to find some "thread of cultural unity to bind together all of the nation's noisy plurality," with the Bible providing the closest source America has to a

---

[5] Hatch, *The Bible in America: Essays in Cultural History,* ed. Nathan O. Hatch and Mark A. Noll (New York/Oxford: Oxford University Press, 1982) 4.

[6] Mark A. Noll, "Bible and American Culture," in *Dictionary of Christianity in America,* ed. Reid, 133.

[7] Ibid.

common set of stories, images, and ideas.[8] Even amid America's social and religious diversity, most Americans believe that the Bible is relevant to today. Gallup polls in 2000–2001 reveal that sixty-five percent of Americans believe that the Bible "answers all or most of the basic questions of life" and approximately half of Americans (forty-nine percent) believe that the Bible "is the inspired word of God."[9] Thus, while America at the dawn of the twenty-first century is certainly not Puritan New England, the Bible remains a respected authority in public life.

Perhaps most importantly, the Bible has influenced Americans' understanding of their nation. For over two centuries, many Americans have believed that their nation is unique, even blessed by God for a special mission to the world. While the United States has no national church, and has a population marked by religious pluralism, many Americans commonly think of their nation in religious terms. The Bible is the primary source of this American "Civil Religion." In his appropriately titled book, *God's New Israel*, Conrad Cherry highlights the biblical images that Americans use to interpret their national status and divine mission. Americans, Cherry argues, have consistently thought of themselves as "God's New Israel, his newly chosen people."[10] In this religious view of the nation, "Washington became both Moses and Joshua, both the deliverer of the American people out of bondage and the leader of the chosen people into the Promised Land of independence." Likewise, "Lincoln assumes the role of a Christ figure in the national memory: one who tragically dedicated himself to the destiny of a united nation and whose death summed up the

---

[8] Edwin Gaustad, "Bible in America," in *Mercer Dictionary of the Bible*, ed. Watson E. Mills et al., (Macon GA: Mercer University Press, 1990) 111.

[9] Alec Gallup and Wendy W. Simmons, "Six in Ten Americans Read Bible at least Occasionally," *Gallup News Service*, 20 October 2000; Gallup and Simmons, "Easter Season Finds a Religious Nation," *Gallup News Service*, 13 April 2001.

[10] Conrad Cherry, *God's New Israel: Religious Interpretations of American Destiny* (Chapel Hill NC: University of North Carolina Press, 1998) 19.

sacrifice that redeemed the nation for that destiny."[11] These are only two examples of a religious view of America that has influenced the relationship between religion and politics in various ways. And Cherry contends that, more often than not, "the belief in America as God's New Israel has come to support America's arrogant self-righteousness."[12]

Roger Williams recognized this arrogant self-righteousness at its colonial birthplace in Massachusetts Bay. In his arguments with the Puritans, he opposed the idea that God still had chosen lands, and he contested this arrogance at its biblical foundations. This book has revealed the major dimensions of Williams's biblical opposition to this national self-understanding, revealing his challenge to any attempt to construct a "Christian nation." This challenge is significant because many Christians continue to dream of the Christian America that mainline Protestants have attempted to construct since the colonial period.[13] Just as in Puritan New England, this vision of a God-endorsed society emphasizes the state's role in protecting the church and the church's duty to guide the state toward righteousness and morality. Undeterred by the two-hundred-year-old arguments of Thomas Jefferson and the constitutional validity of the First Amendment, many political leaders, ministers, and church bodies repeatedly challenge the separation of church and state on religious grounds. Williams's biblical espousal of religious liberty is therefore still relevant because many Americans who contest religious liberty and the separation of church and state do so with Bible in hand. Legal historian Timothy Hall has emphasized the unique contribution that Williams's thought makes to contemporary discourse. Williams "was an apologist for religious freedom to the religiously devout"

---

[11] Ibid., 11.

[12] Ibid., 21.

[13] For the classic examination of this process, see Robert T. Handy, *A Christian America: Protestant Hopes and Historical Realities* (New York/Oxford: Oxford University Press, 1984).

in the seventeenth century and he can be so today.[14] Our evaluation of Williams's biblical thought therefore contributes to current discussions of religious liberty because the Bible retains its political relevance for a broad spectrum of the American population.

Amazingly enough, some of the most visible opponents of the separation of church and state on religious grounds are Baptists—heirs of the tradition that Williams most closely identified with in his lifetime. While Williams was not officially a Baptist for long, he secured his place in history in part by establishing the first Baptist church in America. His eventual rejection of the Baptist church along with all others should not conceal his deep respect for Baptists who had pursued religious liberty in England and the colonies. Several years after he became convinced that all churches were corrupt, Williams continued to praise Baptists and quote from their writings. His affection for Baptists was answered when eighteenth-century Baptists—especially Isaac Backus—summoned Williams's memory, praising him for his courageous advocacy of religious liberty. During the Revolutionary era, when the desire for liberty in church and state pervaded colonial rhetoric, Backus honored Williams as the founder of the first commonwealth ever established on the principle of religious freedom.[15] It also did not hurt Backus's cause that the colonial prophet of religious freedom represented the Baptist tradition.

Yet, if Revolutionary Baptists praised Williams's thought, some modern Baptists have either ignored or rejected it. Many Baptists in the latter twentieth century supported political efforts to restore religious influence and Christian morality to American society. These Baptists, many of whom were members of the Southern Baptist Convention, questioned earlier Baptists' advocacy of the separation of church and state, which they viewed as an atheistic policy that threatened to undermine the Christian foundations of American society. As one Southern Baptist minister

---

[14] Hall, *Separating Church and State*, 147.

[15] Isaac Backus, *A History of New England, With Particular Reference to the Baptists* (New York: Arno Press, 1969) 75–76.

declared on *The CBS Evening News* in 1984, "the separation of church and state was the figment of some infidel's imagination."[16] John Cotton could not have said it better. Such attitudes revealed the ideological chasm that separated Roger Williams from many of his Baptist successors in America. Baptists who continue to defend the separation of church and state, however, have a valuable asset in Williams's biblical thought. His biblical vision of religious liberty challenges Baptists who seek government support for religious institutions and causes. Williams remains, therefore, a valuable resource for Baptists who seek to reassert their historic advocacy of religious liberty on biblical terms.

Williams's perceptive interpretation of scripture also alerts us to the violent potential of Christianity in the seventeenth century—and in the twenty-first. His rejection of the forced conversions of Native Americans is particularly insightful. He recognized that, in most cases, efforts to convert Native Americans to Christianity were coercive acts in which a powerful nation forced its religion on a people. Williams drew this insight into Christian violence from his reading of the Bible. In Paul's description of Christian armor in Ephesians 6, Williams found confirmation that the sword of the spirit, and not the physical sword, was the only weapon that could persuade the conscience. All too often, Williams argued, Christian missionaries came armed with swords of steel, and their efforts to "convert" the Native Americans were thinly-veiled acts of violence. The central problem with Christian violence therefore rested in the so-called "Christian" nations that used their supposed religious superiority to justify both forced conversions and the theft of American territories that rightly belonged to the Native Americans. Williams knew that this notion of "Christian nations" was rooted in a perversion of scripture. In combating this biblical perversion with his interpretation of the Bible, Williams hoped to curtail many of the violent atrocities of the seventeenth century. Even today,

---

[16] William Estep, *The Revolution within the Revolution: the First Amendment in Historical Context, 1612–1789* (Grand Rapids MI: William B. Eerdmans Publishing, 1990) 9.

Williams's biblical witness against "Christian nations" alerts us to the tragic, often violent consequences of uniting coercive power with religious zeal.

This book has revealed Williams as an innovative thinker who engaged perennial issues from his unique perspective. While he was unconventional, Williams was not an isolated radical who drew his convictions from an unmediated reading of scripture—nor was he a biblically-minded Thoreau who crafted his revolutionary ideas solely from meditations in the wilderness. Indeed, in his trips to England to secure the charter for Rhode Island, Williams was a man about town who used his connections with influential people to get results in English politics. Williams had similar connections in his biblical interpretation. At a time when biblical issues had supreme political relevance, he was conversant with various interpreters of scripture. Williams struggled with the Bible, constantly seeking its direction for church and state, and he struggled with his predecessors and contemporaries, repeatedly engaging their views on the scriptures. He found agreement and disagreement at almost every turn. Williams revered Calvin's theological genius and considered him a great man, but he attacked Calvin's biblical interpretation, calling it a dangerous perversion that turned the holy Word into a bloody instrument of persecution. He expressed similar convictions regarding Puritan opponents such as John Cotton. Even Separatists like the Plymouth "Pilgrims," whom Williams admired for their prophetic rejection of the Church of England, fell victim to the devil's snares in their biblical interpretation because, like the Puritans, they believed that the Bible endorsed the magistrate's power to enforce religious policy with the sword. Williams's closest theological colleagues were the Baptists. Though he eventually rejected their church, he shared their biblical augments for religious liberty, which they probably drew in part from sixteenth-century Anabaptists. But Williams developed their arguments in light of his view of religious persecution and biblical error in colonial America. His awareness of perilous misinterpretations of the Bible convinced him that a one-dimensional biblical argument would be powerless against the

Bible Commonwealths of Massachusetts. In order to persuade his opponents in that biblically-saturated society, Williams constructed a biblical arsenal that challenged religious persecution at its strongest defenses: the political interpretation of the Old Testament, Jesus' parable of the weeds, the writings of Paul, and the book of Revelation. Our understanding of Williams, therefore, must account for his biblical acumen, his selective adaptation of traditions, and his creativity with biblical arguments and their implications for violent persecution and religious liberty in colonial America.

&

Imp:
1. First case for religious liberty in USA
2. Biblical nature of his thought
3. Calls for sep. of church + state
4. Alerts us to violent capabilities of Xnity.
5. Source for Baptists wanting to reassert religious liberty.

BIBLIOGRAPHY

A. PRIMARY TEXTS

Ainsworth, Henry. *Arrow Against Idolatry.* N.p., 1640.
———. *Communion of Saints.* London: John Bellamie and Ralph Smith, 1641.
———. *Counterpoyson.* London: n.p., 1642.
———. *A Defence of the Holy Scriptures.* Amsterdam: Giles Thorp, 1613.
Ainsworth, Henry, and John Ainsworth. *The Trying Out of the Truth.* n.p.: N.P., 1615.
Ames, William. *The Marrow of Theology.* Translated by John D. Eusden. Edited by John D. Eusden. Boston: Pilgrim Press, 1968.
The Ancient Bounds. London: Henry Overton, 1645.
An Apologie or Defence of Such True Christians as Are Commonly (but Unjustly) Called Brownists. Amsterdam: n.p., 1604.
Barrow, Henry. *The Writings of Henry Barrow, 1587–1590.* Edited by Leland H. Carlson. London: Allen and Unwin, 1962.
———. *The Writings of Henry Barrow, 1590–1591.* Edited by Leland H. Carlson. London: Allen and Unwin, 1966.
——— and John Greenwood. *The Writings of John Greenwood and Henry Barrow, 1591–1593.* Edited by Leland H. Carlson. London: Allen and Unwin, 1970.
Bradford, William. *Of Plymouth Plantation, 1620–1647.* Edited by Samuel Eliot Morison. New York: Alfred A. Knopf, 1953.
Brightman, Thomas. *The Works of that Famous, Reverend and Learned Divine, Mr. Tho. Brightman.* London: n.p., 1644.
Browne, Robert and Robert Harrison. *The Writings of Robert Harrison and Robert Browne.* Edited by Albert Peel and Leland H. Carlson. London: Allen and Unwin, 1953.
Busher, Leonard. *Religious Peace; or a Plea for Liberty of Conscience.* In *Tracts on Liberty of Conscience and Persecution, 1614–1661,* edited by Edward Bean Underhill, 1–81. New York: Burt Franklin, 1966.
Calvin, John. *The Epistles of Paul the Apostle to the Romans and to the Thessalonians.* Translated by Ross Mackenzie. Edited by David W. Torrance and Thomas F. Torrance, Calvin's Commentaries. Grand Rapids MI: William B. Eerdmans Publishing, 1960.

———. *A Harmony of the Gospels Matthew, Mark and Luke.* Volume 2 of *Calvin's Commentaries.* Translated by T. H. L. Parker. Edited by David W. Torrance and Thomas F. Torrance. Edinburgh: Saint Andrews Press, 1972.

———. *Institutes of the Christian Religion.* 2 volumes. Translated by Ford Lewis Battles. Edited by John T. McNeill. Philadelphia: Westminster Press, 1960.

———. *Iohannis Calvini Commentarius in Epistolam Pauli ad Romanos.* Edited by T. H. L. Parker. Volume 22 of *Studies in the History of Christian Thought.* Leiden: E. J. Brill, 1981.

Canne, John. *A Necessitie of Separation from the Church of England.* Edited by Charles Stovel. London: Hanserd Knollys Society, 1849.

———. *The Snare is Broken.* London: M. Simmons, 1649.

———. *A Stay Against Straying.* Amsterdam: n.p., 1639.

Cotton, John. *An Abstract of the Lawes of New England.* In *John Cotton: The New England Way,* edited by Sacvan Bercovitch. New York: AMS Press, 1983.

———. *The Bloudy Tenent, Washed, And made white in the bloud of the Lambe.* Edited by Richard C. Robey, Research Library of Colonial Americana. London: 1647. Reprint, New York: Arno Press, 1972.

———. *A Briefe Exposition with Practical Observations Upon the Whole Book of Ecclesiastes.* London: Anthony Tuckney, 1654.

———. *A Practical Commentary or an Exposition with Observations, Reasons, and Uses Upon the First Epistle General of John.* 2d edition. London: Thomas Parkhuist, 1658.

———. *The Way of the Congregational Churches Cleared.* In *John Cotton on the Churches of New England,* edited by Larzer Ziff, 167–364. Cambridge: Belknap Press of Harvard University Press, 1968.

Cushman, Robert. *Reasons & Considerations Touching the Lawfulness of Removing out of England into the Parts of America.* In *Mourt's Relation or Journal of the Plantation at Plymouth by William Bradford and Edward Winslow,* edited by Henry Martyn Dexter, 143–54. New York: Garrett Press, 1969.

The Geneva Bible: A Facsimile of the 1560 Edition. Madison: University of Wisconsin Press, 1969.

The Geneva Bible: The Annotated New Testament, 1602 edition. Edited by Gerald T. Sheppard. Cleveland OH: Pilgrim Press, 1989.

Hall, David D., editor. *The Antinomian Controversy, 1636–1638: A Documentary History.* Middletown CT: Wesleyan University Press, 1968.

Haller, William, editor. *Tracts on Liberty in the Puritan Revolution, 1638–1647.* Volumes 2 and 3. New York: Columbia University Press, 1934.

Hawthorne, Nathaniel. *Grandfather's Chair.* In volume 4 of *The Centenary Edition of the Works of Nathaniel Hawthorne,* edited by William Charvat, Roy Harvey Pearce, and Claude M. Simpson. Columbus: Ohio State University Press, 1972.

Heimert, Alan, and Andrew Delbanco, editors. *The Puritans in America: A Narrative Anthology.* Cambridge: Harvard University Press, 1985.

Helwys, Thomas. *An Advertisement or Admonition unto the Congregations.* N.p., 1611.

———. *A Short Declaration of the Mistery of Iniquity.* N.p., 1612.

Hooker, Thomas. *The Application of Redemption.* New York: Arno Press, 1972.

———. *Thomas Hooker: Writings in England and Holland, 1626–1633.* Edited by George H. Williams, Norman Pettit, Winfried Herget, and Sargent Bush, Jr. Cambridge: Harvard University Press, 1975.

Hubmaier, Balthasar. *On Heretics and Those Who Burn Them.* In *Balthasar Hubmaier: Theologian of Anabaptism,* edited by H. Wayne Pipkin and John H. Yoder, 58–66. Scottdale PA: Herald Press, 1989.

Mather, Richard. *Church-Government and Church-Covenant Discussed.* In *Church Covenant: Two Tracts,* edited by Richard C. Robey. New York: Arno Press, 1972.

A Most Humble Supplication of Many of the King's Majesty's Loyal Subjects. In *Tracts on Liberty of Conscience and Persecution, 1614–1661,* edited by Edward Bean Underhill, 181–231. New York: Burt Franklin, 1966.

Objections: Answered by Way of Dialogue. N.p., 1615.

A Paraenetick, Or, Humble Address to the Parliament and Assembly for (Not Loose, But) Christian Libertie. London: Matthew Simmons for Henry Overton, 1644.

Perkins, William. *A Commentary on Galatians.* Edited by Gerald T. Sheppard, Pilgrim Classic Commentaries. New York: The Pilgrim Press, 1989.

———. *A Commentary on Hebrews 11 (1609 Edition).* Edited by John H. Augustine, Pilgrim Classic Commentaries. New York: The Pilgrim Press, 1991.

———. *A Discourse of Conscience.* In *William Perkins, 1558–1602,* edited by Thomas F. Merrill. Nieuwkoop: B. De Graaf, 1966.

Persecution for Religion Judged and Condemned. In *Tracts on Liberty of Conscience,* edited by Edward Bean Underhill, 83–180. New York: Burt Franklin, 1966.

Philips, Dirk. *Enchiridion or Handbook of Christian Doctrine and Religion.* In *The Writings of Dirk Philips,* edited by Cornelius J. Dyck, William E. Keeney, and Alvin J. Beachy, 49–440. Scottdale PA: Herald Press, 1992.

Robinson, John. *The Works of John Robinson.* Edited by Robert Ashton. Boston: Doctrinal Tract and Book Society, 1851.

Shepard, Thomas. *The Parable of the Ten Virgins.* In volume 2 of *The Works of Thomas Shepard.* Boston: Doctrinal Tract and Book Society, 1853. Reprint, New York: AMS Press, 1967.

Simons, Menno. *The Complete Writings of Menno Simons.* Edited by John Christian Wenger. Scottdale PA: Herald Press, 1956.

Smyth, John. *Paralleles, Censures, Observations.* In volume 2 of *The Works of John Smyth,* edited by W. T. Whitley, 327–562. Cambridge MA: Cambridge University Press, 1915.

———. *Propositions and Conclusions Concerning the True Christian Religion, 1612–1614.* In *Baptist Confessions of Faith,* edited by William L. Lumpkin, 123–42. Valley Forge PA: Judson Press, 1969.

Tertullian. *To Scapula.* In volume 10 of *The Fathers of the Church: A New Translation,* edited by Roy J. Deferrari, 147–64. New York: Fathers of the Church, Inc., 1950.

Tombes, John. *Jehova-Jireh; or, God's Providence in Delivering the Godly.* London: Michael Sparkes, Sr., 1643.

A True Confession of the Faith. In *The Creeds and Platforms of Congregationalism,* edited by Williston Walker, 49–74. Philadelphia: Pilgrim Press, 1960.

Ward, Nathaniel. *The Simple Cobbler of Aggawam in America.* Edited by P. M. Zall. Lincoln: University of Nebraska Press, 1969.

Williams, Roger. *The Complete Writings of Roger Williams.* Volume 1. Edited by Reuben Aldridge Guild and James Hammond Trumbull. Providence RI: Narragansett Club Publications, 1866. Reprint, New York: Russell & Russell, 1963.

———. *The Complete Writings of Roger Williams.* Volume 2. Edited by J. Lewis Diman and Reuben Aldridge Guild. Providence RI: Narragansett Club Publications, 1867. Reprint, New York: Russell & Russell, 1963.

———. *The Complete Writings of Roger Williams.* Volume 3. Edited by Samuel L. Caldwell. Providence RI: Narragansett Club Publications, 1867. Reprint, New York: Russell & Russell, 1963.

———. *The Complete Writings of Roger Williams.* Volume 4. Edited by Samuel L. Caldwell. Providence RI: Narragansett Club Publications, 1870. Reprint, New York: Russell & Russell, 1963.

———. *The Complete Writings of Roger Williams.* Volume 5. Edited by J. Lewis Diman. Providence RI: Narragansett Club Publications, 1872. Reprint, New York: Russell & Russell, 1963.

———. *The Complete Writings of Roger Williams.* Volume 7. Edited by Perry Miller. New York: Russell & Russell, 1963.

———. *The Correspondence of Roger Williams.* Edited by Glenn W. LaFantasie. 2 volumes. Hanover NH: Brown University Press, 1988.

Winthrop, John. *The Journal of John Winthrop, 1630–1649.* Edited by Richard S. Dunn, James Savage, and Laetitia Yeandle. Cambridge: Belknap Press of Harvard University Press, 1996.

———. "A Modell of Christian Charity." In *The Puritans: A Sourcebook of Their Writings,* edited by Perry Miller and Thomas H. Johnson, 195–99. New York: Harper & Row Publishers, 1963.

Zeal Examined: or, A Discourse for Liberty of Conscience in Matters of Religion. London: G.D. for Giles Calvert, 1652.

B. SECONDARY STUDIES

Allen, Crawford Leonard. "'The Restauration of Zion': Roger Williams and the Quest for the Primitive Church." Ph.D. dissertation, University of Iowa, 1984.

———. "Roger Williams and 'The Restauration of Zion.'" In *The American Quest for the Primitive Church,* edited by Richard T. Hughes, 33–68. Urbana and Chicago: University of Illinois Press, 1988.

Augustine, John H. "'Notable Precedents': The Vocational Rhetoric of Exemplary Figures." In *William Perkins, A Commentary on Hebrews 11 (1609 Edition),* edited by John H. Augustine, 1–31. New York: The Pilgrim Press, 1991.

Axtell, James. *The Invasion Within: The Contest of Cultures in Colonial North America.* New York/Oxford: Oxford University Press, 1985.

Backus, Isaac. *A History of New England, With Particular Reference to the Baptists.* New York: Arno Press, 1969.

Bainton, Roland H. "The Parable of the Tares as the Proof Text for Religious Liberty to the End of the Sixteenth Century." *Church History* 1/2 (1932): 67–89.

Bellin, Joshua David. "The Demon of the Continent: American Literature, Indian Conversion, and the Dynamics of Cultural Exchange." Ph.D. dissertation, University of Pennsylvania, 1995.

Bercovitch, Sacvan. *The American Jeremiad.* Madison: University of Wisconsin Press, 1978.

———. "New England's Errand Reappraised." In *New Directions in American Intellectual History,* edited by John Higham and Paul K. Conkin, 85–104. Baltimore: Johns Hopkins University Press, 1979.

———. *The Puritan Origins of the American Self.* New Haven CT: Yale University Press, 1975.

———. "Typology in Puritan New England: The Williams-Cotton Controversy Reassessed." *American Quarterly* 19 (1967): 163–91.

Bozeman, Theodore Dwight. "Biblical Primitivism: An Approach to New England Puritanism." In *The American Quest for the Primitive Church,* edited by Richard T. Hughes, 19–32. Urbana and Chicago: University of Illinois Press, 1988.

———. *To Live Ancient Lives: The Primitivist Dimension in Puritanism.* Chapel Hill: University of North Carolina Press, 1988.

Brockunier, Samuel Hugh. *The Irrepressible Democrat: Roger Williams.* New York: Ronald Press, 1940.

Brumm, Ursula. *American Thought and Religious Typology*. Translated by John Hoaglund. New Brunswick NJ: Rutgers University Press, 1970.

Burrage, Champlin. *The Early English Dissenters in the Light of Recent Research (1550–1641)*. 2 volumes. Cambridge MA: Cambridge University Press, 1912.

Butts, Francis T. "The Myth of Perry Miller." *American Historical Review* 87/3 (1982): 665–94.

Caird, G.B. *A Commentary on The Revelation of St. John the Divine*. Edited by Henry Chadwick, Harpers New Testament Commentaries. New York: Harper and Row, 1966.

Calamandrei, Mauro. "Neglected Aspects of Roger Williams' Thought." *Church History* 21 (1952): 239–58.

———. "The Theology and Political Thought of Roger Williams." Ph.D. dissertation, University of Chicago, 1953.

Campbell, Ted A. *Christian Confessions: A Historical Introduction*. Louisville KY: Westminster John Knox Press, 1996.

Cherry, Conrad, editor. *God's New Israel: Religious Interpretations of American Destiny*. Chapel Hill: University of North Carolina Press, 1998.

Coggins, James Robert. *John Smyth's Congregation: English Separatism, Mennonite Influence, and the Elect Nation*. Edited by Cornelius J. Dyck, Studies in Anabaptist and Mennonite History. Scottdale PA: Herald Press, 1991.

Cohen, Charles L. "The Post-Puritan Paradigm of Early American Religious History." *William and Mary Quarterly* 54/4 (1997): 695–722.

Coolidge, John S. *The Pauline Renaissance in England: Puritanism and the Bible*. London: Clarendon Press, 1970.

Cowart, Donald W. "'A Minister I Will Not Be': Historical Ministers in the Works of Nathaniel Hawthorne." Ph.D. dissertation, University of South Florida, 1995.

Coyle, Edward Wallace. "From Sinner to Saint: A Study of the Critical Reputation of Roger Williams With An Annotated Bibliography of Writings About Him." Ph.D. dissertation, University of Massachusetts, 1974.

———. *Roger Williams: A Reference Guide*. Boston: G. K. Hall & Co., 1977.

Davidson, Edward H. "John Cotton's Biblical Exegesis: Method and Purpose." *Early American Literature* 17 (1982): 119–38.

Davis, Jack L. "Roger Williams Among the Narragansett Indians." *New England Quarterly* 43 (1970): 593–604.

Delbanco, Andrew. "The Puritan Errand Re-Viewed." *Journal of American Studies* 18 (1984): 343–60.

———. *The Puritan Ordeal*. Cambridge: Harvard University Press, 1989.

Delfs, Arne. "Anxieties of Influence: Perry Miller and Sacvan Bercovitch." *New England Quarterly* 70/4 (1997): 601–15.

Easton, Emily. *Roger Williams: Prophet and Pioneer.* Boston: Houghton Mifflin, 1930.

Ernst, James E. "The Political Thought of Roger Williams." Ph.D. dissertation, University of Washington, 1928.

———. *Roger Williams: New England Firebrand.* New York: The Macmillan Company, 1932.

Estep, William. "Sixteenth-Century Anabaptism and the Puritan Connections: Reflections upon Baptist Origins." In *Mennonites and Baptists,* edited by Paul Toews, 1–38. Winnipeg: Kindred Press, 1993.

———. *The Revolution within the Revolution: the First Amendment in Historical Context, 1612–1789.* Grand Rapids MI: William B. Eerdmans Publishing, 1990.

———. *The Anabaptist Story: An Introduction to Sixteenth-Century Anabaptism.* 3rd edition. Grand Rapids MI: William B. Eerdmans Publishing, 1996.

Foster, Stephen. "English Puritanism and the Progress of New England Institutions, 1630–1660." In *Saints and Revolutionaries: Essays on Early American History,* edited by David D. Hall, John M. Murrin, and Thad W. Tate, 3–37. New York: W. W. Norton & Company, 1984.

Gallup, Alec and Wendy W. Simmons. "Six in Ten Americans Read Bible at least Occasionally." In *Gallup News Service.* 20 October 2000.

———. "Easter Season Finds a Religious Nation." *Gallup News Service,* 13 April 2001.

Gaustad, Edwin S. *Liberty of Conscience: Roger Williams in America.* Edited by Mark A. Noll and Nathan O. Hatch, Library of Religious Biography. Grand Rapids MI: William B. Eerdmans Publishing, 1991.

———. *Roger Williams: Prophet of Liberty.* Oxford Portraits. Oxford/New York: Oxford University Press, 2001.

———. "Bible in America." In *Mercer Dictionary of the Bible,* edited by Watson E. Mills et al., 109–12. Macon GA: Mercer University Press, 1990.

———. "Review of Hugh Spurgin's *Roger Williams and Puritan Radicalism in the English Separatist Tradition.*" *Church History* 61/4 (1992): 453–54.

———. "Roger Williams and the Principle of Separation." *Foundations* 1 (1958): 55–64.

George, Timothy. "Between Pacifism and Coercion: The English Baptist Doctrine of Religious Toleration." *Mennonite Quarterly Review* 58/1 (1984): 30–49.

———. *John Robinson and the English Separatist Tradition.* Macon GA: Mercer University Press, 1982.

Gilpin, W. Clark. *The Millenarian Piety of Roger Williams.* Chicago: University of Chicago Press, 1979.

————. "Recent Studies of American Protestant Primitivism." *Religious Studies Review* 19/3 (1993): 231–35.

————. "Roger Williams." In *Makers of Christian Theology in America*, edited by Mark G. Toulouse and James O. Duke, 39–44. Nashville: Abingdon Press, 1997.

Greaves, Richard L. "Traditionalism and the Seeds of Revolution in the Social Principles of the Geneva Bible." Paper presented at the Conference on Puritanism in Old and New England, Thomas More College, Ft. Mitchell KY, 1975.

Gummere, Richard M. *The American Colonial Mind and the Classical Tradition: Essays in Comparative Culture.* Cambridge: Harvard University Press, 1963.

————. "Church, State, and the Classics: The Cotton-Williams Debate." *Classical Journal* 54 (1958): 175–83.

Gura, Philip. *A Glimpse of Sion's Glory: Puritan Radicalism in New England, 1620–1660.* Middletown CT: Wesleyan University Press, 1984.

————. "The Study of Colonial American Literature, 1966–1987: A Vade Mecum." *William and Mary Quarterly* 45/2 (1988): 305–41.

Hall, David D. *Puritanism in Seventeenth-Century Massachusetts.* New York: Holt, Rinehart, and Winston, 1968.

Hall, Timothy L. *Separating Church and State: Roger Williams and Religious Liberty.* Urbana: University of Illinois Press, 1998.

Hambrick-Stowe, Charles E. *The Practice of Piety: Puritan Devotional Disciplines in Seventeenth-Century New England.* Chapel Hill: University of North Carolina Press, 1982.

Handy, Robert T. *A Christian America: Protestant Hopes and Historical Realities.* New York/Oxford: Oxford University Press, 1984.

Harlan, David. "A People Blinded from Birth: American History According to Sacvan Bercovitch." *Journal of American History* 78/3 (1991): 949–71.

Heimert, Alan, and Andrew Delbanco, editors. *The Puritans in America: A Narrative Anthology.* Cambridge: Harvard University Press, 1985.

Hill, Christopher. *Antichrist in Seventeenth-Century England.* London: Oxford University Press, 1971.

————. *The English Bible and the Seventeenth-Century Revolution.* London: Penguin Press, 1993.

————. *Society and Puritanism in Pre-Revolutionary England.* Second edition. New York: Schocken Books, 1967.

Hofstadter, Richard. *The Progressive Historians: Turner, Beard, Parrington.* Chicago: University of Chicago Press, 1968.

Holifield, E. Brooks. *Era of Persuasion: American Thought and Culture 1521–1680.* Edited by Lewis Perry, Twayne's American Thought and Culture. Boston: Twayne Publishers, 1989.

Holifield, E. Brooks, and Sidney E. Mead. "Puritan and Enlightenment Primitivism: A Response." In *The American Quest for the Primitive Church*, edited by Richard T. Hughes, 69–77. Urbana and Chicago: University of Illinois Press, 1988.

Hoopes, James. "Art as History: Perry Miller's *New England Mind.*" *American Quarterly* 34 (1982): 3–25.

Howe, Daniel. "Descendants of Perry Miller." *American Quarterly* 34 (1982): 88–94.

Hudson, Winthrop. "Roger Williams, No Secularist." *Christian Century* 68 (1951): 963–64.

————. "Baptists Were Not Anabaptists." *Chronicle* 16 (1953): 171–78.

Hughes, Richard T., and C. Leonard Allen. *Illusions of Innocence: Protestant Primitivism in America, 1630–1875.* Chicago: University of Chicago Press, 1988.

Irwin, Raymond D. "A Man for All Eras: The Changing Historical Image of Roger Williams, 1630–1993." *Fides et Historia* 26/3 (1994): 6–23.

Knight, Janice. *Orthodoxies in Massachusetts: Rereading American Puritanism.* Cambridge: Harvard University Press, 1994.

Knott, John R., Jr. *The Sword of the Spirit: Puritan Responses to the Bible.* Chicago: University of Chicago Press, 1980.

Lovejoy, David S. *Religious Enthusiasm in the New World: Heresy to Revolution.* Cambridge: Harvard University Press, 1985.

————. "Roger Williams and George Fox: The Arrogance of Self-Righteousness." *New England Quarterly* 66/2 (1993): 199–225.

Lowance, Mason I., Jr. *The Language of Canaan: Metaphor and Symbol in New England from the Puritans to the Transcendentalists.* Cambridge: Harvard University Press, 1980.

————. "Typology and the New England Way: Cotton Mather and the Exegesis of Biblical Types." *Early American Literature* 4 (1969): 15–37.

Maclear, James F. "New England and the Fifth Monarchy: The Quest for the Millennium in Early American Puritanism." In *Puritan New England: Essays on Religion, Society, and Culture,* edited by Alden T. Vaughan and Francis J. Bremer, 66–91. New York: St. Martin's Press, 1977.

Marsden, George M. "Perry Miller's Rehabilitation of the Puritans: A Critique." *Church History* 39/1 (1970): 91–105.

McBeth, Leon. *English Baptist Literature on Religious Liberty to 1689.* New York: Arno Press, 1980.

McGiffert, Michael. "American Puritan Studies in the 1960s." *William and Mary Quarterly* 27/1 (1970): 36–67.

McLoughlin, William G. *Soul Liberty: The Baptists' Struggle in New England, 1630–1833.* Hanover NH: Brown University Press, 1991.

Miller, Perry. "Errand Into the Wilderness." In *Errand Into the Wilderness*, 1–15. Cambridge: Belknap Press of Harvard University Press, 1956.

———. "General Introduction." In *The Puritans: A Sourcebook of their Writings*, edited by Perry Miller and Thomas H. Johnson, 1–79. New York: Harper & Row Publishers, 1963.

———. *The New England Mind: The Seventeenth Century*. Cambridge: Belknap Press of Harvard University Press, 1939.

———. *Orthodoxy in Massachusetts, 1630–1650*. Cambridge: Harvard University Press, 1933.

———. *Roger Williams: His Contribution to the American Tradition*. New York: Bobbs-Merrill, 1953.

Moore, Leroy. "Religious Liberty, Roger Williams, and the Revolutionary Era." *Church History* 34/1 (1965): 57–76.

———. "Roger Williams and the Historians." *Church History* 32 (1963): 432–51.

Morgan, Edmund S. "Miller's Williams." *New England Quarterly* 38 (1965): 513–23.

———. *Roger Williams: The Church and the State*. New York: Harcourt Brace, 1967.

———. *Visible Saints: The History of a Puritan Idea*. Ithaca NY: Cornell University Press, 1963.

Mueller, David L. "Roger Williams on the Church and Ministry." *Review and Expositor* 55 (1958): 165–81.

Niebuhr, H. Richard. *The Kingdom of God in America*. New York: Harper and Row Publishers, 1937. [Reprint; Middletown: Wesleyan University Press, 1988.]

Noll, Mark A., George M. Marsden, and Nathan O. Hatch. *The Search for Christian America*. Colorado Springs: Helmers & Howard, 1989.

Noll, Mark A. "Bible and American Culture." In *Dictionary of Christianity in America*, edited by Daniel G. Reid, 132–36. Downers Grove IL: InterVarsity Press, 1990.

Parrington, Vernon L. *Main Currents in American Thought*. Volume 1. New York: Harcourt Brace, 1927.

Peace, Nancy E. "Roger Williams: A Historiographical Essay." *Rhode Island History* 35/4 (1976): 103–13.

Pettit, Norman. *The Heart Prepared: Grace and Conversion in Puritan Spiritual Life*. Second edition. Middletown CT: Wesleyan University Press, 1989.

Reinitz, Richard. "The Separatist Background of Roger Williams' Argument for Religious Toleration." In *Typology and Early American Literature*, edited by Sacvan Bercovitch, 107–37. Amherst MA: University of Massachusetts Press, 1972.

————. "The Typological Argument for Religious Toleration: The Separatist Tradition and Roger Williams." *Early American Literature* 5/4 (1970): 74–110.

————. "Symbolism and Freedom: The Use of Biblical Typology as an Argument for Religious Toleration in Seventeenth Century England and America." Ph.D. dissertation, University of Rochester, 1967.

Roddy, Clarence S. "The Religious Thought of Roger Williams." Ph.D. dissertation, New York University, 1948.

Rosenmeier, Jesper. "The Image of Christ: The Typology of John Cotton." Ph.D. dissertation, Harvard University, 1965.

————. "The Teacher and the Witness: John Cotton and Roger Williams." *William and Mary Quarterly* 25 (1968): 408–31.

————. "Veritas: The Sealing of the Promise." *Harvard Library Bulletin* 16 (1968): 26–37.

Scanlan, Thomas J. "Conversion, Suppression, or Limited Partnership: Problems in the Protestant Colonial Ethic." Ph.D. dissertation, Duke University, 1992.

Scholz, Robert Francis. "'The Reverend Elders': Faith, Fellowship and Politics in the Ministerial Community of Massachusetts Bay, 1630–1710." Ph.D. dissertation, University of Minnesota, 1966.

Seavey, Ormond. "Sacvan Bercovitch and Perry Miller: Perricide Regained." *Studies in Puritan American Spirituality* 3 (1992): 149–64.

Sheppard, Gerald T. "Christian Interpretation of the Old Testament between Reformation and Modernity." In *William Perkins, A Commentary on Hebrews 11 (1609 Edition),* edited by John H. Augustine, 46–70. New York: The Pilgrim Press, 1991.

Simpson, Alan. "How Democratic Was Roger Williams?" *William and Mary Quarterly* 13 (1956): 53–67.

Skaggs, Donald. *Roger Williams' Dream for America.* New York: Peter Lang, 1993.

————. "Roger Williams in History: His Image in the American Mind." Ph.D. dissertation, University of Southern California, 1972.

Smolinski, Reiner. "Israel Redivius: The Eschatological Limits of Puritan Typology in New England." *New England Quarterly* 63 (1990): 357–95.

Spurgin, Hugh. *Roger Williams and Puritan Radicalism in the English Separatist Tradition.* Volume 34, Studies in American Religion. Lewiston NY: Edwin Mellen Press, 1989.

Staloff, Darren. *The Making of an American Thinking Class: Intellectuals and Intelligentsia in Puritan Massachusetts.* New York/Oxford: Oxford University Press, 1998.

Stassen, Glen H. "Anabaptist Influence in the Origin of the Particular Baptists." *Mennonite Quarterly Review,* 36/4 (1962): 322–48.

Stavely, Keith W. F. "Roger Williams and the Enclosed Gardens of New England." In *Puritanism: Transatlantic Perspectives on a Seventeenth-Century Anglo-American Faith,* edited by Francis J. Bremer, 257–74. Boston: Massachusetts Historical Society, 1993.

Steinmetz, David C. *Calvin in Context.* New York/Oxford: Oxford University Press, 1995.

Stout, Harry S. *The New England Soul: Preaching and Religious Culture in Colonial New England.* New York/Oxford: Oxford University Press, 1986.

———. "The Puritans and Edwards." In *Jonathan Edwards and the American Experience,* edited by Nathan O. Hatch and Harry S. Stout, 142–59. New York/Oxford: Oxford University Press, 1988.

———. "Word and Order in Colonial New England." In *The Bible in America: Essays in Cultural History,* edited by Nathan O. Hatch and Mark A. Noll, 19–38. New York/Oxford: Oxford University Press, 1982.

Strickland, Arthur B. *Roger Williams, Prophet and Pioneer of Soul Liberty.* Boston: Judson Press, 1919.

Teunissen, John J., and Evelyn J. Hinz. "Roger Williams, St. Paul, and American Primitivism." *The Canadian Review of American Studies* 4/2 (1973): 121–36.

Vraniak, Leonard J., Jr. "Created Works, Created Selves: Intersections of Genre and Self-Fashioning in the New World." Ph.D. dissertation, Louisiana State University, 1997.

Walker, Williston. "The Second Confession of the London-Amsterdam Church, 1596." In *The Creeds and Platforms of Congregationalism,* edited by Williston Walker, 41–48. Philadelphia: Pilgrim Press, 1960.

Watts, Michael R. *The Dissenters: From the Reformation to the French Revolution.* Oxford: Clarendon Press, 1978.

Winslow, Ola Elizabeth. *Master Roger Williams.* New York: Macmillan, 1957.

Woodhouse, A. S. P., editor. *Puritanism and Liberty.* Second edition. Chicago: University of Chicago Press, 1974.

Wright, Paul Orrin. "Roger Williams: God's Swordsman in Searching Times." Ph.D. dissertation, Dallas Theological Seminary, 1968.

Ziff, Larzer. *The Career of John Cotton: Puritanism and the American Experience.* Princeton NJ: Princeton University Press, 1962.

Appendix

A Reference Guide to Roger Williams's Biblical Interpretation

Introduction

The preceding examination of Williams's biblical interpretation would not have been possible without the contents of this appendix. In the following reference guide, I have classified all of Williams's biblical citations in six volumes of his *Complete Writings*.[1] The indices have been invaluable tools that have enabled me to locate where Williams discussed specific biblical passages in his scattered writings. In addition, the rankings have assisted me in discerning which passages, books, and biblical genre were most cited by Williams in making his arguments.

A few notes of clarification are in order. First, I have listed in italics citations in which Williams discussed passages without explicitly citing chapter and verse in the text. Second, I have listed as chapter "zero" those occasions in which Williams referred to an entire biblical book, rather than a passage within the book.

Publisher Note: This appendix is only one prepared by the author. For a copy of the remainder of the appendixes such as Williams's citation of scripture by his writing, etc., contact the publisher and we will be glad to send you a free copy of the remaining appendixes totalling nearly 100 pages.

---

[1] I have included six of the seven volumes of Williams's writings in the most recent edition, published by Russell & Russell in 1963. I have omitted volume 6, which contains "The Letters of Roger Williams," because a recent two-volume edition of Williams's correspondence that was edited by Glenn LaFantasie has superceded it. See Williams, *Correspondence*.

1. A Scripture Index to
The Complete Writings of Roger Williams

Genesis
Total References: 47

Chap(s)	Verse(s)	Williams Text	Vol.	Page(s)
2	7	George Fox Digg'd out of his Burrowes	5	220
3		George Fox Digg'd out of his Burrowes	5	160
3		*George Fox Digg'd out of his Burrowes*	5	*199*
3		*George Fox Digg'd out of his Burrowes*	5	*442*
3	4-5	*George Fox Digg'd out of his Burrowes*	5	*188*
6	1-7	George Fox Digg'd out of his Burrowes	5	130
6	5	George Fox Digg'd out of his Burrowes	5	425
9	18-28	*Mr. Cotton's Letter Examined*	1	*346*
9	20	Bloody Tenent Yet More Bloody	4	357
9	20-23	*Experiments*	7	*96*
9	27	Bloody Tenent Yet More Bloody	4	528
9	27	*Key into the Language*	1	*87*
13	7	Bloudy Tenent	3	38
13	7	Bloudy Tenent	3	212
14		Bloudy Tenent	3	112
15	1	George Fox Digg'd out of his Burrowes	5	499
15	12-16	Bloudy Tenent	3	112
16	3	Bloudy Tenent	3	38
16	3	Bloudy Tenent	3	212
18	16-33	*Bloudy Tenent*	3	*166*
19		Bloudy Tenent	3	166
19		*Experiments*	7	*58*
20		Bloudy Tenent	3	38
20		Bloudy Tenent	3	212
20		*George Fox Digg'd out of his Burrowes*	5	*325*
21	23-24	Bloudy Tenent	3	212
21	33-34	Bloudy Tenent	3	38
22	1-19	*George Fox Digg'd out of his Burrowes*	5	*63*
22	1-19	*George Fox Digg'd out of his Burrowes*	5	*314*
26		Bloudy Tenent	3	38
26		Bloudy Tenent	3	212
27	11-12	*Experiments*	7	*63*
28	10-22	*George Fox Digg'd out of his Burrowes*	5	*237*
31		Bloudy Tenent	3	38

31		Bloudy Tenent	3	212
32	*22-32*	*Experiments*	*7*	*74*
33	*9*	*Experiments*	*7*	*88*
34		Christenings Make Not Christians	7	38
37	*18-28*	Bloody Tenent Yet More Bloody	4	*36*
38	*24*	*Examiner Defended*	*7*	*245*
39		Bloody Tenent Yet More Bloody	4	420
39		*Bloudy Tenent*	*3*	*96*
39		*Bloudy Tenent*	*3*	*300*
39		*Experiments*	*7*	*97*
39		*George Fox Digg'd out of his Burrowes*	*5*	*172*
39		*George Fox Digg'd out of his Burrowes*	*5*	*325*
39		*George Fox Digg'd out of his Burrowes*	*5*	*436*

Exodus
Total References: 38

Chap	Verse(s)	Williams Text	Volume	Page(s)
2	*11-15*	*George Fox Digg'd out of his Burrowes*	*5*	*314*
2	*11-25*	*George Fox Digg'd out of his Burrowes*	*5*	*280-81*
4		*George Fox Digg'd out of his Burrowes*	*5*	*335*
5	*8*	*Bloudy Tenent*	*3*	*82*
7	3	Bloody Tenent Yet More Bloody	4	148
9	*27-28*	*George Fox Digg'd out of his Burrowes*	*5*	*441*
12		Bloudy Tenent	3	38
12		Bloudy Tenent	3	212
18		Bloudy Tenent	3	414
18	21	Bloudy Tenent	3	412-13
19	5	Bloudy Tenent	3	327
19	6	Bloudy Tenent	3	328
20		Bloody Tenent Yet More Bloody	4	368-69
20		Bloody Tenent Yet More Bloody	4	397-98
20		Bloody Tenent Yet More Bloody	4	416
20		*Bloody Tenent Yet More Bloody*	*4*	*485*
20		*Bloody Tenent Yet More Bloody*	*4*	*490*
20		George Fox Digg'd out of his Burrowes	5	219
20		George Fox Digg'd out of his Burrowes	5	281
20		*George Fox Digg'd out of his Burrowes*	*5*	*374*
20		*George Fox Digg'd out of his Burrowes*	*5*	*387*
20	*1-17*	*Bloudy Tenent*	*3*	*151-55*
20	*1-17*	*Bloudy Tenent*	*3*	*162*
20	*1-17*	*Bloudy Tenent*	*3*	*177*
20	*1-17*	*Bloudy Tenent*	*3*	*229*

20	1-17	*Bloudy Tenent*	3	235-241
20	1-17	*Bloudy Tenent*	3	243
20	1-17	*Bloudy Tenent*	3	250
20	1-21	*Examiner Defended*	7	235
20	3-17	Bloody Tenent Yet More Bloody	4	263-65
20	7	*Hireling Ministry None of Christs*	7	188
22	20	Bloudy Tenent	3	269
30	22-38	Experiments	7	52
32		*Examiner Defended*	7	256
32		*Examiner Defended*	7	262
32	1-6	Bloody Tenent Yet More Bloody	4	36
32	1-28	Bloody Tenent Yet More Bloody	4	448
32	32	*Experiments*	7	99

Leviticus
Total References: 11

Chap.	Verse(s)	Williams Text	Volume	Page(s)
10	3	*Experiments*	7	80
16		Mr. Cotton's Letter Examined	1	373
20		Examiner Defended	7	251
20	25-26	Examiner Defended	7	251-52
20	26	Bloudy Tenent	3	324
24	1-9	Bloody Tenent Yet More Bloody	4	153
24	13-23	Bloody Tenent Yet More Bloody	4	448
24	16	Bloody Tenent Yet More Bloody	4	153
24	16	Bloudy Tenent	3	269
25	23	Bloudy Tenent	3	320-21
26		Bloudy Tenent	3	358

Numbers
Total References: 14

Chap.	Verse(s)	Williams Text	Volume	Page(s)
6		Bloody Tenent Yet More Bloody	4	66
12		Bloody Tenent Yet More Bloody	4	36
14	1–5	Bloody Tenent Yet More Bloody	4	36
16		*George Fox Digg'd out of his Burrowes*	5	395
16		George Fox Digg'd out of his Burrowes	5	460-63
16	41	Bloody Tenent Yet More Bloody	4	36
19		Mr. Cotton's Letter Examined	1	373
20	1–11	Bloody Tenent Yet More Bloody	4	66
23	10	*Experiments*	7	69
24	13	*Experiments*	7	63

25		*Bloudy Tenent*	3	*210*
25	*6– 13*	*Bloody Tenent Yet More Bloody*	4	*448-49*
30		Bloody Tenent Yet More Bloody	4	401
30		Examiner Defended	7	223

Deuteronomy
Total References: 42

Chap.	Verse(s)	Williams Text	Volume	Page(s)
4	32-34	Bloudy Tenent	3	325
7		Bloudy Tenent	3	318
7	25-26	Bloudy Tenent	3	319
8		Bloudy Tenent	3	327
8	3	George Fox Digg'd out of his Burrowes	5	52
10		Bloudy Tenent	3	358
13		Bloody Tenent Yet More Bloody	4	110
13		Bloody Tenent Yet More Bloody	4	185-186
13		Bloody Tenent Yet More Bloody	4	286
13		Bloudy Tenent	3	270
13		Bloudy Tenent	3	359
13		George Fox Digg'd out of his Burrowes	5	254
13		George Fox Digg'd out of his Burrowes	5	270
13		Mr. Cotton's Letter Examined	1	332
13	1-11	Bloody Tenent Yet More Bloody	4	245
13	1-11	Bloody Tenent Yet More Bloody	4	250
13	3	Bloody Tenent Yet More Bloody	4	362
13	5	Bloody Tenent Yet More Bloody	4	153
13	5	Bloody Tenent Yet More Bloody	4	346-347
13	5	Bloudy Tenent	3	91
13	5	Bloudy Tenent	3	269
13	6-10	Bloody Tenent Yet More Bloody	4	88
13	6-11	Bloudy Tenent	3	210
13	10	Bloody Tenent Yet More Bloody	4	286-287
13	10	Bloody Tenent Yet More Bloody	4	434
17		Bloudy Tenent	3	414
17		Bloudy Tenent	3	416
17	15	Bloudy Tenent	3	406
17	15	Bloudy Tenent	3	412-413
18		Bloudy Tenent	3	270
18		Bloudy Tenent	3	357
18		Bloudy Tenent	3	414
18		Bloudy Tenent	3	416
18		Bloudy Tenent	3	416

18	10	Bloudy Tenent	3	269
18	15-22	George Fox Digg'd out of his Burrowes	5	56
18	15-22	George Fox Digg'd out of his Burrowes	5	101
23	12	Bloudy Tenent	3	364
24	1-4	Bloudy Tenent	3	166
28		Bloudy Tenent	3	358
33	8-11	Examiner Defended	7	264
34		Mr. Cotton's Letter Examined	1	357

Joshua
Total References: 3

Chap.	Verse(s)	Williams Text	Volume	Page(s)
6		Bloudy Tenent	3	318
7	25-26	Bloody Tenent Yet More Bloody	4	250
10		Bloudy Tenent	3	318

Judges
Total References: 23

Chap.	Verse(s)	Williams Text	Volume	Page(s)
3	12-30	Bloudy Tenent	3	288
3	12-30	George Fox Digg'd out of his Burrowes	5	314
3	20	Bloudy Tenent	3	279
3	20	Bloudy Tenent	3	287
5	23	Mr. Cotton's Letter Examined	1	391
6		Bloody Tenent Yet More Bloody	4	36
7		Bloody Tenent Yet More Bloody	4	36
7		Bloody Tenent Yet More Bloody	4	277
8		Bloudy Tenent	3	247
8		Bloudy Tenent	3	251
12		Bloody Tenent Yet More Bloody	4	182
14		George Fox Digg'd out of his Burrowes	5	87
15		George Fox Digg'd out of his Burrowes	5	335
15	9-13	Bloody Tenent Yet More Bloody	4	37
16		Experiments	7	64
16		George Fox Digg'd out of his Burrowes	5	434
16	23-30	Bloody Tenent Yet More Bloody	4	316
17	5-6	Bloudy Tenent	3	312
17-18		Hireling Ministry None of Christs	7	164
18		Bloody Tenent Yet More Bloody	4	175
18		Bloody Tenent Yet More Bloody	4	178-179
20		Bloody Tenent Yet More Bloody	4	37
21	25	Bloody Tenent Yet More Bloody	4	377

Ruth
Total References: 3

Chap.	Verse(s)	Williams Text	Volume	Page(s)
1	16-17	*Experiments*	7	*93*
2	4	*Experiments*	7	*90*
3		*Experiments*	7	*91*

1 Samuel
Total References: 30

Chap.	Verse(s)	Williams Text	Volume	Page(s)
1		*Experiments*	7	*98*
3	18	*Experiments*	7	*65*
8		Bloody Tenent Yet More Bloody	4	37
8		*Bloudy Tenent*	3	*122*
8		*Bloudy Tenent*	3	*169*
8		Experiments	7	81
8	5	Bloudy Tenent	3	262
10-11		*George Fox Digg'd out of his Burrowes*	5	*329*
13		Bloudy Tenent	3	200
13	19	Bloody Tenent Yet More Bloody	4	392
13	19	Bloody Tenent Yet More Bloody	4	394
14	1-23	Bloody Tenent Yet More Bloody	4	394
15	32-34	*George Fox Digg'd out of his Burrowes*	5	*314*
17		Bloody Tenent Yet More Bloody	4	316
17		*George Fox Digg'd out of his Burrowes*	5	*202-203*
17	28	Bloody Tenent Yet More Bloody	4	37
17	40-51	Bloody Tenent Yet More Bloody	4	296
17	51	*George Fox Digg'd out of his Burrowes*	5	*456*
19	8-17	*George Fox Digg'd out of his Burrowes*	5	*68*
19	11-17	*George Fox Digg'd out of his Burrowes*	5	*368*
20	3	*Key into the Language*	1	*273*
20	37	Bloody Tenent Yet More Bloody	4	36
26		Experiments	7	97
26	20	Bloody Tenent Yet More Bloody	4	37
28		*George Fox Digg'd out of his Burrowes*	5	*443*
28	3-25	*George Fox Digg'd out of his Burrowes*	5	*275*
28	3-25	*George Fox Digg'd out of his Burrowes*	5	*408*
28	14	Bloody Tenent Yet More Bloody	4	169
28	14	*George Fox Digg'd out of his Burrowes*	5	*162*
30		*Experiments*	7	*58*

2 Samuel

Total References: 37

Chap.	Verse(s)	Williams Text	Volume	Page(s)
2		Bloody Tenent Yet More Bloody	4	37
3		Bloody Tenent Yet More Bloody	4	37
4		Bloody Tenent Yet More Bloody	4	37
6		Bloudy Tenent	3	183
6		*Examiner Defended*	7	*256-257*
6		*Experiments*	7	*96*
6		*Mr. Cotton's Letter Examined*	1	*322-323*
6		*Mr. Cotton's Letter Examined*	1	*383*
6		*Mr. Cotton's Letter Examined*	1	*383-384*
6	12	Bloody Tenent Yet More Bloody	4	172
7		*George Fox Digg'd out of his Burrowes*	5	*272*
7		Mr. Cotton's Letter Examined	1	321
7	1-17	Bloudy Tenent	3	183
7	7	Christenings Make Not Christians	7	40
9	8	*Experiments*	7	*77*
11		Bloody Tenent Yet More Bloody	4	357
11		*Bloody Tenent Yet More Bloody*	4	*463*
11		*Experiments*	7	*94*
11		*George Fox Digg'd out of his Burrowes*	5	*199*
11		*George Fox Digg'd out of his Burrowes*	5	*280*
11		*George Fox Digg'd out of his Burrowes*	5	*496*
11		*Mr. Cotton's Letter Examined*	1	*328*
11	1-13	Bloody Tenent Yet More Bloody	4	358
11	14-27	*Bloody Tenent Yet More Bloody*	4	*512*
11	14-27	*George Fox Digg'd out of his Burrowes*	5	*271*
11	15	Bloody Tenent Yet More Bloody 4	37-38	
11-12		*George Fox Digg'd out of his Burrowes*	5	*432*
12		Bloudy Tenent	3	166
12		*Experiments*	7	*94*
13		Bloody Tenent Yet More Bloody	4	325-326
13	1-22	*Bloudy Tenent*	3	*300*
14	9	*Bloody Tenent Yet More Bloody*	4	*504*
15	11	*George Fox Digg'd out of his Burrowes*	5	*479*
15-20		*George Fox Digg'd out of his Burrowes*	5	*262*
16	5-14	*Experiments*	7	*99*
21		*Bloody Tenent Yet More Bloody*	4	*91*
21		Bloudy Tenent	3	82

1 Kings

Total References: 43

Chap.	Verse(s)	Williams Text	Volume	Page(s)
1		Bloudy Tenent	3	80
2	26-27	Bloudy Tenent	3	24
2	26-27	Bloudy Tenent	3	339-340
3	1-15	Key into the Language	1	140
5		Bloudy Tenent	3	36
11		Examiner Defended	7	256
12		Bloody Tenent Yet More Bloody	4	59
12		Christenings Make Not Christians	7	38
12	16-20	Bloody Tenent Yet More Bloody	4	38
12	25-33	Bloody Tenent Yet More Bloody	4	325
12	25-33	Bloody Tenent Yet More Bloody	4	512
12	25-33	Examiner Defended	7	210
12	25-33	Examiner Defended	7	214
12	25-33	Examiner Defended	7	256
15	5	Mr. Cotton's Letter Examined	1	343
15	9-15	Examiner Defended	7	236
18		Bloudy Tenent	3	210
18	17-18	Bloudy Tenent	3	75
18	19-22	Mr. Cotton's Letter Examined	1	322
18	20-40	Bloody Tenent Yet More Bloody	4	152-153
18	20-40	Bloody Tenent Yet More Bloody	4	215
18	20-40	Bloody Tenent Yet More Bloody	4	392
18	20-40	Bloody Tenent Yet More Bloody	4	449
18	20-40	Bloody Tenent Yet More Bloody	4	451-455
18	20-40	Examiner Defended	7	262
18	20-40	George Fox Digg'd out of his Burrowes	5	41
18	40	Bloody Tenent Yet More Bloody	4	418
18	40	Bloudy Tenent	3	116
18	40-41	Bloody Tenent Yet More Bloody	4	348
20	42	Bloody Tenent Yet More Bloody	4	153
21		Bloody Tenent Yet More Bloody	4	308
21		Bloody Tenent Yet More Bloody	4	467
21		Bloudy Tenent	3	278
21		Examiner Defended	7	233
21	1-16	Bloudy Tenent	3	336
21	8	Bloudy Tenent	3	263
21	13	Bloudy Tenent	3	83
21	27-29	Queries of Highest Consideration	2	271

22		Mr. Cotton's Letter Examined	1	322
22	8	Examiner Defended	7	199
22	8	Examiner Defended	7	201
22	8	Experiments	7	64
22	13-28	Experiments	7	98

2 Kings
Total References: 25

Chap.	Verse(s)	Williams Text	Volume	Page(s)
1		Bloudy Tenent	3	115
1	9-12	Bloudy Tenent	3	210
1	10	Bloody Tenent Yet More Bloody	4	383
3		Queries of Highest Consideration	2	270
6	33	Experiments	7	77
7		Queries of Highest Consideration	2	270
9		Bloody Tenent Yet More Bloody	4	128-129
9	22	Bloody Tenent Yet More Bloody	4	315
10		Bloody Tenent Yet More Bloody	4	27
10		Bloody Tenent Yet More Bloody	4	128-129
10		Queries of Highest Consideration	2	270
10	16	Bloody Tenent Yet More Bloody	4	17-18
10	16	Experiments	7	73
10	31-32	Bloody Tenent Yet More Bloody	4	73
10	32	Bloody Tenent Yet More Bloody	4	79
17		Christenings Make Not Christians	7	38
17		Examiner Defended	7	268
17		George Fox Digg'd out of his Burrowes	5	148
17		Mr. Cotton's Letter Examined	1	372
17		Queries of Highest Consideration	2	271
17	6	Bloody Tenent Yet More Bloody	4	153
17	23	Bloudy Tenent	3	359
18	9-12	Bloody Tenent Yet More Bloody	4	38
18	13-37	Experiments	7	99
23	24-25	George Fox Digg'd out of his Burrowes	5	141

1 Chronicles
Total References: 6

Chap.	Verse(s)	Williams Text	Volume	Page(s)
13		Queries of Highest Consideration	2	263
13	9-11	Experiments	7	67
15		Queries of Highest Consideration	2	263
16	4-6	Bloody Tenent Yet More Bloody	4	172-173

| 21 | 9-13 | *Examiner Defended* | 7 | *264* |
| 28 | 11-13 | Bloudy Tenent | 3 | 339 |

2 Chronicles
Total References: 26

Chap.	Verse(s)	Williams Text	Volume	Page(s)
12		Bloody Tenent Yet More Bloody	4	65
13	9	Bloody Tenent Yet More Bloody	4	65
14		Bloudy Tenent	3	361
14	5	Bloody Tenent Yet More Bloody	4	65
15	3	Bloudy Tenent	3	247
15	3	Bloudy Tenent	3	251
15	5-6	Bloudy Tenent	3	247
15	5-6	Bloudy Tenent	3	251
15	12-13	Bloudy Tenent	3	329
16	*1-10*	*George Fox Digg'd out of his Burrowes*	*5*	*271*
16	*7-10*	Bloody Tenent Yet More Bloody	4	38
16	*7-10*	*Experiments*	*7*	*94*
16	*7-10*	*Experiments*	*7*	*97*
16	*7-10*	*Experiments*	*7*	*98*
16	10	Bloody Tenent Yet More Bloody	4	357
16	10	Bloody Tenent Yet More Bloody	4	357
16	*10*	*Mr. Cotton's Letter Examined*	*1*	*328*
17		Bloudy Tenent	3	23
17		Bloudy Tenent	3	297
20	3	Bloudy Tenent	3	341
30	18-19	Bloody Tenent Yet More Bloody	4	63
30	*18-19*	*Experiments*	*7*	*84*
31		Bloudy Tenent	3	302
31	4	Bloudy Tenent	3	292
36		Bloudy Tenent	3	38
36		Bloudy Tenent	3	212

Ezra
Total References: 21

Chap.	Verse(s)	Williams Text	Volume	Page(s)
0		Mr. Cotton's Letter Examined	1	348
1		Bloudy Tenent	3	266
1		Examiner Defended	7	276
4-5		Examiner Defended	7	275
6		Examiner Defended	7	276
6	11	Examiner Defended	7	276

6	19-22	Bloudy Tenent	3	324
7		Bloudy Tenent	3	266
7		Examiner Defended	7	227
7		Examiner Defended	7	274-277
7	13	Examiner Defended	7	227
7	23	Bloody Tenent Yet More Bloody	4	200
7	23	Bloudy Tenent	3	261-262
7	23	Bloudy Tenent	3	264
7	23	Bloudy Tenent	3	312
7	23	Bloudy Tenent	3	390
7	23	Bloudy Tenent	3	396
7	24	Bloudy Tenent	3	252
7	24	Examiner Defended	7	275-276
7	27-28	Bloudy Tenent	3	266-267
9	1-2	Bloudy Tenent	3	327

Nehemiah
Total References: 7

Chap.	Verse(s)	Williams Text	Volume	Page(s)
0		Mr. Cotton's Letter Examined	1	348
1	11	Experiments	7	62
8		George Fox Digg'd out of his Burrowes	5	75
9		George Fox Digg'd out of his Burrowes	5	75
9	1-4	Bloudy Tenent	3	324
13		Bloudy Tenent	3	302
13	10-11	Bloudy Tenent	3	291

Job
Total References: 30

Chap.	Verse(s)	Williams Text	Volume	Page(s)
1		George Fox Digg'd out of his Burrowes	5	502
1	21	Experiments	7	80
2	9-10	Experiments	7	64
2	9-10	Experiments	7	96
5	19	Mr. Cotton's Letter Examined	1	342
6	24	Experiments	7	66
8	13-15	George Fox Digg'd out of his Burrowes	5	185
12	5	Mr. Cotton's Letter Examined	1	338
13	28	Bloody Tenent Yet More Bloody	4	35
23	15	Experiments	7	106
26		Bloudy Tenent	3	145
26		Bloudy Tenent	3	149

Psalms

Total References: 96

39	6	Bloudy Tenent	3	81
39	9	Experiments	7	80
40	7-8	Experiments	7	85
40	8	Experiments	7	79
42	*1*	*Experiments*	*7*	*78*
42	5	Experiments	7	89
42	11	Experiments	7	89
43	5	Experiments	7	89
45		Bloudy Tenent	3	337
45	4	Hireling Ministry None of Christs	7	158
45	4-5	Bloudy Tenent	3	220
45	6	Bloody Tenent Yet More Bloody	4	278
46	8	Experiments	7	109
50		Bloudy Tenent	3	418
50	16	Hireling Ministry None of Christs	7	171
50	16-23	Queries of Highest Consideration	2	261
51		Experiments	7	94
51	*5*	*George Fox Digg'd out of his Burrowes*	*5*	*424-425*
51	*10-11*	*George Fox Digg'd out of his Burrowes*	*5*	*162*
51	*14*	*Experiments*	*7*	*95*
53		George Fox Digg'd out of his Burrowes	5	480
57	*4*	*George Fox Digg'd out of his Burrowes*	*5*	*458*
63	*1*	*Experiments*	*7*	*78*
66	*12*	*Mr. Cotton's Letter Examined*	*1*	*342*
69		Experiments	7	101
73		Bloudy Tenent	3	59
73	21-22	Experiments	7	86
74		Bloudy Tenent	3	371
74	4-8	George Fox Digg'd out of his Burrowes	5	340
74	9-11	Queries of Highest Consideration	2	268
82		Bloody Tenent Yet More Bloody	4	158
83		Bloudy Tenent	3	360
84	*10*	*Experiments*	*7*	*82*
89		Bloody Tenent Yet More Bloody	4	353
89	20	Bloudy Tenent	3	336
92		Bloudy Tenent	3	370
101		Bloudy Tenent	3	282
101	8	Bloudy Tenent	3	22
101	8	Bloudy Tenent	3	278
101	8	Bloudy Tenent	3	280
102	26	Bloudy Tenent	3	56
103	1-4	Experiments	7	55

103	1-5	Experiments	7	48
103	11	Bloudy Tenent	3	94
104	24	Experiments	7	71
105		Bloudy Tenent	3	337
105	6	Bloudy Tenent	3	323
107		George Fox Digg'd out of his Burrowes	5	446
110		George Fox Digg'd out of his Burrowes	5	446
119		Experiments	7	76
119	19	Examiner Defended	7	202
119	45	Experiments	7	79-80
119	62	Key into the Language	1	108
119	73	Experiments	7	72
119	75	Experiments	7	80
119	*105*	*George Fox Digg'd out of his Burrowes*	*5*	*289*
119	120	Experiments	7	106
119	147	Key into the Language	1	108
122		Bloudy Tenent	3	246
122		Bloudy Tenent	3	318
122	6	Bloody Tenent Yet More Bloody	4	75
132	*3-5*	*Bloody Tenent Yet More Bloody*	*4*	*518*
139	13-14	Experiments	7	71
139	23-24	Experiments	7	63
139	23-24	Experiments	7	85
139	23-24	Experiments	7	100-101
141	5	Bloudy Tenent	3	407
141	5	Mr. Cotton's Letter Examined	1	341
143	2	George Fox Digg'd out of his Burrowes	5	497
143	10	Experiments	7	85
146		Bloudy Tenent	3	251
147		Bloudy Tenent	3	358
147	18	George Fox Digg'd out of his Burrowes	5	445
149		Bloudy Tenent	3	356
149	6-9	Bloudy Tenent	3	145
149	8	Bloudy Tenent	3	158

Proverbs
Total References: 32

Chap.	Verse(s)	Williams Text	Volume	Page(s)
1	17	Bloudy Tenent	3	84
1	28	Mr. Cotton's Letter Examined	1	316
6	*16-19*	*George Fox Digg'd out of his Burrowes*	*5*	*161*
7		Bloudy Tenent	3	300

7	10-27	*George Fox Digg'd out of his Burrowes*	5	408
9		Hireling Ministry None of Christs	7	157
9	1-6	Bloudy Tenent	3	301
9	1-6	Examiner Defended	7	269
9	3	Bloody Tenent Yet More Bloody	4	152
9	8	*Experiments*	7	98
9	13-18	*George Fox Digg'd out of his Burrowes*	5	57
11	26	Mr. Cotton's Letter Examined	1	329-331
12	27	Key into the Language	1	253
17	14	*Bloudy Tenent*	3	58-59
18	21	*George Fox Digg'd out of his Burrowes*	5	149
19	29	Bloudy Tenent	3	413
20	27	*Examiner Defended*	7	241
20	28	Examiner Defended	7	216
21		Experiments	7	51
26	6	Bloody Tenent Yet More Bloody	4	269
26	7	*George Fox Digg'd out of his Burrowes*	5	300
26	18	*Examiner Defended*	7	246-247
27	5	Bloody Tenent Yet More Bloody	4	28
28	5	George Fox Digg'd out of his Burrowes	5	323-324
28	12	Bloody Tenent Yet More Bloody	4	75
28	26	George Fox Digg'd out of his Burrowes	5	132
29	2	Bloudy Tenent	3	412-413
30	12	*George Fox Digg'd out of his Burrowes*	5	302
30	13	*George Fox Digg'd out of his Burrowes*	5	246
30	14	*George Fox Digg'd out of his Burrowes*	5	458
30	28	Bloody Tenent Yet More Bloody	4	455
31	26	Bloudy Tenent	3	276

Ecclesiastes

Total References: 6

Chap.	Verse(s)	Williams Text	Volume	Page(s)
1	6	Key into the Language	1	171
2		George Fox Digg'd out of his Burrowes	5	451
3	16	*Bloody Tenent Yet More Bloody*	4	469
7	7	Bloody Tenent Yet More Bloody	4	313
7	16	Bloody Tenent Yet More Bloody	4	110
9	11	*Queries of Highest Consideration*	2	270

Song of Songs
Total References: 57

Chap.	Verse(s)	Williams Text	Volume	Page(s)
1		Bloody Tenent Yet More Bloody	4	325
1		Bloody Tenent Yet More Bloody	4	336
1		Bloudy Tenent	3	64
1		Examiner Defended	7	268
1	2	Experiments	7	62
1	2	Mr. Cotton's Letter Examined	1	389
1	3	George Fox Digg'd out of his Burrowes	5	480
1	4	Bloody Tenent Yet More Bloody	4	122
1	7	Experiments	7	61-62
1	*7*	*George Fox Digg'd out of his Burrowes*	*5*	*103-104*
1	8	Bloudy Tenent	3	64
1	8	Mr. Cotton's Letter Examined	1	389
1	11	Bloudy Tenent	3	78-79
1	16	Bloody Tenent Yet More Bloody	4	406
1	16	Bloudy Tenent	3	59
1	16	Bloudy Tenent	3	259
1	16	Mr. Cotton's Letter Examined	1	363
1	16	Mr. Cotton's Letter Examined	1	389
2	7	Bloody Tenent Yet More Bloody	4	34
2	8	Examiner Defended	7	200
2	15	George Fox Digg'd out of his Burrowes	5	225
3		Bloody Tenent Yet More Bloody	4	336
3		Bloudy Tenent	3	64
3	*1-3*	*Experiments*	*7*	*68*
4		Bloody Tenent Yet More Bloody	4	122
4		Bloudy Tenent	3	245
4		Mr. Cotton's Letter Examined	1	389
4	4	Bloody Tenent Yet More Bloody	4	145
4	4	Bloudy Tenent	3	100
4	4	Bloudy Tenent	3	111
4	4	Bloudy Tenent	3	256
4	8	Bloody Tenent Yet More Bloody	4	9
4	8	Bloudy Tenent	3	205
5		Bloody Tenent Yet More Bloody	4	102
5		Bloody Tenent Yet More Bloody	4	336
5		Bloudy Tenent	3	64
5		Mr. Cotton's Letter Examined	1	352
5	2	Bloody Tenent Yet More Bloody	4	94
5	2	Bloudy Tenent	3	65

5	2	Bloudy Tenent	3	134
5	2	Bloudy Tenent	3	184
5	2	Bloudy Tenent	3	192
5	2	Bloudy Tenent	3	368
5	2	Experiments	7	66
5	2	Mr. Cotton's Letter Examined	1	346-347
5	2-8	Bloudy Tenent	3	89
5	2-8	Examiner Defended	7	257
5	3	Examiner Defended	7	200
5	8	*Experiments*	7	83
5	11	Bloody Tenent Yet More Bloody	4	361
6	1	Experiments	7	68
6	9	Queries of Highest Consideration	2	265
6	10	*George Fox Digg'd out of his Burrowes*	5	401
8		Bloudy Tenent	3	335
8	1	*Experiments*	7	83
8	9	Bloudy Tenent	3	22
8	9	Bloudy Tenent	3	286

Isaiah

Total References: 78

Chap.	Verse(s)	Williams Text	Volume	Page(s)
1	15	Bloody Tenent Yet More Bloody	4	31
1	15-16	Bloody Tenent Yet More Bloody	4	58
2	3-4	Bloudy Tenent	3	232
2	4	Bloody Tenent Yet More Bloody	4	234
2	4	Bloody Tenent Yet More Bloody	4	295
2	4	Bloudy Tenent	3	17
2	4	Bloudy Tenent	3	30
2	4	Bloudy Tenent	3	45
2	4	Bloudy Tenent	3	139-141
6	8	*Experiments*	7	79
6	9-13	Bloudy Tenent	3	273
7		Examiner Defended	7	274
8		George Fox Digg'd out of his Burrowes	5	155
8	8	Bloudy Tenent	3	320
8	16-22	George Fox Digg'd out of his Burrowes	5	254
8	19-22	George Fox Digg'd out of his Burrowes	5	190
9		Bloudy Tenent	3	357
9	6	George Fox Digg'd out of his Burrowes	5	95
9	6-7	Bloudy Tenent	3	314
9	6-7	Bloudy Tenent	3	373

9	7	Bloudy Tenent	3	232
9	20-21	Bloody Tenent Yet More Bloody	4	35
10		Bloudy Tenent	3	17
10		Bloudy Tenent	3	136
10	1	Bloudy Tenent	3	407
11		George Fox Digg'd out of his Burrowes	5	119-120
11		George Fox Digg'd out of his Burrowes	5	128
11	9	Bloudy Tenent	3	30
11	9	Bloudy Tenent	3	45
11	9	Bloudy Tenent	3	140
20		George Fox Digg'd out of his Burrowes	5	61
20		George Fox Digg'd out of his Burrowes	5	310
26	9	Bloody Tenent Yet More Bloody	4	87-88
38		Experiments	7	56
40		Examiner Defended	7	208
40	6	*Bloudy Tenent*	3	*176*
40	6	Mr. Cotton's Letter Examined	1	323
40	12	Experiments	7	51
40	15	Queries of Highest Consideration	2	254
45	1	Bloody Tenent Yet More Bloody	4	213
49		Bloudy Tenent	3	316
49		Bloudy Tenent	3	372
49	6	*George Fox Digg'd out of his Burrowes*	5	*331*
49	22-23	Examiner Defended	7	207-208
49	23	Bloudy Tenent	3	20
49	23	Bloudy Tenent	3	26
49	23	Bloudy Tenent	3	121
49	23	*Bloudy Tenent*	3	*177*
49	23	Bloudy Tenent	3	222-223
49	23	Bloudy Tenent	3	226
49	23	Bloudy Tenent	3	312
49	23	Bloudy Tenent	3	371
49	23	Bloudy Tenent	3	410
49	23	*Hireling Ministry None of Christs*	7	*178*
52	11	Mr. Cotton's Letter Examined	1	345
52	11	Mr. Cotton's Letter Examined	1	358-360
54	5	Experiments	7	51
56	4-7	Bloody Tenent Yet More Bloody	4	376
58	3-5	Experiments	7	77
59	20-21	George Fox Digg'd out of his Burrowes	5	251
59	21	Bloudy Tenent	3	323
59	21	George Fox Digg'd out of his Burrowes	5	132

59	21	George Fox Digg'd out of his Burrowes	5	190
59	21	George Fox Digg'd out of his Burrowes	5	199
59	21	George Fox Digg'd out of his Burrowes	5	453
59	21	George Fox Digg'd out of his Burrowes	5	457
59	21	George Fox Digg'd out of his Burrowes	5	501
59	21	Hireling Ministry None of Christs	7	180
61	1	Bloudy Tenent	3	337
63		Mr. Cotton's Letter Examined	1	363
63	15-19	Experiments	7	60
63	17	Examiner Defended	7	264
66	1-2	Experiments	7	72
66	1-2	Experiments	7	85
66	2	George Fox Digg'd out of his Burrowes	5	48
66	3	Bloudy Tenent	3	138
66	5	Experiments	7	64
66	5	Experiments	7	72-73

Jeremiah
Total References: 38

Chap.	Verse(s)	Williams Text	Volume	Page(s)
1	10	Bloudy Tenent	3	115
3	10	Bloody Tenent Yet More Bloody	4	216-217
5		Bloudy Tenent	3	166
7		Examiner Defended	7	263
9	7-9	George Fox Digg'd out of his Burrowes	5	66
12	1-4	Bloudy Tenent	3	167
12	4	*George Fox Digg'd out of his Burrowes*	5	409
14		Mr. Cotton's Letter Examined	1	316
14	8	George Fox Digg'd out of his Burrowes	5	186
14	11	Bloudy Tenent	3	115
16	14-15	*Mr. Cotton's Letter Examined*	1	350-351
17	5-6	Bloudy Tenent	3	264
22		George Fox Digg'd out of his Burrowes	5	148
22	15-17	Bloody Tenent Yet More Bloody	4	350
24		Bloudy Tenent	3	115
24		Mr. Cotton's Letter Examined	1	317
25		Bloudy Tenent	3	115
26		Bloudy Tenent	3	116
27		Mr. Cotton's Letter Examined	1	336
29		Bloudy Tenent	3	241
29	7	Bloody Tenent Yet More Bloody	4	174
29	7	Bloudy Tenent	3	72

29	7	Bloudy Tenent	3	112
29	7	Bloudy Tenent	3	115
29	7	Bloudy Tenent	3	223
29	7	Bloudy Tenent	3	225
29	7	Bloudy Tenent	3	236
29	7	Examiner Defended	7	221
29	7	Major Butler	7	133
31		Bloudy Tenent	3	358
33	8	Bloody Tenent Yet More Bloody	4	63
37		Bloudy Tenent	3	77
38		Bloudy Tenent	3	77
42		Mr. Cotton's Letter Examined	1	317
42-43		*Examiner Defended*	7	*200*
45		Experiments	7	93
50	6	Bloody Tenent Yet More Bloody	4	391
51		Bloudy Tenent	3	278

Lamentations

Total References: 13

Chap.	Verse(s)	Williams Text	Volume	Page(s)
1		Mr. Cotton's Letter Examined	1	363
1		Mr. Cotton's Letter Examined	1	383
1	6	Bloody Tenent Yet More Bloody	4	224
1	10	Bloody Tenent Yet More Bloody	4	76
1	12	Christenings Make Not Christians	7	41
1	*18*	*Experiments*	*7*	*78*
1	18	Experiments	7	80
2	18	Experiments	7	77
3	*22*	*Experiments*	*7*	*78*
3	24	George Fox Digg'd out of his Burrowes	5	26
3	40	Experiments	7	100
3	66	Bloudy Tenent	3	115
4	20	Bloudy Tenent	3	337

Ezekiel

Total References: 14

Chap.	Verse(s)	Williams Text	Volume	Page(s)
3		*George Fox Digg'd out of his Burrowes*	*5*	*141*
6	9	Experiments	7	86
6	9	Mr. Cotton's Letter Examined	1	350
9		Christenings Make Not Christians	7	41
14		Mr. Cotton's Letter Examined	1	316

16	44	*Bloudy Tenent*	3	*275*
16	49-50	Bloody Tenent Yet More Bloody	4	174
18	21-29	George Fox Digg'd out of his Burrowes	5	487-490
20		Bloudy Tenent	3	327
20	6	Bloudy Tenent	3	317
21	26-27	Bloudy Tenent	3	338
36		Experiments	7	105
43		Christenings Make Not Christians	7	41
43	11	Mr. Cotton's Letter Examined	1	350

Daniel

Total References: 56

Chap.	Verse(s)	Williams Text	Volume	Page(s)
0		Mr. Cotton's Letter Examined	1	348
2		Mr. Cotton's Letter Examined	1	355
2	45	Bloudy Tenent	3	174
2-3		*George Fox Digg'd out of his Burrowes*	5	*441*
3		Bloody Tenent Yet More Bloody	4	59
3		Bloody Tenent Yet More Bloody	4	262
3		Bloody Tenent Yet More Bloody	4	283
3		Bloudy Tenent	3	72
3		Bloudy Tenent	3	76
3		Bloudy Tenent	3	137
3		Bloudy Tenent	3	266
3		Bloudy Tenent	3	300
3		Christenings Make Not Christians	7	38
3		Queries of Highest Consideration	2	258
3	1-18	Bloody Tenent Yet More Bloody	4	358
3	*1-18*	*Bloudy Tenent*	*3*	*157*
3	1-18	Bloudy Tenent	3	237
3	*1-18*	*Examiner Defended*	*7*	*210*
3	*1-18*	*Examiner Defended*	*7*	*214*
3	*19-30*	*George Fox Digg'd out of his Burrowes*	*5*	*243-244*
3	21	Bloudy Tenent	3	63
4		Bloudy Tenent	3	6
4	27	Examiner Defended	7	230
5		Bloody Tenent Yet More Bloody	4	320-321
5		Bloudy Tenent	3	265
5		Bloudy Tenent	3	330
6		Bloudy Tenent	3	63
6		Bloudy Tenent	3	72
6		Bloudy Tenent	3	266

6		Bloudy Tenent	3	278
6		*Examiner Defended*	7	277
6	10-18	Bloody Tenent Yet More Bloody	4	148
7		*Bloody Tenent Yet More Bloody*	4	45-46
7		Bloody Tenent Yet More Bloody	4	46
7		Bloody Tenent Yet More Bloody	4	412
7		Bloudy Tenent	3	6
7		Bloudy Tenent	3	265
7		Bloudy Tenent	3	357
7		Mr. Cotton's Letter Examined	1	355
7	7	Bloudy Tenent	3	333
7	19-21	Bloody Tenent Yet More Bloody	4	27
7	25	Bloudy Tenent	3	349
8		Bloudy Tenent	3	189
8		Bloudy Tenent	3	265
8		Bloudy Tenent	3	349
8		Queries of Highest Consideration	2	268
9		Christenings Make Not Christians	7	41
9		Bloudy Tenent	3	189
11		Bloudy Tenent	3	349
11		Hireling Ministry None of Christs	7	173
11		Hireling Ministry None of Christs	7	184
11		Queries of Highest Consideration	2	270
11	36	Bloudy Tenent	3	349
12		Bloudy Tenent	3	189
12		Queries of Highest Consideration	2	268

Hosea
Total References: 8

Chap.	Verse(s)	Williams Text	Volume	Page(s)
1	4	Examiner Defended	7	253
2	7	Bloody Tenent Yet More Bloody	4	78
6	2-3	Bloody Tenent Yet More Bloody	4	87-88
7		Bloudy Tenent	3	123
7	14	Experiments	7	66
7	14	Experiments	7	76
9	3	Bloudy Tenent	3	320
10	1	Experiments	7	87

Joel
Total References: 2

Chap.	Verse(s)	Williams Text	Volume	Page(s)
2	28-29	*George Fox Digg'd out of his Burrowes*	5	*475-477*
2	28-32	George Fox Digg'd out of his Burrowes	5	359-362

Obadiah
Total References: 1

Chap.	Verse(s)	Williams Text	Volume	Page(s)
1	4	Bloody Tenent Yet More Bloody	4	12

Jonah
Total References: 6

Chap.	Verse(s)	Williams Text	Volume	Page(s)
1		Bloody Tenent Yet More Bloody	4	86-87
1		*Queries of Highest Consideration*	2	*271*
1	6	Examiner Defended	7	228
3		Bloudy Tenent	3	279
3		Bloudy Tenent	3	417
3	*6-10*	*Examiner Defended*	7	*227-229*

Micah
Total References: 9

Chap.	Verse(s)	Williams Text	Volume	Page(s)
3	1	Bloudy Tenent	3	407
3	10-11	Bloody Tenent Yet More Bloody	4	31
4		Bloudy Tenent	3	357
4	3	Bloody Tenent Yet More Bloody	4	234
4	3	Bloody Tenent Yet More Bloody	4	295
4	3	Bloudy Tenent	3	17
4	3	Bloudy Tenent	3	139
4	3-4	Bloudy Tenent	3	30
4	3-4	Bloudy Tenent	3	45

Nahum
Total References: 1

Chap.	Verse(s)	Williams Text	Volume	Page(s)
1	9	Bloody Tenent Yet More Bloody	4	187-188

Habakkuk
Total References: 5

Chap.	Verse(s)	Williams Text	Volume	Page(s)
1	6	Bloody Tenent Yet More Bloody	4	31

1	14-17	Bloudy Tenent	3	167
1	14-17	*Key into the Language*	1	202
3	17-18	*Experiments*	7	78
3	17-18	*Experiments*	7	88

Haggai
Total References: 2

Chap.	Verse(s)	Williams Text	Volume	Page(s)
0		Mr. Cotton's Letter Examined	1	348
2	13-15	Mr. Cotton's Letter Examined	1	371-373

Zechariah
Total References: 8

Chap.	Verse(s)	Williams Text	Volume	Page(s)
1	19	Bloody Tenent Yet More Bloody	4	76
2	12	Bloudy Tenent	3	319
3	3-5	Bloody Tenent Yet More Bloody	4	64-65
4	6	Bloody Tenent Yet More Bloody	4	392-394
8	16	Bloudy Tenent	3	56
13	4-6	Bloody Tenent Yet More Bloody	4	347
13	6	Bloody Tenent Yet More Bloody	4	78
13	6	Bloody Tenent Yet More Bloody	4	87-88

Malachi
Total References: 2

Chap.	Verse(s)	Williams Text	Volume	Page(s)
1	8	Bloody Tenent Yet More Bloody	4	193
1	11	*Key into the Language*	1	88

Matthew
Total References: 214

Chap.	Verse(s)	Williams Text	Volume	Page(s)
3	1-17	*George Fox Digg'd out of his Burrowes*	5	141-142
3	6	Mr. Cotton's Letter Examined	1	366
3	6	*Mr. Cotton's Letter Examined*	1	368
4	1-11	George Fox Digg'd out of his Burrowes	5	52
4	1-11	*George Fox Digg'd out of his Burrowes*	5	63
4	1-11	*George Fox Digg'd out of his Burrowes*	5	143-144
4	1-11	*George Fox Digg'd out of his Burrowes*	5	203
4	1-11	*George Fox Digg'd out of his Burrowes*	5	456
4	4	*George Fox Digg'd out of his Burrowes*	5	158-159
4	5-6	*George Fox Digg'd out of his Burrowes*	5	162

4	8-10	*Experiments*	7	73
4	16	*George Fox Digg'd out of his Burrowes*	5	481
5		*Bloody Tenent Yet More Bloody*	4	8
5		Bloudy Tenent	3	30
5		Bloudy Tenent	3	359
5		George Fox Digg'd out of his Burrowes	5	412-413
5	3	*Experiments*	7	52
5	3	George Fox Digg'd out of his Burrowes	5	459
5	5	Bloudy Tenent	3	318
5	7	Bloudy Tenent	3	95
5	9-10	Examiner Defended	7	279
5	14-16	George Fox Digg'd out of his Burrowes	5	330
5	20	*George Fox Digg'd out of his Burrowes*	5	490
5	21-26	Bloudy Tenent	3	273
5	33-37	George Fox Digg'd out of his Burrowes	5	409
5	33-37	*George Fox Digg'd out of his Burrowes*	5	412
5	43-48	*Bloudy Tenent*	3	164
5	43-48	*Key into the Language*	1	96
5	44-45	*Queries of Highest Consideration*	2	270
5	48	*George Fox Digg'd out of his Burrowes*	5	226
5	48	George Fox Digg'd out of his Burrowes	5	302
6	5-6	*Experiments*	7	76
6	13	*George Fox Digg'd out of his Burrowes*	5	432
6	22-23	*George Fox Digg'd out of his Burrowes*	5	481
6	33	Bloody Tenent Yet More Bloody	4	408-409
7	15	*Bloody Tenent Yet More Bloody*	4	521
7	15-20	Bloody Tenent Yet More Bloody	4	225
7	15-20	*Examiner Defended*	7	254
7	15-20	*George Fox Digg'd out of his Burrowes*	5	400
7	15-20	George Fox Digg'd out of his Burrowes	5	427
7	21-23	Experiments	7	60
7	21-23	George Fox Digg'd out of his Burrowes	5	495
8	5-13	*George Fox Digg'd out of his Burrowes*	5	459
8	8	Experiments	7	77
8	12	Bloudy Tenent	3	107
8	28-34	*George Fox Digg'd out of his Burrowes*	5	376
8	29	*George Fox Digg'd out of his Burrowes*	5	86
9	5	Bloody Tenent Yet More Bloody	4	91
9	18-26	*Bloody Tenent Yet More Bloody*	4	507
10		Hireling Ministry None of Christs	7	175
10		Major Butler	7	131
10	5-15	*Bloody Tenent Yet More Bloody*	4	486

10	12	Bloody Tenent Yet More Bloody	4	420
10	12	Bloudy Tenent	3	37
10	*14*	*Mr. Cotton's Letter Examined*	*1*	*331*
10	14-15	Bloudy Tenent	3	288
10	16	Bloody Tenent Yet More Bloody	4	156
10	16	Bloody Tenent Yet More Bloody	4	418
10	16	Bloudy Tenent	3	37
10	16-23	Bloody Tenent Yet More Bloody	4	419
10	17	Bloudy Tenent	3	37
10	18	Bloudy Tenent	3	222
10	34-39	Examiner Defended	7	223
11	*13*	*Bloody Tenent Yet More Bloody*	*4*	*119*
11	20-24	Queries of Highest Consideration	2	271
11	*23-24*	*George Fox Digg'd out of his Burrowes*	*5*	*393*
11	*23-24*	*George Fox Digg'd out of his Burrowes*	*5*	*436*
11	*30*	*George Fox Digg'd out of his Burrowes*	*5*	*68*
12		Bloudy Tenent	3	417
12	22-32	Bloudy Tenent	3	246
12	24	Bloody Tenent Yet More Bloody	4	158-159
13	1-9	Bloody Tenent Yet More Bloody	4	131-134
13	*1-9*	*Bloudy Tenent*	*3*	*105-108*
13	1-9	Bloudy Tenent	3	298
13	10-17	Bloudy Tenent	3	273
13	18-19	Key into the Language	1	174
13	18-23	Bloody Tenent Yet More Bloody	4	131-134
13	*18-23*	*Bloudy Tenent*	*3*	*105-108*
13	24-30	Bloody Tenent Yet More Bloody	4	114-155
13	24-30	Bloody Tenent Yet More Bloody	4	340
13	24-30	Bloody Tenent Yet More Bloody	4	437
13	24-30	Bloudy Tenent	3	16-17
13	24-30	Bloudy Tenent	3	29
13	24-30	Bloudy Tenent	3	97-119
13	24-30	Bloudy Tenent	3	168-170
13	24-30	Bloudy Tenent	3	178-179
13	24-30	Bloudy Tenent	3	184-185
13	24-30	Bloudy Tenent	3	208
13	24-30	Bloudy Tenent	3	285
13	24-30	Bloudy Tenent	3	373
13	24-30	George Fox Digg'd out of his Burrowes	5	196
13	24-30	George Fox Digg'd out of his Burrowes	5	207
13	24-30	Queries of Highest Consideration	2	274
13	26-27	Bloudy Tenent	3	102

18	20	Bloudy Tenent	3	27
18	*20*	*Bloudy Tenent*	*3*	*293*
18	*20*	*George Fox Digg'd out of his Burrowes*	*5*	*77*
19	7-9	Bloudy Tenent	3	18
19	7-9	Bloudy Tenent	3	167
19	*17*	*George Fox Digg'd out of his Burrowes*	*5*	*491*
20	6	Bloudy Tenent	3	31
20	6	Bloudy Tenent	3	164
20	6-7	Key into the Language	1	136
21	38	Bloudy Tenent	3	80
21	43	Bloudy Tenent	3	107
22	1-14	Bloudy Tenent	3	294
22	*15-22*	*Examiner Defended*	*7*	*232*
22	21	Bloody Tenent Yet More Bloody	4	110-111
22	21	Bloody Tenent Yet More Bloody	4	222
23		Bloody Tenent Yet More Bloody	4	158
23	*1-3*	*George Fox Digg'd out of his Burrowes*	*5*	*452*
23	*1-36*	*George Fox Digg'd out of his Burrowes*	*5*	*285*
23	*8-12*	*Hireling Ministry None of Christs*	*7*	*170*
23	15	Bloody Tenent Yet More Bloody	4	182
23	*27-28*	*George Fox Digg'd out of his Burrowes*	*5*	*55*
23	*27-28*	*George Fox Digg'd out of his Burrowes*	*5*	*174*
23	29-31	Bloody Tenent Yet More Bloody	4	95
23	*30*	*Bloudy Tenent*	*3*	*79*
23	37	Bloody Tenent Yet More Bloody	4	179-180
23	*37-39*	*Examiner Defended*	*7*	*249*
24		Bloudy Tenent	3	138
24		Bloudy Tenent	3	361
24	*23-28*	*George Fox Digg'd out of his Burrowes*	*5*	*103*
25	1-13	Bloody Tenent Yet More Bloody	4	121-122
25	*1-13*	*George Fox Digg'd out of his Burrowes*	*5*	*490*
25	*31-46*	*Bloudy Tenent*	*3*	*105*
25	*31-46*	*George Fox Digg'd out of his Burrowes*	*5*	*185*
25	31-46	George Fox Digg'd out of his Burrowes	5	245
25	32-33	Bloody Tenent Yet More Bloody	4	125
25	34	Bloody Tenent Yet More Bloody	4	18
25	41	Bloody Tenent Yet More Bloody	4	17
25	*41*	*Experiments*	*7*	*111*
25	*41*	*George Fox Digg'd out of his Burrowes*	*5*	*392*
25	*41-43*	*George Fox Digg'd out of his Burrowes*	*5*	*19*
25	*41-46*	*Bloody Tenent Yet More Bloody*	*4*	*517*
26		Bloudy Tenent	3	420

Mark

7	1-23	George Fox Digg'd out of his Burrowes	5	180
7	6-8	Bloody Tenent Yet More Bloody	4	350
7	21-22	George Fox Digg'd out of his Burrowes	5	425
7	24-30	George Fox Digg'd out of his Burrowes	5	459
9	24	Experiments	7	63
9	24	George Fox Digg'd out of his Burrowes	5	468
9	44	Experiments	7	111
10	29-31	Bloody Tenent Yet More Bloody	4	349
12	28-34	*George Fox Digg'd out of his Burrowes*	5	486
13	34	Bloudy Tenent	3	240
13	34	Bloudy Tenent	3	357
15	43	*Bloody Tenent Yet More Bloody*	4	529
16		Mr. Cotton's Letter Examined	1	317
16	15-16	Bloudy Tenent	3	288
16	15-16	Bloudy Tenent	3	293
16	16	Bloudy Tenent	3	12
16	16	Examiner Defended	7	271
16	16	Queries of Highest Consideration	2	272

Luke
Total References: 88

Chap.	Verse(s)	Williams Text	Volume	Page(s)
1		George Fox Digg'd out of his Burrowes	5	140
1		George Fox Digg'd out of his Burrowes	5	446
1	30-32	Examiner Defended	7	231
1	32	Bloudy Tenent	3	343
1	32	Bloudy Tenent	3	348
1	32	Bloudy Tenent	3	357
1	43	Experiments	7	77
1	47	George Fox Digg'd out of his Burrowes	5	472
1	70	George Fox Digg'd out of his Burrowes	5	152-153
2	10-12	George Fox Digg'd out of his Burrowes	5	469
4	18	George Fox Digg'd out of his Burrowes	5	443
4	18-19	Bloudy Tenent	3	337
4	18-19	George Fox Digg'd out of his Burrowes	5	304
5	8	*George Fox Digg'd out of his Burrowes*	5	503
6		Bloudy Tenent	3	359
6	22	Key into the Language	1	94-95
6	27-28	Bloody Tenent Yet More Bloody	4	285
6	27-28	Bloody Tenent Yet More Bloody	4	296
8		Bloudy Tenent	3	418
8	3	Bloudy Tenent	3	305

14	23	Bloudy Tenent	3	299-301
14	25-26	Bloudy Tenent	3	325
16	1-9	Bloody Tenent Yet More Bloody	4	104
16	1-13	Bloody Tenent Yet More Bloody	4	303-304
16	14-15	Bloody Tenent Yet More Bloody	4	511
16	15	Bloody Tenent Yet More Bloody	4	20
16	*19-31*	*George Fox Digg'd out of his Burrowes*	*5*	*153*
16	19-31	George Fox Digg'd out of his Burrowes	5	375
17	3	Examiner Defended	7	226
17	*20-21*	*George Fox Digg'd out of his Burrowes*	*5*	*231*
18	2-8	Bloody Tenent Yet More Bloody	4	166
18	*9-14*	*George Fox Digg'd out of his Burrowes*	*5*	*180*
19	17	Bloudy Tenent	3	407
19	27	Bloody Tenent Yet More Bloody	4	478
21	12	Bloody Tenent Yet More Bloody	4	105
21	*18*	*George Fox Digg'd out of his Burrowes*	*5*	*362*
21	22	Bloody Tenent Yet More Bloody	4	359
21	34-38	George Fox Digg'd out of his Burrowes	5	494
22		Bloody Tenent Yet More Bloody	4	297
22		Bloudy Tenent	3	36
22		Bloudy Tenent	3	419
22	36	Bloody Tenent Yet More Bloody	4	306
22	36	Bloudy Tenent	3	419
24		Christenings Make Not Christians	7	39
24	27	Bloody Tenent Yet More Bloody	4	448
24	44-49	George Fox Digg'd out of his Burrowes	5	178

John
Total References: 84

Chap.	Verse(s)	Williams Text	Volume	Page(s)
1		George Fox Digg'd out of his Burrowes	5	329-330
1		*George Fox Digg'd out of his Burrowes*	*5*	*446*
1	5	George Fox Digg'd out of his Burrowes	5	327
1	*5*	*George Fox Digg'd out of his Burrowes*	*5*	*380*
1	*9*	*George Fox Digg'd out of his Burrowes*	*5*	*329-330*
1	9	George Fox Digg'd out of his Burrowes	5	481
1	*9*	*George Fox Digg'd out of his Burrowes*	*5*	*502*
1	12	Experiments	7	56
1	12	Mr. Cotton's Letter Examined	1	351
1	*16-18*	*George Fox Digg'd out of his Burrowes*	*5*	*438-439*
1	17	Bloody Tenent Yet More Bloody	4	447
1	*19-34*	*George Fox Digg'd out of his Burrowes*	*5*	*439*

14		George Fox Digg'd out of his Burrowes	5	182
15	*4*	*George Fox Digg'd out of his Burrowes*	*5*	*77*
16		Bloudy Tenent	3	361
16		George Fox Digg'd out of his Burrowes	5	418
16	2	Bloody Tenent Yet More Bloody	4	105
16	*13*	*George Fox Digg'd out of his Burrowes*	*5*	*476*
16	16-20	Bloudy Tenent	3	251
16	16-24	Bloody Tenent Yet More Bloody	4	242-243
17		Bloudy Tenent	3	77
17		Experiments	7	76
17		George Fox Digg'd out of his Burrowes	5	351
17	4	Experiments	7	72
17	9	Bloody Tenent Yet More Bloody	4	130
18	*10-11*	*George Fox Digg'd out of his Burrowes*	*5*	*271*
18	36	Bloody Tenent Yet More Bloody	4	186
18	36	Bloudy Tenent	3	223-224
18	*36*	*George Fox Digg'd out of his Burrowes*	*5*	*379*
18	36	Queries of Highest Consideration	2	267
18	37	Bloudy Tenent	3	13
18	37	Experiments	7	72
19	19	Bloudy Tenent	3	76
19	*19-20*	*Examiner Defended*	*7*	*231*
19	39-40	Bloody Tenent Yet More Bloody	4	529
20	13	Experiments	7	101
20	*22*	*George Fox Digg'd out of his Burrowes*	*5*	*121*
20	23	Bloudy Tenent	3	222
20	*28*	*George Fox Digg'd out of his Burrowes*	*5*	*27*
20	30-31	George Fox Digg'd out of his Burrowes	5	311
20	31	George Fox Digg'd out of his Burrowes	5	144
21	*17*	*Hireling Ministry None of Christs*	*7*	*182*

Acts
Total References: 186

Chap.	Verse(s)	Williams Text	Volume	Page(s)
1		Bloudy Tenent	3	341
1		Bloudy Tenent	3	354
1		Examiner Defended	7	232
1	6-11	George Fox Digg'd out of his Burrowes	5	321
1	11	George Fox Digg'd out of his Burrowes	5	407
2		Bloody Tenent Yet More Bloody	4	60
2		Hireling Ministry None of Christs	7	167
2		Mr. Cotton's Letter Examined	1	367-368

13	9-11	Bloody Tenent Yet More Bloody	4	418
13	13-52	George Fox Digg'd out of his Burrowes	5	93-94
13	13-52	Major Butler	7	131
13	38-39	George Fox Digg'd out of his Burrowes	5	93-94
13	51	Bloudy Tenent	3	288
13	51	Mr. Cotton's Letter Examined	1	331
14		Bloudy Tenent	3	341
14		George Fox Digg'd out of his Burrowes	5	120-121
14		George Fox Digg'd out of his Burrowes	5	347
14	4	Bloudy Tenent	3	78
14	11	George Fox Digg'd out of his Burrowes	5	418
14	16-17	George Fox Digg'd out of his Burrowes	5	479-480
15		Bloudy Tenent	3	27
15		Bloudy Tenent	3	222
15		Bloudy Tenent	3	404-406
15		Queries of Highest Consideration	2	257-258
15	10	Bloudy Tenent	3	7
15	24-26	Bloody Tenent Yet More Bloody	4	86
15	39	Bloody Tenent Yet More Bloody	4	38
16		Bloudy Tenent	3	159
16		George Fox Digg'd out of his Burrowes	5	347
16		Queries of Highest Consideration	2	257-258
16	3	Mr. Cotton's Letter Examined	1	357
16	11-15	George Fox Digg'd out of his Burrowes	5	121
16	11-15	George Fox Digg'd out of his Burrowes	5	198-199
16	14	George Fox Digg'd out of his Burrowes	5	58-59
16	16-40	George Fox Digg'd out of his Burrowes	5	291
16	29-30	George Fox Digg'd out of his Burrowes	5	441
17		George Fox Digg'd out of his Burrowes	5	199
17		George Fox Digg'd out of his Burrowes	5	483
17	1-9	George Fox Digg'd out of his Burrowes	5	304
17	2	Bloudy Tenent	3	75
17	6	Bloody Tenent Yet More Bloody	4	112
17	7	Bloudy Tenent	3	76
17	17	Bloudy Tenent	3	75
17	21	Bloody Tenent Yet More Bloody	4	39
17	22-31	Key into the Language	1	141
17	24-28	George Fox Digg'd out of his Burrowes	5	386
17	30	Examiner Defended	7	252
18	12-17	Bloudy Tenent	3	312
18	14	Bloudy Tenent	3	39
18	14	Bloudy Tenent	3	213

18	*24-28*	*George Fox Digg'd out of his Burrowes*	5	*304*
19		George Fox Digg'd out of his Burrowes	5	52
19		Mr. Cotton's Letter Examined	1	357
19	18	Mr. Cotton's Letter Examined	1	366
19	18	Mr. Cotton's Letter Examined	1	369
19	21-41	Bloody Tenent Yet More Bloody	4	112
19	*21-41*	*Bloudy Tenent*	*3*	*73*
19	27	Bloody Tenent Yet More Bloody	4	337
19	27	Bloudy Tenent	3	39
19	27	Bloudy Tenent	3	213
19	28	Bloudy Tenent	3	298
19	29	Bloudy Tenent	3	78
19	35	Bloudy Tenent	3	39
19	35	Bloudy Tenent	3	213
19	40	Bloudy Tenent	3	78
20		Bloudy Tenent	3	403
20		Bloudy Tenent	3	408
20	17-38	Bloody Tenent Yet More Bloody	4	347
20	17-38	George Fox Digg'd out of his Burrowes	5	110
20	25-28	George Fox Digg'd out of his Burrowes	5	417
20	26-27	Bloudy Tenent	3	129
20	28	Bloudy Tenent	3	240
20	28-30	Bloody Tenent Yet More Bloody	4	203-204
20	28-30	Bloody Tenent Yet More Bloody	4	239-240
20	28-31	Bloudy Tenent	3	99
20	28-31	George Fox Digg'd out of his Burrowes	5	427
20	28-31	Mr. Cotton's Letter Examined	1	387
20	29	Bloudy Tenent	3	17
20	29-31	Bloudy Tenent	3	141-142
20	*29-31*	*Bloudy Tenent*	*3*	*145*
21	7-16	George Fox Digg'd out of his Burrowes	5	310
21	20	Mr. Cotton's Letter Examined	1	353
21	30-31	Bloudy Tenent	3	78
23	1	Bloody Tenent Yet More Bloody	4	442
23	*2-3*	*Bloudy Tenent*	*3*	*76*
23	12-22	Examiner Defended	7	201
24		Bloody Tenent Yet More Bloody	4	273
25		Bloody Tenent Yet More Bloody	4	273-275
25		Bloudy Tenent	3	157
25	8	Bloody Tenent Yet More Bloody	4	423
25	9	Bloody Tenent Yet More Bloody	4	161
25	11	Bloody Tenent Yet More Bloody	4	110

25	11	Bloody Tenent Yet More Bloody	4	160-168
25	11	Bloudy Tenent	3	96
25	11	Bloudy Tenent	3	231
26		Christenings Make Not Christians	7	39
26		George Fox Digg'd out of his Burrowes	5	351
26		George Fox Digg'd out of his Burrowes	5	457
27		Bloudy Tenent	3	166
28		George Fox Digg'd out of his Burrowes	5	483
28	*1-10*	*George Fox Digg'd out of his Burrowes*	5	*396*
28	26-28	Bloudy Tenent	3	273

Romans
Total References: 146

Chap.	Verse(s)	Williams Text	Volume	Page(s)
1		Examiner Defended	7	241
1		George Fox Digg'd out of his Burrowes	5	123
1	2-3	Bloudy Tenent	3	224
1	3-4	Experiments	7	52
1	16	George Fox Digg'd out of his Burrowes	5	293
1	16-17	George Fox Digg'd out of his Burrowes	5	468
1	18-23	George Fox Digg'd out of his Burrowes	5	434
1	18-32	Examiner Defended	7	242-244
1	18-32	Examiner Defended	7	250
1	*18-32*	*Examiner Defended*	7	*255-256*
1	19-20	George Fox Digg'd out of his Burrowes	5	355
1	19-20	George Fox Digg'd out of his Burrowes	5	363
1	21	Examiner Defended	7	241
1	24-32	Examiner Defended	7	264
1-2		George Fox Digg'd out of his Burrowes	5	327-328
2		Examiner Defended	7	257
2		George Fox Digg'd out of his Burrowes	5	344
2	15-16	George Fox Digg'd out of his Burrowes	5	294
2	15-16	George Fox Digg'd out of his Burrowes	5	324
2	*15-16*	*George Fox Digg'd out of his Burrowes*	5	*328*
2	16	George Fox Digg'd out of his Burrowes	5	471
2	17-24	Bloody Tenent Yet More Bloody	4	486
3		George Fox Digg'd out of his Burrowes	5	191
3		George Fox Digg'd out of his Burrowes	5	194-195
3-4		George Fox Digg'd out of his Burrowes	5	298
5	12-21	George Fox Digg'd out of his Burrowes	5	425
6		Examiner Defended	7	221
6		Experiments	7	57

6		Experiments	7	58
6	1-11	Bloudy Tenent	3	209
6	1-14	George Fox Digg'd out of his Burrowes	5	351
7		Bloudy Tenent	3	322
7		George Fox Digg'd out of his Burrowes	5	425
7	4	Experiments	7	84
7	14-25	*George Fox Digg'd out of his Burrowes*	5	*426*
7	14-25	George Fox Digg'd out of his Burrowes	5	467
7	14-25	George Fox Digg'd out of his Burrowes	5	484-485
7	14-25	George Fox Digg'd out of his Burrowes	5	493
7	14-25	*George Fox Digg'd out of his Burrowes*	5	*498*
7	17	*George Fox Digg'd out of his Burrowes*	5	*432*
7	21	Experiments	7	74
7	24	Experiments	7	58
7	24	*Mr. Cotton's Letter Examined*	1	*342*
8		Bloudy Tenent	3	363
8		George Fox Digg'd out of his Burrowes	5	120
8		George Fox Digg'd out of his Burrowes	5	300
8		George Fox Digg'd out of his Burrowes	5	383
8		Queries of Highest Consideration	2	262
8	14	*George Fox Digg'd out of his Burrowes*	5	*124*
8	14	*George Fox Digg'd out of his Burrowes*	5	*126*
8	15-17	Bloudy Tenent	3	318
8	18-25	*George Fox Digg'd out of his Burrowes*	5	*186*
8	24	Bloody Tenent Yet More Bloody	4	60
8	24	*George Fox Digg'd out of his Burrowes*	5	*151*
8	29-30	George Fox Digg'd out of his Burrowes	5	474
9		Bloudy Tenent	3	126
9		Bloudy Tenent	3	251
9		George Fox Digg'd out of his Burrowes	5	186
9		Hireling Ministry None of Christs	7	169
9	1-18	George Fox Digg'd out of his Burrowes	5	199
9	3	*Experiments*	7	*99*
9	3	Mr. Cotton's Letter Examined	1	333
9	16-18	*George Fox Digg'd out of his Burrowes*	5	*332-333*
9	22-24	Bloudy Tenent	3	166
10		Bloudy Tenent	3	360
10		George Fox Digg'd out of his Burrowes	5	120
10		George Fox Digg'd out of his Burrowes	5	192
10	4	Bloudy Tenent	3	360
10	4	George Fox Digg'd out of his Burrowes	5	483
10	5-21	George Fox Digg'd out of his Burrowes	5	381

10	9-10	Examiner Defended	7	225
10	14-15	Christenings Make Not Christians	7	39
10	14-17	Bloudy Tenent	3	293-294
10	14-17	George Fox Digg'd out of his Burrowes	5	190
10	14-17	George Fox Digg'd out of his Burrowes	5	198
10	15	Bloody Tenent Yet More Bloody	4	133
10	15	Christenings Make Not Christians	7	41
10	15	Major Butler	7	130
11		Hireling Ministry None of Christs	7	159
11	20	George Fox Digg'd out of his Burrowes	5	483
11	*28-29*	*Major Butler*	*7*	*136*
12		Bloudy Tenent	3	151
12		Bloudy Tenent	3	162
12		Bloudy Tenent	3	163
12	1	Bloudy Tenent	3	95
12	4-8	George Fox Digg'd out of his Burrowes	5	476
12	*15*	*Experiments*	*7*	*109*
12	18	Bloody Tenent Yet More Bloody	4	314
13		Bloody Tenent Yet More Bloody	4	144
13		Bloody Tenent Yet More Bloody	4	262-272
13		Bloody Tenent Yet More Bloody	4	284
13		Bloudy Tenent	3	18
13		Bloudy Tenent	3	45
13		Bloudy Tenent	3	59
13		Bloudy Tenent	3	146-147
13		Bloudy Tenent	3	150-164
13		Bloudy Tenent	3	211
13		Bloudy Tenent	3	232
13		Bloudy Tenent	3	355
13		Bloudy Tenent	3	373
13		Bloudy Tenent	3	387-389
13		Bloudy Tenent	3	398
13		Bloudy Tenent	3	403
13		Examiner Defended	7	232
13		Hireling Ministry None of Christs	7	180
13		Queries of Highest Consideration	2	266
13	1	Bloudy Tenent	3	222
13	1	Bloudy Tenent	3	226
13	1	Bloudy Tenent	3	268
13	1-4	Bloody Tenent Yet More Bloody	4	243-244
13	1-7	Bloudy Tenent	3	109
13	3	Bloudy Tenent	3	226

13	4	Bloody Tenent Yet More Bloody	4	266
13	4	Bloody Tenent Yet More Bloody	4	420
13	4	Bloody Tenent Yet More Bloody	4	440-441
13	4	Bloody Tenent Yet More Bloody	4	447
13	4	Bloudy Tenent	3	18
13	4	Bloudy Tenent	3	46
13	4	Bloudy Tenent	3	159
13	4	Bloudy Tenent	3	162
13	4	Bloudy Tenent	3	312
13	5-6	Bloudy Tenent	3	226
13	5-6	Bloudy Tenent	3	226
13	6	Bloudy Tenent	3	161
13	6-7	Bloody Tenent Yet More Bloody	4	280-283
13	7-8	Bloudy Tenent	3	151
13	*8*	*Key into the Language*	*1*	*248*
13	9-10	Bloudy Tenent	3	152
14		Bloudy Tenent	3	93
14		Bloudy Tenent	3	100
14	1	Bloudy Tenent	3	101
14	1-4	Bloody Tenent Yet More Bloody	4	108
14	1-4	Bloudy Tenent	3	43
14	1-6	Bloudy Tenent	3	260
14	1-6	Mr. Cotton's Letter Examined	1	353
14	14	Bloudy Tenent	3	256
14	23	Bloudy Tenent	3	138
14	23	Bloudy Tenent	3	256
14	23	Bloudy Tenent	3	258
15	4	Bloudy Tenent	3	263
15	4	George Fox Digg'd out of his Burrowes	5	144
16		Experiments	7	92
16		George Fox Digg'd out of his Burrowes	5	153
16	17	Bloody Tenent Yet More Bloody	4	106
16	17	Bloody Tenent Yet More Bloody	4	240
16	17	Bloudy Tenent	3	91

1 Corinthians
Total References: 124

Chap.	Verse(s)	Williams Text	Volume	Page(s)
1		Bloudy Tenent	3	414
1	12	Bloody Tenent Yet More Bloody	4	38
1	18-31	Examiner Defended	7	241
1	18-31	George Fox Digg'd out of his Burrowes	5	355

5	9-10	Bloody Tenent Yet More Bloody	4	124
5	9-10	Examiner Defended	7	251
5	9-13	Bloudy Tenent	3	17
5	9-13	Bloudy Tenent	3	299
5	10	Bloudy Tenent	3	175
5	10-13	Bloudy Tenent	3	116-117
5	11	Bloody Tenent Yet More Bloody	4	143
5	13	Bloody Tenent Yet More Bloody	4	120-121
5	13	Bloudy Tenent	3	91
6		Bloudy Tenent	3	382
6		Examiner Defended	7	251
6	2	Bloudy Tenent	3	226
6	9	Bloudy Tenent	3	30-31
6	9-11	Mr. Cotton's Letter Examined	1	355
6	17-19	George Fox Digg'd out of his Burrowes	5	286
6	19	George Fox Digg'd out of his Burrowes	5	288
7	1-16	Bloudy Tenent	3	242
7	1-16	Bloudy Tenent	3	324
7	5	Experiments	7	102
7	16	Bloody Tenent Yet More Bloody	4	401
7	*16*	*Examiner Defended*	*7*	*224*
7	*16*	*George Fox Digg'd out of his Burrowes*	*5*	*151*
7	23	Bloudy Tenent	3	13
7	23	Bloudy Tenent	3	255
7	23	Bloudy Tenent	3	354
7	23	Examiner Defended	7	232
8	1-3	George Fox Digg'd out of his Burrowes	5	434
8	3	Mr. Cotton's Letter Examined	1	342-343
8	7-13	Bloudy Tenent	3	207
8	11	Bloody Tenent Yet More Bloody	4	437-438
8	13	Bloudy Tenent	3	256
9		Bloudy Tenent	3	298
9		Mr. Cotton's Letter Examined	1	333
10		Bloudy Tenent	3	327
10		Bloudy Tenent	3	362
10		Bloudy Tenent	3	371
10		George Fox Digg'd out of his Burrowes	5	93
10	1-22	Examiner Defended	7	275
10	13	George Fox Digg'd out of his Burrowes	5	80
10	31	Bloudy Tenent	3	256
10	33	Bloudy Tenent	3	392
10	33	Bloudy Tenent	3	401-402

2 Corinthians
Total References: 64

2	6-7	Bloudy Tenent	3	208
2	16-17	*Major Butler*	7	*121*
3		George Fox Digg'd out of his Burrowes	5	149
3		George Fox Digg'd out of his Burrowes	5	198
4		Examiner Defended	7	230
4		George Fox Digg'd out of his Burrowes	5	381
4	3	George Fox Digg'd out of his Burrowes	5	471
4	6	George Fox Digg'd out of his Burrowes	5	130
4	6	George Fox Digg'd out of his Burrowes	5	482
4	7	*Examiner Defended*	7	*224*
4	16	Experiments	7	56
5	11	Bloudy Tenent	3	301
5	19	Bloudy Tenent Yet More Bloody	4	130
5	19	*George Fox Digg'd out of his Burrowes*	5	*228*
6	2	Bloudy Tenent	3	318
6	14	Mr. Cotton's Letter Examined	1	373
6	14-15	*George Fox Digg'd out of his Burrowes*	5	*379-380*
6	14-18	Bloudy Tenent	3	324
6	17	Mr. Cotton's Letter Examined	1	345
6	17	Mr. Cotton's Letter Examined	1	358-359
6	17	Mr. Cotton's Letter Examined	1	362-365
7		George Fox Digg'd out of his Burrowes	5	237
7		George Fox Digg'd out of his Burrowes	5	494
7	13-16	*George Fox Digg'd out of his Burrowes*	5	*44*
9	5-7	Bloudy Tenent	3	292
10		Bloudy Tenent	3	262
10		Bloudy Tenent	3	357
10	3-4	Bloudy Tenent Yet More Bloody	4	256-258
10	3-4	Bloudy Tenent	3	90
10	3-4	Bloudy Tenent	3	111
10	3-4	Bloudy Tenent	3	146-148
10	3-4	Bloudy Tenent	3	199
10	3-4	*Bloudy Tenent*	3	*363*
10	3-4	Examiner Defended	7	265
10	3-5	Bloudy Tenent Yet More Bloody	4	393-394
10	3-5	Bloudy Tenent	3	285
10	3-5	Examiner Defended	7	218
10	3-6	Bloudy Tenent Yet More Bloody	4	379
10	4	Bloudy Tenent Yet More Bloody	4	145
10	4	Bloudy Tenent Yet More Bloody	4	223
10	4	Bloudy Tenent	3	18
10	4	Bloudy Tenent	3	30

10	4	Bloudy Tenent	3	45
10	4-5	Bloody Tenent Yet More Bloody	4	89
10	6	Bloudy Tenent	3	46
10	6	Bloudy Tenent	3	146
11		Bloudy Tenent	3	294
11	1	Mr. Cotton's Letter Examined	1	365
11	14-15	George Fox Digg'd out of his Burrowes	5	162
11	14-15	George Fox Digg'd out of his Burrowes	5	227
11	23	Bloudy Tenent	3	392
11	23	Bloudy Tenent	3	401-402
12	1-10	George Fox Digg'd out of his Burrowes	5	376
12	10	Experiments	7	88
13	5	George Fox Digg'd out of his Burrowes	5	82
13	5	George Fox Digg'd out of his Burrowes	5	88
13	5	George Fox Digg'd out of his Burrowes	5	92
13	5	George Fox Digg'd out of his Burrowes	5	94-95
13	5	George Fox Digg'd out of his Burrowes	5	283
13	5	George Fox Digg'd out of his Burrowes	5	413
13	5	George Fox Digg'd out of his Burrowes	5	417
13	5	George Fox Digg'd out of his Burrowes	5	500

Galatians
Total References: 47

Chap.	Verse(s)	Williams Text	Volume	Page(s)
0		George Fox Digg'd out of his Burrowes	5	298
1	6-9	Bloody Tenent Yet More Bloody	4	349
1	6-9	Examiner Defended	7	273
1	8	Bloudy Tenent	3	59
1	8	Bloudy Tenent	3	212
2	20	George Fox Digg'd out of his Burrowes	5	406
3	15-18	George Fox Digg'd out of his Burrowes	5	491
3	19-29	George Fox Digg'd out of his Burrowes	5	300
3	28	Bloudy Tenent	3	222
3	28	Bloudy Tenent	3	240
3	28	Bloudy Tenent	3	406
3	28	Examiner Defended	7	224
3	28	George Fox Digg'd out of his Burrowes	5	19
3	28	George Fox Digg'd out of his Burrowes	5	305
3	28-29	Bloudy Tenent	3	328
3	29	Bloudy Tenent	3	323
4	4-5	George Fox Digg'd out of his Burrowes	5	160
4	6	George Fox Digg'd out of his Burrowes	5	119

4	6-7	Experiments	7	60
4	*21-31*	*Bloody Tenent Yet More Bloody*	*4*	*450*
4	21-31	Bloudy Tenent	3	281
4	21-31	Bloudy Tenent	3	320
5		Bloody Tenent Yet More Bloody	4	379
5		Bloudy Tenent	3	199
5		Bloudy Tenent	3	207
5		Bloudy Tenent	3	359
5		George Fox Digg'd out of his Burrowes	5	426
5	2	Mr. Cotton's Letter Examined	1	354
5	2	Mr. Cotton's Letter Examined	1	357
5	*5*	*George Fox Digg'd out of his Burrowes*	*5*	*186*
5	9	Bloudy Tenent	3	198-199
5	9	Bloudy Tenent	3	244
5	9	Bloudy Tenent	3	285
5	12	Bloody Tenent Yet More Bloody	4	86
5	12	Bloody Tenent Yet More Bloody	4	393
5	16-20	George Fox Digg'd out of his Burrowes	5	493
5	16-26	Experiments	7	63
6		Bloudy Tenent	3	362
6	4	Experiments	7	70
6	4	Mr. Cotton's Letter Examined	1	342
6	6	Bloudy Tenent	3	23
6	6	Bloudy Tenent	3	291
6	6	Bloudy Tenent	3	298
6	8	Experiments	7	114
6	14	Mr. Cotton's Letter Examined	1	373
6	15-16	Bloudy Tenent	3	328
6	16	Bloudy Tenent	3	359

Ephesians
Total References: 68

Chap.	Verse(s)	Williams Text	Volume	Page(s)
1		George Fox Digg'd out of his Burrowes	5	474
1	3	Bloody Tenent Yet More Bloody	4	351
1	3-4	Bloody Tenent Yet More Bloody	4	349
1	3-14	George Fox Digg'd out of his Burrowes	5	151
1	11	Experiments	7	106
1	20-21	George Fox Digg'd out of his Burrowes	5	480
2		Bloudy Tenent	3	246
2		Examiner Defended	7	220
2		George Fox Digg'd out of his Burrowes	5	190

5	8-9	George Fox Digg'd out of his Burrowes	5	198
5	11	Key into the Language	1	212
5	11	Mr. Cotton's Letter Examined	1	373
5	21-33	Bloudy Tenent	3	114
6		Bloudy Tenent	3	149-150
6		Bloudy Tenent	3	361-363
6	1-19	Bloudy Tenent	3	114
6	5-8	Bloody Tenent Yet More Bloody	4	278
6	6	Bloudy Tenent	3	255
6	10-17	Bloudy Tenent	3	149-150
6	10-20	Bloody Tenent Yet More Bloody	4	248
6	10-20	Bloudy Tenent	3	18
6	10-20	George Fox Digg'd out of his Burrowes	5	494
6	10-20	Queries of Highest Consideration	2	269
6	17	Bloody Tenent Yet More Bloody	4	88
6	17	Bloudy Tenent	3	160
6	17	George Fox Digg'd out of his Burrowes	5	456

Philippians

Total References: 23

Chap.	Verse(s)	Williams Text	Volume	Page(s)
1	3	Mr. Cotton's Letter Examined	1	389
1	*23-28*	*Experiments*	*7*	*87*
1	29	Bloudy Tenent	3	138
2	*12*	*Examiner Defended*	*7*	*271*
2	*12*	*Mr. Cotton's Letter Examined*	*1*	*344*
2	*12-13*	*Experiments*	*7*	*53*
2	*12-13*	*George Fox Digg'd out of his Burrowes*	*5*	*44*
2	12-13	George Fox Digg'd out of his Burrowes	5	46
2	12-13	George Fox Digg'd out of his Burrowes	5	198
2	12-18	Examiner Defended	7	240
2	13	Bloudy Tenent	3	258
2	25-30	Experiments	7	87
3		Bloudy Tenent	3	93
3		George Fox Digg'd out of his Burrowes	5	302
3	*2*	*George Fox Digg'd out of his Burrowes*	*5*	*225*
3	7-21	Experiments	7	87
3	8	Key into the Language	1	258
3	15-17	Bloudy Tenent	3	43
3	17-21	Bloody Tenent Yet More Bloody	4	108
4	*11-12*	*Experiments*	*7*	*88*
4	13	George Fox Digg'd out of his Burrowes	5	323

| 4 | 18 | Bloudy Tenent | 3 | 301 |
| 4 | 22 | Examiner Defended | 7 | 225 |

Colossians
Total References: 23

Chap.	Verse(s)	Williams Text	Volume	Page(s)
1		George Fox Digg'd out of his Burrowes	5	436-438
1	13-14	George Fox Digg'd out of his Burrowes	5	436-437
1	15	George Fox Digg'd out of his Burrowes	5	438
1	15-23	George Fox Digg'd out of his Burrowes	5	436-437
1	18-19	George Fox Digg'd out of his Burrowes	5	438
1	20	George Fox Digg'd out of his Burrowes	5	437
1	24-29	Queries of Highest Consideration	2	267
1	27	George Fox Digg'd out of his Burrowes	5	185
1	28	George Fox Digg'd out of his Burrowes	5	13
1	28	George Fox Digg'd out of his Burrowes	5	330
2		Mr. Cotton's Letter Examined	1	320
2	5	Bloody Tenent Yet More Bloody	4	62-63
2	6-19	George Fox Digg'd out of his Burrowes	5	82
2	9	*George Fox Digg'd out of his Burrowes*	5	394
2	15-18	Bloudy Tenent	3	354
2	16	Examiner Defended	7	239
2	21-22	Bloudy Tenent	3	255
3	11	Bloudy Tenent	3	406
3	16	George Fox Digg'd out of his Burrowes	5	456
3	18-25	Bloudy Tenent	3	114
4		Bloudy Tenent	3	408
4	1	Bloudy Tenent	3	114
4	17	Mr. Cotton's Letter Examined	1	322

1 Thessalonians
Total References: 11

Chap.	Verse(s)	Williams Text	Volume	Page(s)
1	2-10	Bloody Tenent Yet More Bloody	4	336
1	9	Bloudy Tenent	3	294
1	9	Christenings Make Not Christians	7	39
1	9	Key into the Language	1	221
1	9	Mr. Cotton's Letter Examined	1	355
2		George Fox Digg'd out of his Burrowes	5	120
2	13	George Fox Digg'd out of his Burrowes	5	52
4	11-12	Bloudy Tenent	3	305
5	4-5	*George Fox Digg'd out of his Burrowes*	5	169

| 5 | 19 | *George Fox Digg'd out of his Burrowes* | 5 | *419* |
| 5 | 21 | Bloudy Tenent | 3 | 13 |

2 Thessalonians
Total References: 14

Chap.	Verse(s)	Williams Text	Volume	Page(s)
1		Mr. Cotton's Letter Examined	1	318
1	8	Bloody Tenent Yet More Bloody	4	323
1	8	Key into the Language	1	222
2		Bloody Tenent Yet More Bloody	4	135
2		Bloudy Tenent	3	273
2		Bloudy Tenent	3	349
2		George Fox Digg'd out of his Burrowes	5	143
2		George Fox Digg'd out of his Burrowes	5	267
2	1-12	Bloudy Tenent	3	112
2	8	Bloody Tenent Yet More Bloody	4	149-149
2	9-12	Bloody Tenent Yet More Bloody	4	327
3	2	George Fox Digg'd out of his Burrowes	5	486
3	6	Bloody Tenent Yet More Bloody	4	142
3	*6-13*	*Bloudy Tenent*	*3*	*305*

1 Timothy
Total References: 33

Chap.	Verse(s)	Williams Text	Volume	Page(s)
1		Bloudy Tenent	3	341
1	4	Bloudy Tenent	3	86
1	19-20	Major Butler	7	132
2	1-2	Bloody Tenent Yet More Bloody	4	72-73
2	1-2	Bloody Tenent Yet More Bloody	4	281
2	1-2	Bloody Tenent Yet More Bloody	4	422-424
2	1-2	Bloudy Tenent	3	112
2	1-2	Bloudy Tenent	3	224
2	1-2	Bloudy Tenent	3	235-236
2	*1-2*	*Bloudy Tenent*	*3*	*244*
2	1-2	Bloudy Tenent	3	312
2	1-2	Major Butler	7	133
2	1-3	Examiner Defended	7	221
2	2	Bloody Tenent Yet More Bloody	4	78
2	15	George Fox Digg'd out of his Burrowes	5	151
3		Bloudy Tenent	3	416
3	1-13	Mr. Cotton's Letter Examined	1	390
3	14-16	George Fox Digg'd out of his Burrowes	5	223

3	16	George Fox Digg'd out of his Burrowes		65
4	1-2	*Bloody Tenent Yet More Bloody*	4	467
4	4-5	Bloudy Tenent	3	319
4	7-8	Bloody Tenent Yet More Bloody	4	403
4	16	Bloudy Tenent	3	209
5	20	Bloody Tenent Yet More Bloody	4	347
5	20	Bloudy Tenent	3	127-128
5	23	*Experiments*	7	103
6	4-5	Bloudy Tenent	3	86
6	11-16	George Fox Digg'd out of his Burrowes	5	286-287
6	12	*Experiments*	7	103
6	14	Bloudy Tenent	3	240
6	14-15	Bloudy Tenent	3	259
6	16	George Fox Digg'd out of his Burrowes	5	352
6	18-19	Bloudy Tenent	3	65

2 Timothy
Total References: 38

Chap.	Verse(s)	Williams Text	Volume	Page(s)
1	6-7	*George Fox Digg'd out of his Burrowes*	5	123
1	10	George Fox Digg'd out of his Burrowes	5	352
1	15	*Experiments*	7	93
2		Bloudy Tenent	3	92
2		Bloudy Tenent	3	173
2		Bloudy Tenent	3	240
2	1-2	Bloudy Tenent	3	232
2	3	Bloudy Tenent	3	133
2	15	*Bloudy Tenent*	3	113
2	15	*Mr. Cotton's Letter Examined*	1	346
2	16	Bloody Tenent Yet More Bloody	4	346-347
2	16-19	Bloody Tenent Yet More Bloody	4	184
2	23-26	Bloody Tenent Yet More Bloody	4	109
2	23-26	Bloody Tenent Yet More Bloody	4	184-185
2	24	Bloudy Tenent	3	30
2	24-25	Bloody Tenent Yet More Bloody	4	152
2	24-26	Bloody Tenent Yet More Bloody	4	150
2	24-26	Bloody Tenent Yet More Bloody	4	216
2	24-26	Bloody Tenent Yet More Bloody	4	218
2	24-26	Bloody Tenent Yet More Bloody	4	225
2	24-26	Bloudy Tenent	3	130
2	24-26	Bloudy Tenent	3	133
2	24-26	Bloudy Tenent	3	135

2	24-26	Bloudy Tenent	3	207
2	24-26	Bloudy Tenent	3	275-276
2	24-26	Experiments	7	95
2	25-26	Bloudy Tenent	3	17
2	25-26	Examiner Defended	7	250
3	2-5	Bloudy Tenent Yet More Bloody	4	143
3	5	Bloudy Tenent Yet More Bloody	4	141
3	5	Examiner Defended	7	272
3	12	Bloudy Tenent	3	361
3	16	George Fox Digg'd out of his Burrowes	5	157-158
3	17	Bloudy Tenent	3	259
4	1-8	Queries of Highest Consideration	2	267
4	3	Bloudy Tenent Yet More Bloody	4	39
4	3-4	Bloudy Tenent Yet More Bloody	4	418
4	17	Bloudy Tenent	3	75

Titus

Total References: 32

Chap.	Verse(s)	Williams Text	Volume	Page(s)
1		Bloudy Tenent	3	298
1		Bloudy Tenent	3	341
1		Bloudy Tenent	3	416
1	5-9	Mr. Cotton's Letter Examined	1	390
1	9	Bloudy Tenent	3	276
1	9-11	Bloudy Tenent	3	18
1	9-11	Bloudy Tenent	3	144-145
1	13	George Fox Digg'd out of his Burrowes	5	110
1	15	Bloudy Tenent	3	319
1	16	Examiner Defended	7	268
1	16	George Fox Digg'd out of his Burrowes	5	50
2	7	Bloudy Tenent	3	235-236
2	11	George Fox Digg'd out of his Burrowes	5	331
2	12	Experiments	7	71
2	14	Bloudy Tenent	3	327
3		Examiner Defended	7	263
3	1	Bloudy Tenent	3	222
3	10	Bloody Tenent Yet More Bloody	4	43
3	10-11	Bloody Tenent Yet More Bloody	4	98-102
3	10-11	Bloody Tenent Yet More Bloody	4	105-106
3	10-11	Bloody Tenent Yet More Bloody	4	239
3	10-11	Bloody Tenent Yet More Bloody	4	247
3	10-11	Bloody Tenent Yet More Bloody	4	325

3	10-11	Bloody Tenent Yet More Bloody	4	418
3	10-11	Bloudy Tenent	3	16
3	10-11	Bloudy Tenent	3	42
3	10-11	Bloudy Tenent	3	84-88
3	10-11	Bloudy Tenent	3	90-91
3	10-11	Bloudy Tenent	3	127
3	*10-11*	*Bloudy Tenent*	*3*	*130*
3	10-11	Bloudy Tenent	3	192
3	10-11	Bloudy Tenent	3	271

Hebrews
Total References: 57

Chap.	Verse(s)	Williams Text	Volume	Page(s)
1		Queries of Highest Consideration	2	264
1	1-2	George Fox Digg'd out of his Burrowes	5	153
1	1-4	Examiner Defended	7	231
1	1-4	George Fox Digg'd out of his Burrowes	5	52
1	1-4	George Fox Digg'd out of his Burrowes	5	338
1	8	Bloody Tenent Yet More Bloody	4	278
4	8	Bloudy Tenent	3	322
4	12	Bloudy Tenent	3	160
4	12	Bloudy Tenent	3	303
4	12	George Fox Digg'd out of his Burrowes	5	456
6		Bloody Tenent Yet More Bloody	4	63
6	1-2	Bloody Tenent Yet More Bloody	4	21-22
6	1-2	Bloody Tenent Yet More Bloody	4	62
6	1-2	Bloody Tenent Yet More Bloody	4	300-301
6	1-2	Bloudy Tenent	3	65
6	1-2	Bloudy Tenent	3	67
6	1-2	Bloudy Tenent	3	87
6	1-2	Examiner Defended	7	269
6	1-2	Examiner Defended	7	271-272
6	*1-2*	*George Fox Digg'd out of his Burrowes*	*5*	*177*
6	1-2	George Fox Digg'd out of his Burrowes	5	344
6	1-2	Hireling Ministry None of Christs	7	162
6	1-2	Key into the Language	1	221
6	1-2	Queries of Highest Consideration	2	272
6	1-8	Queries of Highest Consideration	2	262
6	2	Bloody Tenent Yet More Bloody	4	64
6	4-8	George Fox Digg'd out of his Burrowes	5	482
6	16	Bloudy Tenent	3	383
7		Bloudy Tenent	3	303

7		Examiner Defended	7	275
7		Mr. Cotton's Letter Examined	1	317
8		Bloody Tenent Yet More Bloody	4	383
8		Bloudy Tenent	3	358
9		George Fox Digg'd out of his Burrowes	5	320
9		George Fox Digg'd out of his Burrowes	5	344
10		Bloody Tenent Yet More Bloody	4	383
10		Bloudy Tenent	3	358
10	25	Bloudy Tenent	3	390
10	28-29	Bloudy Tenent	3	12
10	34	Experiments	7	88
11	6	Bloudy Tenent	3	138
11	6	Examiner Defended	7	271
11	6	Key into the Language	1	207
11	7	Bloudy Tenent	3	318
11	9-10	Bloudy Tenent	3	322
12		Bloudy Tenent	3	209-210
12		Bloudy Tenent	3	281
12		Bloudy Tenent	3	320
12		George Fox Digg'd out of his Burrowes	5	472
12		Queries of Highest Consideration	2	264
12	1-2	*George Fox Digg'd out of his Burrowes*	5	188
12	2	*George Fox Digg'd out of his Burrowes*	5	439
12	2	*George Fox Digg'd out of his Burrowes*	5	456
12	22-24	Bloudy Tenent	3	328
12	28	Mr. Cotton's Letter Examined	1	356
13	17	Bloudy Tenent	3	406
13	17	Bloudy Tenent	3	408

James
Total References: 18

Chap.	Verse(s)	Williams Text	Volume	Page(s)
1	5	*George Fox Digg'd out of his Burrowes*	5	127
2		Bloudy Tenent	3	360
2		Bloudy Tenent	3	414
2	1	Examiner Defended	7	225
2	1-7	Bloudy Tenent	3	245
2	1-13	Experiments	7	48
2	5	Examiner Defended	7	224
2	26	Examiner Defended	7	272
3	1	Bloudy Tenent	3	240
3	2	*George Fox Digg'd out of his Burrowes*	5	468

3	10	Bloody Tenent Yet More Bloody	4	413
3	10	Bloudy Tenent	3	140
3	10	*Bloudy Tenent*	3	*140*
3	10-11	Bloody Tenent Yet More Bloody	4	264-265
4	1-10	Mr. Cotton's Letter Examined	1	374
4	4	Bloody Tenent Yet More Bloody	4	381
4	15	*Experiments*	7	*90*
5	12	*George Fox Digg'd out of his Burrowes*	5	*409*

1 Peter
Total References: 38

Chap.	Verse(s)	Williams Text	Volume	Page(s)
1	3-5	George Fox Digg'd out of his Burrowes	5	186
1	*10-12*	*George Fox Digg'd out of his Burrowes*	*5*	*357-358*
1	15	Bloudy Tenent	3	324
1	15	Bloudy Tenent	3	400
1	*24-25*	*Mr. Cotton's Letter Examined*	*1*	*323*
2		Queries of Highest Consideration	2	264
2	1-10	Bloudy Tenent	3	246
2	2	Experiments	7	62
2	2-3	Experiments	7	61
2	4-9	Bloudy Tenent	3	66-67
2	4-10	Queries of Highest Consideration	2	261
2	8	Bloudy Tenent	3	126
2	9	Bloudy Tenent	3	116
2	9	Bloudy Tenent	3	281
2	9	Bloudy Tenent	3	322
2	9	Bloudy Tenent	3	327
2	9	Bloudy Tenent	3	328
2	9	Christenings Make Not Christians	7	32
2	9	Examiner Defended	7	215
2	9	Queries of Highest Consideration	2	260
2	13	Bloudy Tenent	3	398
2	13-14	Bloody Tenent Yet More Bloody	4	487
2	13-14	Bloudy Tenent	3	161
2	13-17	Examiner Defended	7	239
2	17	Bloudy Tenent	3	36-37
2	20	Bloudy Tenent	3	31
2	20	Bloudy Tenent	3	164
3	8-22	George Fox Digg'd out of his Burrowes	5	308
3	18-21	George Fox Digg'd out of his Burrowes	5	472-473
3	*18-22*	*George Fox Digg'd out of his Burrowes*	*5*	*122*

3	19	Bloudy Tenent	3	273
3	21	Bloudy Tenent Yet More Bloody	4	60
3	21-22	George Fox Digg'd out of his Burrowes	5	151
4		Examiner Defended	7	233
5		Bloudy Tenent	3	403
5	13	Bloudy Tenent	3	320
5	13	Mr. Cotton's Letter Examined	1	336
5	13	Mr. Cotton's Letter Examined	1	360

2 Peter
Total References: 13

Chap.	Verse(s)	Williams Text	Volume	Page(s)
1	16-21	George Fox Digg'd out of his Burrowes	5	153
2		Bloody Tenent Yet More Bloody	4	349
2		Bloudy Tenent	3	176
2		George Fox Digg'd out of his Burrowes	5	110
2		George Fox Digg'd out of his Burrowes	5	428
2		George Fox Digg'd out of his Burrowes	5	493
2	3	Major Butler	7	133
2	13	Bloudy Tenent	3	364
2	19	George Fox Digg'd out of his Burrowes	5	429
3	11-13	Bloudy Tenent	3	56
3	18	Experiments	7	52
3	18	George Fox Digg'd out of his Burrowes	5	170
3	18	George Fox Digg'd out of his Burrowes	5	369

1 John
Total References: 22

Chap.	Verse(s)	Williams Text	Volume	Page(s)
1		George Fox Digg'd out of his Burrowes	5	286
1	9	George Fox Digg'd out of his Burrowes	5	468
1	9	George Fox Digg'd out of his Burrowes	5	498
2		Bloudy Tenent	3	337
2	2	Bloody Tenent Yet More Bloody	4	122
2	12-14	Experiments	7	59-60
2	15-16	Queries of Highest Consideration	2	264
2	27	George Fox Digg'd out of his Burrowes	5	323
3		Examiner Defended	7	221
3		George Fox Digg'd out of his Burrowes	5	135
3	1	George Fox Digg'd out of his Burrowes	5	186
4		George Fox Digg'd out of his Burrowes	5	135
4	1	Bloody Tenent Yet More Bloody	4	29

4	1-6	Experiments	7	51
4	2-3	Bloody Tenent Yet More Bloody	4	337
4	13	George Fox Digg'd out of his Burrowes	5	254
4	*18*	*Experiments*	*7*	*106*
5		Bloudy Tenent	3	356
5		Bloudy Tenent	3	360
5		Examiner Defended	7	221
5	9	Bloudy Tenent	3	267
5	18	Experiments	7	63

Jude
Total References: 8

Chap.	Verse(s)	Williams Text	Volume	Page(s)
1	3	Bloody Tenent Yet More Bloody	4	63
1	4	Bloody Tenent	3	59
1	4	Bloody Tenent	3	126
1	*4*	*Major Butler*	*7*	*133*
1	5-13	Bloody Tenent Yet More Bloody	4	262
1	14-16	George Fox Digg'd out of his Burrowes	5	344-345
1	*16*	*George Fox Digg'd out of his Burrowes*	*5*	*143*
1	*23*	*Bloudy Tenent*	*3*	*301*

Revelation
Total References: 306

Chap.	Verse(s)	Williams Text	Volume	Page(s)
0		George Fox Digg'd out of his Burrowes	5	375
0		George Fox Digg'd out of his Burrowes	5	427
0		George Fox Digg'd out of his Burrowes	5	460
1		Bloody Tenent Yet More Bloody	4	383
1		Bloudy Tenent	3	354
1		Christenings Make Not Christians	7	41
1		Mr. Cotton's Letter Examined	1	356
1		Queries of Highest Consideration	2	265
1	1	Christenings Make Not Christians	7	33
1	12-20	Bloody Tenent Yet More Bloody	4	210
1	16	Bloody Tenent Yet More Bloody	4	88
1	16	Bloody Tenent Yet More Bloody	4	154
1	16	Bloody Tenent Yet More Bloody	4	186
1	16	Bloody Tenent Yet More Bloody	4	248
1	16	Bloody Tenent Yet More Bloody	4	261
1	16	Bloody Tenent Yet More Bloody	4	275
1	16	Bloody Tenent Yet More Bloody	4	292

6	4	Key into the Language	1	266
6	9	*Bloody Tenent Yet More Bloody*	4	*25*
6	9	*Bloody Tenent Yet More Bloody*	4	*42*
6	9	Bloody Tenent Yet More Bloody	4	98
6	9	*George Fox Digg'd out of his Burrowes*	5	*272-273*
6	9-10	Bloody Tenent Yet More Bloody	4	33
6	9-10	Bloody Tenent Yet More Bloody	4	409
6	9-11	*Bloudy Tenent*	3	*3*
6	9-11	*Bloudy Tenent*	3	*219*
6	9-11	*Examiner Defended*	7	*199*
6	9-11	*Examiner Defended*	7	*215*
6	9-11	*George Fox Digg'd out of his Burrowes*	5	*172*
6-19		Hireling Ministry None of Christs	7	158
7		Hireling Ministry None of Christs	7	159
7	9	Hireling Ministry None of Christs	7	159
7	9-17	Hireling Ministry None of Christs	7	169
7	14	Bloody Tenent Yet More Bloody	4	58
9		Bloody Tenent Yet More Bloody	4	189
9		George Fox Digg'd out of his Burrowes	5	350
9	14-21	Bloody Tenent Yet More Bloody	4	169-170
9	14-21	Bloody Tenent Yet More Bloody	4	179
9	15-21	Bloody Tenent Yet More Bloody	4	241-242
9	21	Examiner Defended	7	249
10		Bloody Tenent Yet More Bloody	4	423
10		George Fox Digg'd out of his Burrowes	5	409-410
10	*8-10*	*George Fox Digg'd out of his Burrowes*	5	*141*
10	8-11	George Fox Digg'd out of his Burrowes	5	145
10-11		Hireling Ministry None of Christs	7	158
10-11		Hireling Ministry None of Christs	7	161
10-11		Major Butler	7	131
11		Bloody Tenent Yet More Bloody	4	46-47
11		Bloody Tenent Yet More Bloody	4	191
11		Bloody Tenent Yet More Bloody	4	196
11		Bloody Tenent Yet More Bloody	4	260
11		Bloody Tenent Yet More Bloody	4	350
11		Bloody Tenent Yet More Bloody	4	351
11		Bloudy Tenent	3	11
11		Bloudy Tenent	3	57
11		Bloudy Tenent	3	189
11		*George Fox Digg'd out of his Burrowes*	5	*145*
11		*George Fox Digg'd out of his Burrowes*	5	*263*
11		George Fox Digg'd out of his Burrowes	5	337

18	24	Bloody Tenent Yet More Bloody	4	179
18-19		Hireling Ministry None of Christs	7	159
19		Bloody Tenent Yet More Bloody	4	127
19		Bloudy Tenent	3	149
19		Bloudy Tenent	3	363
19		George Fox Digg'd out of his Burrowes	5	49
19		Hireling Ministry None of Christs	7	176
19	7-8	Bloody Tenent Yet More Bloody	4	354
19	7-8	Bloudy Tenent	3	62
19	9-10	George Fox Digg'd out of his Burrowes	5	154
19	11-16	Queries of Highest Consideration	2	269
19	11-21	Bloudy Tenent	3	62
19	11-21	Bloudy Tenent	3	219
19	11-21	Bloudy Tenent	3	262
19	14	Bloody Tenent Yet More Bloody	4	353-354
19	19-20	Bloody Tenent Yet More Bloody	4	354
20		Bloody Tenent Yet More Bloody	4	127-128
20		Bloody Tenent Yet More Bloody	4	129
20		Bloody Tenent Yet More Bloody	4	317-318
20		Bloudy Tenent	3	56
20		Bloudy Tenent	3	181
20		Bloudy Tenent	3	186
20		Bloudy Tenent	3	191
20		Bloudy Tenent	3	361
20		Queries of Highest Consideration	2	273
20	1-3	Bloudy Tenent	3	274
20	1-6	Queries of Highest Consideration	2	268
20	*7-10*	*Experiments*	*7*	*110*
20	7-10	Queries of Highest Consideration	2	269
20	11-12	Hireling Ministry None of Christs	7	160
21		Bloody Tenent Yet More Bloody	4	127-128
21		Bloudy Tenent	3	281
21		Bloudy Tenent	3	371-372
21	9-21	Bloudy Tenent	3	240
22		Bloody Tenent Yet More Bloody	4	127-128
22	18-19	George Fox Digg'd out of his Burrowes	5	154
22	19	George Fox Digg'd out of his Burrowes	5	488

2. Ranking of Biblical Chapter Citations in Williams's Complete Writings

Book	Chapter	Number of References
Revelation	2	48
Romans	13	40
Revelation	17	37
Matthew	13	36
Revelation	11	35
1 Corinthians	5	32
2 Timothy	2	25
Revelation	1	24
Revelation	6	23
1 Peter	2	22
2 Corinthians	10	21
Luke	9	21
Matthew	28	20
Revelation	13	20
Deuteronomy	13	19
Exodus	20	19
Matthew	5	19
Revelation	12	19
Hebrews	6	18
Song of Songs	1	18
Daniel	3	17
John	1	17
Song of Songs	5	17
Titus	3	17
Acts	2	16
Acts	9	16
Acts	20	15
Ephesians	4	15
Galatians	5	15
Romans	1	15
Acts	19	14
Isaiah	49	14
John	3	14
Matthew	10	14
Matthew	18	14
Revelation	19	14
Revelation	20	14

Romans	10	14
1 Corinthians	12	13
1 Kings	18	13
Acts	10	13
Ephesians	6	13
Ezra	7	13
Revelation	18	13
1 Timothy	2	12
2 Samuel	11	12
Ephesians	2	12
Ephesians	5	12
Matthew	16	12
Matthew	25	12
Revelation	3	12
Romans	7	12
Romans	8	12
Acts	5	11
Acts	17	11
Matthew	23	11
Romans	14	11
Titus	1	11
1 Corinthians	7	10
1 Corinthians	14	10
Colossians	1	10
Daniel	7	10
Ephesians	3	10
Galatians	3	10
Galatians	6	10
Hebrews	12	10
Jeremiah	29	10

3. Ranking of Biblical Genre Citations in Williams's Complete Writings

Biblical Genre	Number of References
Pauline epistles	680
Gospels	406
Writings	353
Prophets	335
Revelation	306
Acts and Catholic	285
Law	152

4. Ranking of Citations of Biblical Books in Williams's Complete Writings

Book	Number of References
Revelation	306
Matthew	214
Acts	186
Romans	146
1 Corinthians	124
Psalms	96
Luke	88
John	84
Isaiah	78
Ephesians	68
2 Corinthians	64
Hebrews	57
Song of Songs	57
Daniel	56
Galatians	47
Genesis	47
1 Kings	43
Deuteronomy	42
1 Peter	38
2 Timothy	38
Exodus	38
Jeremiah	38
2 Samuel	37
1 Timothy	33
Proverbs	32
Titus	32
1 Samuel	30
Job	30
2 Chronicles	26
2 Kings	25
Colossians	23
Philippians	23
1 John	22
Ezra	21
Mark	20
James	18
2 Thessalonians	14

Ezekiel	14
Numbers	14
2 Peter	13
Lamentations	13
1 Thessalonians	11
Leviticus	11
Micah	9
Hosea	8
Jude	8
Zechariah	8
Nehemiah	7
1 Chronicles	6
Ecclesiastes	6
Jonah	6
Habakkuk	5
Joshua	3
Ruth	3
Haggai	2
Joel	2
Malachi	2
Nahum	1
Obadiah	1

INDEX

Morgan, Edmund S.: on Barrow's
view of church and state, 103;
on Henry Barrow's zealous
Separatism, 99; on the
religious nature of Williams's
thought, 32; on Williams's
"intellectual courage," 25; on
Williams's denial of America's
"divine mission," 40
Moses: as model for Puritan
political officers, 53, 59, 60
n.11, 62
Moslems: religious liberty of, 153
Murton, John: on 2 Corinthians
10, 148 n.50; and Revelation 2,
159
Naboth, 3, 58, 72, 79-86 passim;
Williams's identification with,
83
Narragansett peoples, 13, 14, 24,
130
National covenant: Puritan
understanding of, 36-37;
Williams's understanding of,
69-70
Native Americans, 2, 8, 13, 14, 24;
and Williams's view of
civility, 74 n.46; as proof that
civil peace thrives without
Christian establishment, 169;
missions to, 2, 15, 74-75, 189-
190; opinions of English and
Dutch toward, 15; unjust
seizure of their lands, 174-175,
181-182
Nebuchadnezzar, 3, 58, 69, 85-86;
Anabaptist interpretations of,
76n; and forced conversions of
Native Americans to
Christianity, 74; as biblical
example of a religious
persecutor, 71-79; William

Perkins's interpretation of, 73
n.43
Nero, 82; compared with
Constantine, 114-115, 176;
persecution of the church: 114
New Testament: and typological
interpretation, 38; as model
for church government, 16;
Williams's interpretation of, 8
Niebuhr, H. Richard: on modern
misinterpretations of
Williams, 31
Noah, 109
Oaths, 13
Old Testament, 51, 183; Puritan
interpretation of, 8, 53-54;
typological interpretation of,
38-39, 43; Williams's
interpretation of, 9, 53-86
Paine, Thomas: Williams as
forerunner of, 29
Parable of the weeds (Mt 13:24-30,
36-43), 183, 191; and
Anabaptists, 95-97; and
English Separatism, 97-104;
and New England Puritanism,
104-110; and the Reformation,
92-97; as directive for civil
peace, 120-121; Henry
Barrow's interpretation of,
99-104; John Cotton's
interpretation of, 104-110;
perverted to violent ends, 88-
89; Williams's interpretation
of, 9, 86, 110-127
*Paraenetick, or, Humble Address
to the Parliament*: Williams's
probable authorship of, 70
n.40
Parliament, 6, 14, 16, 17, 18, 19,
70
Parrington, Vernon Louis, 26, 31,
40; interpretation of Williams,